THE PIEBALD STANDARD

A Biography of the Knights Templars

From Les Croniques de Jherusalem abregies, *Österreichische National-Bibliothek*

Battle scene — progress of Saladin

The Piebald Standard

A Biography of the Knights Templars

Edith Simon

WHITE LION PUBLISHERS LIMITED
London, New York, Sydney and Toronto

First published in Great Britain by
Cassell and Co. Ltd., 1959

Copyright © Edith Simon 1959

White Lion edition, 1976

ISBN 85617 208 1

Made and printed in Great Britain
for White Lion Publishers Limited
138 Park Lane, London W1Y 3DD
by Hendington Limited
Deadbrook Lane, Aldershot, Hampshire

Foreword

The more I became involved in reading and writing about the Templars, the more I had to wonder at the obscurity which has engulfed them. To most people they are barely more than a name today — and a vaguely worthy, faintly stodgy one at that, where once it was a name which rang throughout Europe and the East, echoing every virtue, vice, glory and corruption of the Crusades which it epitomized. As for their story, which has all the elements of both classical tragedy and the unsolved mystery, it has virtually lapsed from popular knowledge, merely dug up at long intervals to serve as a bone of scholarly contention, and buried again, the more securely, in respectability.

Partly this may be due to the impersonal air apt to grow up about a corporate body, with a life span of two hundred years, as compared with short-lived individuals on whom individual imagination can fasten with readier sympathy. Partly, however, I am sure, a certain confusion of assessment is responsible, which has affected the intrinsic deserts of the Templars and which has thus befogged the causes, the pattern and the significance of their rise and downfall.

Were the Templars "good" or were they "bad," and therefore, was their extraordinary power a good thing or an ill, their end a matter for satisfaction or an unpardonable injustice? In the repeated endeavor to settle this question first and foremost, as a basis from which investigation might be launched, the subject seems to have become detached from its general context, in which alone it can be understood: the context of the life, institutions and ideas, as well as the military events and manifold political import, of the crusading era.

Suspending judgment of the Temple's development in order to appraise it as a phenomenon pure and simple from every relevant aspect, one finds a distinct law and order of growth and decline, cause and effect, in what had appeared a chaos of turbid contradictions. And while from the moral point of view we still look in vain for black or white, a comprehensive spectrum of grays is revealed, such as we have learned to recognize as the palette of truth — notwithstanding the colorful background of the age and the remaining gaps in our information.

To do justice to both background and theme in one limited framework, a great deal of fascinating material had necessarily to be sacrificed, and the reader's indulgence is asked, should he miss in these pages some favorite incident or personage. Throughout, I have given preference to salient detail, typifying the particular always in relation to the general. To assist anyone wishing to fill in the rest, I have given a list of the main works consulted, at the end of the book. For a complete picture of the Crusades one cannot do better than read Sir Steven Runciman's great work and its exhaustive bibliography, with supplementary reference to the *Historical Atlas of the Muslim Peoples* by R. Roolvink, which provides most graphic and dynamic illustration.

In the interests of clarity, I have kept down the number of proper names to a minimum, only giving those of persons who figure prominently in the story. This applies especially to the names of Arabic, Persian and Mongol origin with their unfamiliar constellations of letters, a profusion of which tends to confound their purpose of distinctive identification. Christian names are generally given in their English version. As for the suffix "de," I have differentiated between designations which, though still referring to a man's place of origin, are in effect surnames, and the titles of princes and other sovereign rulers of given territories. In the case of the former, "de" is used, and in the latter's, "of." Spelling of names varies a great deal, almost from book to book, and I have adopted whichever variant seemed to me the most simple phonetically and the best calculated to distinguish characters from one another.

The Christian year was yet far from standardized in the Middle Ages; indeed, the Gregorian Calendar was not devised until the sixteenth century and not universally embraced until the nineteenth. My dates follow present-day reckoning, taking January 1 as the beginning of each year.

Assessing ancient currencies in modern terms is a precarious undertaking, even when the weights of the different coins are accurately known, because of infinite variations in purchasing power, and it can never be more than approximate. In view of the constant rapid changes in contemporary monetary values, the validity of any comparative tables also is extremely fleeting. I have therefore leveled dinars, besants, florins, francs and the rest to "gold pieces" for the most part — a term which will always convey the desired idea even without an exact equivalent.

Of the illustrations, few are strictly contemporary with the subjects, and few of the portraits would seem to be actual likenesses. But although most of the representations, of people and places and scenes, are imaginary, they were made within a few hundred years (frequently less) of the events depicted, in times more slow-moving than ours with regard to engines, tools, costume and the like; and apart from their beauty and the devoted workmanship of the day, they communicate to us the impact of those events on the medieval Western imagination — purveying, one might say, realism in another dimension.

My friend Joan Feisenberger was responsible for unearthing the majority of them, and I am happy to acknowledge my debt to her generous and perceptive labors. The index also is her work.

I wish to thank the following for their courteous co-operation: the Trustees of the British Museum; la Biblioteca Apostolica Vaticana; die Österreichische National-Bibliothek; Monsieur O. Estrade-Fuerra of the Bibliothèque Nationale; H. A. C. Sturgess, Esq., Librarian of the Honorable Society of the Middle Temple; Miss Edmonds, Librarian of the Order of St. John of Jerusalem; Sir Steven Runciman; the Director-General of the Papal Monuments, Museums and Galleries; Monsieur Louradour of Maissonises, Creuse, Secretary of the Archaeological Society of Creuse; la Bibliothèque Nationale (Caisse Nationale des Monuments Historiques); also Messieurs Methuen and Company, the Cambridge University Press, and the Golden Cockerel Press and Professor Arnold Lawrence, for permission to quote from, respectively, Charles Oman's *A History of the Art of War in the Middle Ages,* Steven Runciman's *A History of the Crusades* and T. E. Lawrence's *Crusader Castles.*

I am very grateful to my sister, Inge Goodwin, for her admirable translations of the verse appearing on pp. 145 and 165–166; and as always my greatest thanks must go to my husband, Eric Reeve, for his constant support, inspiration and forbearance.

E. S.

Contents

ILLUSTRATIONS

Photographs appear between pages 166-167

MAPS AND PLANS

Part One

The Creators

1 The Age

By A.D. 1118 in Christian reckoning, it was obvious that the end of the world, originally expected for the year 1000, had been postponed, perhaps indefinitely. Anticlimax and relief had had time enough to settle. The second coming of Christ and the millennium of His reign on earth no longer figured in human calculations for the immediate future. When nothing happened upon the completion of the first thousand years, it had been reasoned that naturally the Saviour would not return so long as His native resorts were under occupation by the Infidel. But the Holy City had fallen to the Christian armies under Godfrey de Bouillon in 1099, and the Kingdom of Jerusalem was nearly twenty years old. So the concept of the New Jerusalem, an ideal, spiritual realm representing perfection, consolation and paradise, had become confused with the actual earthly city; it had gone under in the precarious reality of a commonwealth maintained on enemy territory. The millennium had been replaced by the Crusades as a factor in the world.

Peace had returned to the status of a metaphysical condition. Peace was in Heaven, to be achieved by the disembodied soul. On earth there was no peace. Wars great and petty were periodically concluded, that was all. Even the "Truce of God," imposed by the Church in France to reduce the perpetual bloodshed in the land with a prohibition of all fighting from Thursday evenings to Tuesday mornings, during Lent and on every holy day, had more or less lapsed again. To the knowledge of men everywhere, war was a concomitant of existence, feudal society organized for a state of permanent general mobilization.

Warfare laid the ground plan of cottage and castle; towns, few and far between, grew in accordance with the needs of it; human relations and standards of behavior were regulated thereby; fashions in clothes, of women and burgesses as of warriors, closely mirrored the development of armor. Life had few elements of certainty, uncertainty itself being perhaps the most positive of these. Death was one: teeming, besetting, familiar component of everyday. Heaven was another, and with it went Hell. Men might sin, but knew that they were sinning.

They also knew that if they did not eat, they died; that without land for crops and cattle there could be no food, and that all mundane power was derived from land and rested in its possession. They knew the wheel, the plough, the arts of weaving, building in stone and working metal. They did not know the eating fork, the button, the cultivation of root crops; the arts of knitting, printing and manufacturing explosives; the nature and prevention of disease.

They knew a certain heathen superstition that the earth was spherical to have been discredited long since, though neither was it true that the earth terminated in a sheer abyss beyond the Pillars of Hercules at Gibraltar, as had once been believed. They knew of a species of goose born of barnacles, they knew that in some part of Africa lived a race of two-headed men, that there were mermaids, homicidal trees and dragons — none any more incredible, surely, than hermits spending their lives immured with their own dung, vast elaborate cathedrals erected virtually with bare hands, strange Eastern sects such as the Assassins — or, for that matter, caterpillars turning into butterflies, to say nothing of electricity and other dynamic forces whose fantastic evidence many of us take on trust in our own day.

Of their day, they were the modern men.

About 1118, a knight from Champagne named Hugh de Payens founded a new movement, of the utmost modernity, in that it responded precisely to the particular requirements of time and place which had inspired it. He formed a fellowship for the protection of pilgrims and of the roads in the Holy Land.

It was one of those conceptions, strikingly simple and obvious once they become fact.

The stream of pilgrims from all over Europe was unceasing, coming singly, in pairs, by groups and entire uprooted communities sometimes, sometimes accompanying merchant caravans, and sometimes in straggling bodies of as many as a thousand men, women and even children. The roads, such as they were, could hardly have been more insecure.

They led along the stormy coast, through desert without shelter and treacherous rocky terrain, through wilderness of thorn, ideal for ambush, at the mercy alike of friend and foe: friend being rather a loose term, applied to soldiers for whom pillage was the normal course of forage and the harrying of the helpless a traditional outlet. And flying patrols of the enemy were everywhere.

The road tolls were the chief revenue of the Kingdom of Jerusalem, and safe pilgrimage had been a prime inspiration of the earliest Crusades, an inalienable part of the Advocacy of the Holy Sepulchre, which was the very basis of the King's title. Yet so far the pilgrims had been nobody's responsibility. To all intents and purposes they were on their own; they could on occasion get in the way of troop movements, aggravate the trials of a siege, and when they were captured but not killed added to the burden of ransoming transactions.

As so often, humanitarian considerations held a reward of practical profit.

But while this might partly motivate the support with which the new movement was to meet, it was as yet outside the range of vision of the obscure knights who first promoted it. Their intentions were simple and benevolent, their zeal had all the freshness of beginning, piety showed the way in which some personal tragedy or disappointment, perhaps Christian fury, or even purely chivalric aspirations might be visited on the Saracen in the service of others. However, something more than a common purpose was needed to hold them together.

The monastic brotherhoods furnished a model of close-knit permanence transcending individual instability. Hugh de Payens and his companions bound themselves by solemn vow to live after the manner of regular canons and fight for the King of Heaven in chastity, obedience and self-denial. They cropped their hair and let their beards grow long and unkempt, foreswore the pride and distraction of all personal property save their arms, and for food and clothing confined themselves to the charity of the faithful. As far as possible they followed the Rule of St. Augustine, the inventor of collegiate monasticism.

There was, then, nothing particularly new about their pledged way of life — except in the emphasis on fighting, on armed combat in the literal sense. Here there was novelty indeed. Ever since their inception, more than seven hundred years before, such orders had been of their very essence pacifist. Moreover, St. Augustine had expressly laid it down that all bloodshed was mortal sin and that no cause, however good, however sacred, could under any circumstances justify war as such. But the Church and its dogma had come a long way since then.

Even so, an *order* of fighting men must at first have seemed a contradiction in terms. Yet here in this combination was the answer to more than one problem. Composed of many nationalities, speaking diverse languages, activated by every shade of impulse, commanded by leaders in virtually constant mutual rivalry, the Crusaders had hitherto lacked any, as it were, independent contingent to co-ordinate all those with axes to grind of varying ambition and political alignment. The priests and monks who accompanied them but who did not bear arms (except in isolated cases of emergency) could never constitute such a body; for all their spiritual authority, they carried little weight outside their province. A fraternity of warriors linked under a strict religious rule provided an admirable corps of liaison. Also, if such a fraternity attained definite canonical standing, it would once and for all vindicate the profession of arms, hitherto merely licensed, not sanctified, by the cross which all Crusaders wore upon their mantles. Lastly, the ordinary crusader could at any time tear off his badge and go home, generally having given his oath of service for a limited period. A military order formed to guard the roads of the Holy Land must stay, having no reason for existence elsewhere; old members might die and new ones join up, but at last there would be a nucleus embodying continuity of policy.

The cogent attractions of a scheme will shine luminously to the eye of hindsight in the light of success. No matter how speedy and spectacular its success, in the beginning the possibility of failure is counterpoised with it. The first and not the least part of Hugh de Payens' success was that his fellows accepted him as their leader. All of them were knights, and knighthood was as yet inseparable from feudal benefice. No one could be a knight who held no land, and a knight's leader was the lord from whom he had his land in fief. But there was no tie of tenure and service, feudal rights and obligations, between Hugh and his chosen band: in their dedication as well as by rank they were only equals.

Success in their immediate chosen activity gave less cause for wonder. Such men as they were practiced in all branches of arms from their youth and had had some experience of warfare in these parts; both their estate and their devotion would help to impose confident discipline on their charges.

The fellowship rapidly expanded and soon found support in the most powerful circles. Princes, prelates and high officials rallied to their assistance with a rare unanimity, rare despatch, and to an altogether astonishing extent. Within ten years — and in those days of slow communications, of slow, confused and erratic developments, ten years was very little time indeed — this collection of obscure knights had become a force, recognized and honored.

Granted that they filled a need, that the time was ripe, the end righteous, the means accounted noble, and the result useful — still this could not wholly account for so rapid a rise. Who and what was Hugh de Payens that he should have won success so wide and varied, including the respect of the common soldiery and the affectionate regard of the most influential and most personally good of clerics in all Christendom, St. Bernard of Clairvaux, who referred to him as *carissimus meus Hugo,* "my own dearest Hugh"?

He was the son of a small noble owing fealty and service to the counts of Champagne. He was born in a fortified manor, at the core of the concentric zones of such a place: the keep, that strongest tower where they kept the stores, the treasure and the women; last line of defense in the event of assault, just as the stagnant moat around the outer curtain wall was the first. He was born in straw spread for his mother's travail, he was swaddled tight as a prisoner to make his limbs grow straight, duly cleansed of original sin by baptism, acclaimed by the serfs of his father, suckled by a low-born nurse who for a time would be his cradle and constant conveyance also. He was then a creature of small consequence, except among the women, and even they had seen too many like him die in the first few months of life to regard him as much more than an egg, a larva, a bud which might or might not be spared to ripen into a person. The anthropologist of today would have a good deal to say about the shaping of personality by this general pattern of upbringing, with its dual effect of restraint and aggression, methodically thwarted impulse and admiration of force. In fact this forms a discernible tributary to the background currents of the whole Crusades, helping to exalt land hunger and lust for adventure into a tremendous campaign for an ultimate, and loftier, peace; and also helping to pervert the genuine ideals which played a large part in the original impetus.

The education of the child proceeded, from the bottom up. When he began to crawl and stagger on two feet, he would roll in the thick litter of the floor, mixed with bones and other food remains and indeed the refuse of every domestic activity, the dogs his playmates and competitors. He learned to know the men mainly by their feet — entering booted, splashed and caked with mud, heavy spurs strapped to them and blood upon the spikes; changing into sandals, high-soled pattens, brocaded shoes set with jewels, or else to pad along bare, or in laced leather hose, or strips of cloth bound with thongs, in accordance with their degree.

He ate wheaten bread sometimes when the fortunes of the house warranted it; otherwise there was mainly meat: pork, beef and vension, the cheeses furnished by the villagers, and rye or barley for both food and drink. Towards the end of winter and in spring he did not fare very well, better in summer, and gloriously at harvest time and after the autumn slaughtering.

During the cold season he lived in a damp twilight among fierce draughts, hangings, full of vermin and constant smoke from the fire. So the release of spring made him one with all nature in a joy as compelling and instinctive as the sheer bodily shiver of cold or a sneeze. Man's independence from his environment was yet small, for good and for ill.

He passed the first grade of the school for manhood: he had survived. He was acknowledged as a forked creature and breeched, he was ac-

knowledged as a male and taken away from the women. Now he began
to learn to know men by their condition and to judge it by their gait.
For their garments did not always give reliable indication, save on feast
days and in war, and even then hazard could easily deprive anyone of
his accoutrements; while, under penitential vow, the mightiest would go
in sackcloth and ashes. The Emperor Henry IV had done homage to
Pope Gregory VII, standing barefoot in the snow before the fortress of
Canossa, until the Holy Father relented and let him in; and pilgrims were
to be met on every road. (For the matter of that, it was on the whole to
the pilgrim's advantage to walk in poverty — or he might fall victim to
robbery and torture not so very far from home. Many of the nobles in
their castles habitually supplemented their incomes in this fashion; merchants and other travelers were fair game. To go on a journey, it needed
courage, or sufficient means to hire armed protection, and pressing compulsion besides.)

Nothing could disguise the stoop of the husbandman or the equestrian
walk of the noble, accustomed as he was from childhood to spending
a considerable portion of his life on horseback. Quite apart from their
divergent activities, an entirely different set of muscles would tend to be
developed, according as a man shambled furtively in the constant insecurity of helplessness, or, sword in hand, knew himself free and proud
and fearless.

The growing lad was trained in running, leaping, climbing, swim-
ming, as well as learning to handle all the weapons of his era; he was
introduced to the elements of that most highly esteemed of recreations,
the chase, which, especially in its branch of falconry, also furnished the
aristocracy with its chief subject of intellectual application and of small
talk. Horsemanship in itself was a complete branch of education. The
warhorse was bred for viciousness and fire, taught to savage the opponent's mount even as his rider attacked the other, and took much
strength and skill to handle, in or out of battle.

By the time that, still a child, the cadet was taken from his home to
serve as a page elsewhere — in the household of the family's overlord if
he was lucky — he was a man and knight in miniature, imbued with the

nature and the standards of his world, which (comparably to the three R's of later ages) would technically fit him to acquire all such skills and wisdom as remained, so long as he had the quality for it.

This was perhaps the hardest stage of his career, the first loneliness and apprehension of the child the least of his trials — for all that any good-by might as likely as not be final, since sudden death in every form lurked everywhere, for everyone. In the noble household, the page was the lowest form of life, not counting servants; at the tail end of a chain each link of which visited on the next the superior power, wit, caprice and harshness of the one above.

When he was considered fit, he became a squire, privileged to bear his lord's cup and cut his meat for him, take messages and act as standard bearer, all the while continuing in the pursuit of his own proficiency. It might fall to his share of duty to assist his lord into armor — no light task, although armor had not yet developed to that stage where every man was, so to speak, his own tank, where knights appeared as robot-like cylindrical specters, yet were so heavy that it would require engines to hoist them into the saddle. Altogether, this was his term of most concentrated practice in the principles of fidelity, that oath-bound cement of the entire structure of society. Only death or formal release could free the vassal, and even then he must find a new liege: the masterless man was no more viable than the lord without servants. His lord's interests transcended his own and those of any higher authority. He stayed the lord in battle, raised him up if he was unhorsed, yielding up his own mount if the lord's had been disabled; he must bend all his energy on rescuing the lord if he was captured, carry him to safety if wounded, bury him honorably if killed.

When after some years he was judged to have passed every test, he crossed the final threshold of initiation, in a long vigil before God's altar, concluded by priestly blessing of his sword. Then, decked in new clothes and equipped with shield and armor of his very own, he took his place within the ranks of chivalry, his great bridal day made memorable with every ceremony of consecration and of knightly entertainments.

For there was this, too: religion entered into everything. God was omnipresent, an incongruous guest even where the deeds of men most diligently denied Him. The sky was near as yet, not infinite, the ceiling of the world and by that token the floor of Heaven — with the deity ever spying through the chinks. He might be flouted, but was palpable in pursuit. The less they served Him, the more men must propitiate Him. The cross was the only charm that availed against the inimical magic of sorcery and demons infesting the universe.

So while fear of hellfire did not prevent transgression, the sinner was prepared to undergo any penance in atonement. He could not live cut off from God and men. For to be excommunicate meant being shunned by all, debarred from all human dealings whatsoever as well as from the ministrations of the Church, in the most thoroughgoing boycott, with international effect, moreover, at least wherever the Roman faith prevailed. A great magnate, all-powerful within the orbit of his sword and by virtue of it economically self-contained, might be able for a time to ignore the social pressure (although the ban dissolved all bonds of fealty also). But the sense of imminent disaster inevitably brought on by the spiritual isolation, of hopeless conflict with a power against which even he would never have a chance, exerted pressure inescapable in the long run.

Few men would not have had occasion to bid farewell to people sent on pilgrimage by ecclesiastical dictate or by their own vow. Whether consciously or no, few would have failed to note the beneficial outcome. Removed from the scene of his misdeeds and from the routine concerns of his ordinary life, the penitent returned cleansed, refreshed, at peace with his Maker, his horizon enlarged, his soul swept and garnished, his repute increased — and having been away long enough for any local excitement about him to have died down. If he did not return, the probabilities were that he had either gone straight up to Heaven, all his sins remitted, or else made his fortune overseas. It was emigration with a difference, combining merit with improved prospects.

In the meantime the daily round went on at home. Every community was an island hacked and burned out of the forests densely covering most of Western Europe, and liable at any moment to being cut off from the rest. Each had to be as far as possible self-sufficient. Farmstead, village, town or castle, each had its first seed in the water supply, though the ground where it was placed would naturally vary in point of quality or strategic considerations. It was not the thickness of its walls alone, nor its position on a rocky eminence, that would make a fortress impregnable, but the possession of a spring within.

Produce was brought in by the serfs: so much grain in rent per so much arable, so many days of labor service per pair of hands, annually; straw, wool, flax, hides, firewood and winter fodder, beasts and fowl and fish in season; cured meat, cheese, ale according to assessment, likewise men to act as infantry in the lord's campaigns or be at the disposal of the lord's lord. The value of a domain was denominated by these fixed dues. For all the stress on land, therefore, wealth and strength were reckoned in terms of human beings. For all the rigid stratification of society, human interdependence was close-knit and constantly in evidence. And for all that manual work was low-esteemed, the product of craftsmanship, always personal, would communicate the maker's satisfaction to the owner, too.

The isolated farmer's comforts and potentialities were limited by what he happened to be able to turn his hand to. The castle must have its own artisans on the premises: farrier, tanner, carpenter, mason and armorer, or men combining these trades with other, routine duties. Yet where labor is the cheapest of commodities, the number of servants restricted only by the master's capacity of feeding them, the tendency will be for overstaffing. The great feudal household was wasteful and inefficient; for the servant, it was full of arbitrariness but also full of sinecures. The day was ample, although dusk was bedtime; though play could easily be fatal, there was plenty of it.

The world, vaster and more mysterious than ours since so much of it was unknown, was nonetheless more manageable; it was still possible for the single mind to encompass most aspects of life and to gain at least a smattering of them. A member of the lord's mesne would see the law in action, and absorb the first principles of engineering as he watched a wagon being made, it might be, or the mangonel in operation. He was acquainted with the chemistry of brewing and of atmospheric conditions which must be taken into account with regard to the storage and care of arms. He was familiar with textile manufacture, the work of the women, from carding, spinning, weaving to the most intricate embroidery.

Ecclesiastical vestments had only recently emerged as an exclusive uniform, but yet continued to follow the fashions in secular festive and ceremonial robes which eventually they would preserve even into our day. The bishop's cope that we know is a guide to the mantle of the medieval prince, example of the artistry, patience and precious materials lavished on it.

However, feast days excepted, the nobleman's apparel was determined by the need to wear armor. He had to have clothes suitable to being worn underneath and others to go on top; clothes to protect the body against the very impact of encasing mail under the blow it held off; clothes serving the dual purpose of identification and of overawing the foe in combat. Tunics of linen and of wool were customary, with jacket and breeches of sheepskins under the hauberk, though crusaders returned from the Orient were popularizing quilted fabrics as used by the Saracen. The veil of Eastern womanhood and the home-grown masculine helmet of iron merged their discrepant textures in the form of wimples, coverchiefs and very gorgets which became the mode for ladies. In the same way, the flamboyant surcoat of the knight embattled reappeared, exaggerated and sometimes so low-cut as to resemble the merest harness, over the gown of his consort. With slashes in sleeves and chausses and fantastic crenellations of the skirt hem, both sexes in their leisure hours paid tribute still to the merit of battle damage. At the same time, as throughout the ages, the rich and mighty would dissociate themselves from all toil by means of extravagancies in dress hindering movement and quite prohibitive of menial pursuits. Sleeves swept the floor, shoes ran to points so elongated they had to be tied back to the ankle by little chains. Attempts were made to restrict such features of distinction to persons of noble estate. Nonetheless those who could afford it would reflect the high fashions. You scarcely hanged a man for wearing velvet:

to carry sword and blazoned shield without title would be another matter.

But velvet and silks, damask and cloth of gold could not be made at home, nor could any good armor other than ring mail, good weapons other than bow and arrow, nor raw metal, usually, gems, glass and, a further Eastern importation, sugar. Such commodities had to be brought in from outside. To buy, one needs to own surplus of goods, and ready money. To obtain surplus of wealth beyond consumption, one might grant to a villein exemption from services against special payment, or sell various rights to some community as a whole — the right, say, to build and man its own enclosing wall, the right to control its own toll gate and mill its own flour, the right to admit new settlers, the right of association in trade guilds, and so forth. Thus, step by hard-wrung step, a town began to grow, with institutions no longer exclusively subservient to the interests of the lord.

Pursuing his own interest without overmuch theoretical forethought, the lord was caught unawares in the interaction here of gain to him and loss. Not many had the vision to see the loss in immediate power as an ultimate investment which would bring dividends in the shape of untold material benefit as well as civilization in a seemingly more abstract sense. Not a few raged and struggled against a process of emancipation they had themselves helped to instigate and which they continued to advance at the same time as they opposed its manifestations. A handful of the great did appreciate the trend, and favored it in active policy. But the majority went so far as to obstruct the clearance of more land for cultivation although this could only have increased their revenues: fundamentally a blind, emotional reaction, which, however, in the usual way, might arm itself with a full arsenal of good reasons. These ranged from the danger of strengthening the commonalty to the decay of hunting if the great forests were to become any smaller.

A vassal with eyes to see would be confronted with illustrations of each point of view, as he rode in his lord's train, on progress through the lord's lands once a year. Everywhere it was the duty of the inhabitants to furnish sustenance, shelter, change of horses, and any necessary repair services to the lord with his entire household. Cases are on record, of the population with much of its stores and livestock taking to the hills until the visitants had passed.

But that was only one side of the event. For an event it was, alike for high and low: a break, excitement, news, excursion, high living; song and sport and dance. Disputes and probate would be settled, marriages having had to wait the lord's approval might be concluded; and so in many respects the date was anxiously awaited.

The love match, the legal union of a man and a woman on a basis of purely personal desires, played a greater part among the people than where property and alliances were primarily involved. Just as the villein's costume had no function other than utility and had remained roughly the same since time immemorial, so might his private life run along more straightforward, timeless lines — though of course it ceased to be private when the seigneur's concerns cut across it.

In practice love, in and outside marriage, did have its place among the higher strata also — which reservation is neither superfluous nor satirical. There are cultures on a hardly more primitive level where love in our comprehensive meaning is as unknown as the science of astronomy and no less inconceivable than the universe, and in fact there was no, as it were, official provision for it in the feudal scheme of things. But the very negative preoccupation of the religious with woman as the representative of earthly lusts and ties, on the one hand, and on the other, the cult of the Virgin Mary, which was gaining ground, had begun to enlarge the contemporary view of sexual relations. The day was not yet when adultery, spiritualized and glorified, would come to stand for the finest flower of human relations altogether — but that day was not far off.

Peasant and noble married young, often at puberty and, for reasons of state, sometimes in infancy. Disparity in ages was no hindrance where both men and women must count on being widowed, perhaps more than once in a lifetime, mortality in warfare being quite as high as in childbirth, and recovery from illness the exception rather than the rule. There were no old maids and no bachelors except in convents.

In the lord's castle girls were schooled as well as boys: orphan heiresses under his guardianship, poor relations, daughters of the house, and the wives of his retinue, all surrounding the lady with her own hierarchical court. The young knight grew to manhood with plenty of feminine company to draw on, be he never so bashful or haughty in his pride of sex. Life was at all times gregarious. In persons of importance, even birth would be a public affair, and the nuptial bed, if not actually beset by witnesses, would be inspected and displayed for evidence of consummation as a matter of course. As for death — how could that be solitary, save by accident, where a person was either so great as to command the same attendance at his passing as in life, or else would not possess a bed, much less a room, to himself?

Death in bed, from sickness or old age, indeed was an object lesson in the aspirant warrior's curriculum. If his valor were imperfect, he need only observe the misery of the invalid in a day that knew no bedsprings and no bedpans, no antiseptics, deodorants, insecticides, painstilling drugs, false teeth, nor bandages other than rags, and precious little kindness lingering beyond any creature's usefulness: need he see more to know it in his very bones that death in battle was the most desirable?

Hugh de Payens was a widower when first he came to the attention of the chroniclers — whether his wife died while he was away or whether her death had influenced his decision to go. He was already middle-aged when he set out, and his one son of whom we know had embraced the religious life. So there is a hint of family troubles, or at least domestic calamity, such as not infrequently helped to speed the crusader. A case in point was Hugh's liege, the Count of Champagne (also named Hugh), who disinherited his son and left his lands to a nephew before embarking on his pious adventure.

But Hugh de Payens had not waited for the count. Pilgrimage was one activity overriding the obligations of fealty — another attraction. No man needed the permission of his master, and no man could command his servants to accompany him. There were always plenty importuning him to take them.

Preparations were extensive, when absence might run into years, or be for good. Not only had a man to order his affairs, but he must raise funds for his following, men, horses and equipment, enough to see them through the long ride overland and provide for their transport by sea. Among men of high degree as of low, both Hughs were by no means exceptional in abandoning all worldly goods that they could not take with them to Palestine. Never had the French Crown held so much territory as now, when many nobles sold their lands to finance their expeditions; never had the Church received so much in gifts; and never had it been so profitable to take in pledge anything from a hovel to a dukedom. Never, also, had it been so feasible to make the wrench away from everything familiar, binding and oppressive.

At last the great day came, of departure under solemn priestly benediction, amid prayer, weeping and acclaim, respect and envy, the cross flying ahead on the banner, the cross on every cloak; behind them the deluge, for all that they would know about it, before them the extraordinary experience of meeting up in actuality with places that were landmarks of the spirit, names identified with myths, the stuff of visions indescribable by the vocabulary of physical comparisons.

Although ever since the time of Charlemagne the Frankish states, which had formed the heart of his empire, had held themselves peculiarly associated with the protection of the Holy Land, the Provençal seaports had not yet become the chief stapling places of the crusading traffic. The merchant cities of the Italian coast had the most developed harbors and the most ships for hire. The land route, through Byzantium via the Balkans, was cheaper — cheaper in the short run, however, for the journey then might take years instead of months, and the chances of ever reaching one's destination were not good.

The great hordes of the First Crusade had gone overland, and all along those regions had acted as a fine strainer, passing only a small proportion of pilgrims (armed or unarmed) and retaining a thick sediment of the bones of thousands.

There was one other passage, leading from the British Isles around the Iberian seaboard. But here the Straits of Gibraltar, harried by Moslem pirates, formed an even more stringent filter. It was advisable for the

English crusader, and for the Scandinavian, to make his way through France and Italy.

The way from the Seine valley across the Alps was hazardous enough. It led through marsh and forest, rivers and mountainland, along roads which often were little more than a convention like the network of meridians and parallels that marks our globe, save where the ruts graven by the traffic between given communities rendered them unmistakable, or where the highway owed its origin to the old Roman Empire. Inns were rare and in the main an urban feature. At best the travelers could hope to be the guests of local seigneurs, at worst expect to kill or be killed for what they needed. Dust and mire, skirmish and evasion, barter and feast days would slow them down, and it would be most unusual if here and there the train was not swelled by strangers offering their oath, pilgrims who had been awaiting such an opportunity, and loose women smuggled along in the baggage train.

Arrived at the coast, the travelers would be fortunate to find a vessel ready to convey them across the Mediterranean immediately. They might have to wait months. They might have to charter a whole ship, or split up to go as passengers. Often an interpreter would be needed to strike a bargain with some ship's master who did not speak their language — by which the chance of being cheated was increased.

Here was a form of robbery they were not inured to. There were the negotiations for lodgings and converting currency, the tempting markets, streets thronged with pickpockets, cutthroats, confidence tricksters, besides jugglers, mendicants, a large selection of prostitutes, and tokens in every form, living and inanimate, of commerce with the Orient. Here was not only a port of embarkation, but also a trap for purpose and pocket which not every traveler succeeded in eluding. Holiday recklessness was framed to quick irascibility and swagger by a mixture of mistrust and overconfidence. Already the unknown had been braved and numerous vicissitudes lay behind; already old-accustomed rules of conduct seemed less valid.

The voyage was made by sailing ship or galley, exposed to ills against which valor could not guard: seasickness, storms, pirates, shipwreck, monsters or misnavigation. The rolling of those small vessels was fearful, the calking inadequate, their stench infernal; and instruments like compass and astrolabe were only beginning to come into Western use. Sun, moon and stars were yet the mariner's most reliable aids, out of action on cloudy nights and in bad weather, experience his best sextant. To replace drinking water, sheets were spread to catch the rain and then wrung out into containers. The horses stowed below the waterline added to the cramped confusion and suffered pitifully, with only a percentage surviving to land. Yet men were conditioned to take such things in their stride. Everything in their nurture and outlook inclined them to meet hardship as a test — when they were not thoroughly habituated to it.

All being well, the sacred land of Outremer, the land Across-the-Sea, would be sighted after four or five weeks. Acre, with its sheltered harbor and strong fortifications, not long in Christian hands, had by this time become the principal port. The town of Acre might in part resemble a gigantic fairground, like the places of embarkation, but, dominated by its military functions, was still more like a garrison on a grandiose scale. One could get one's bearings soon and feel at home, in spite of the alien environment. Strange, arid, hallowed, arousing every emotion from astonishment to deepest religious feeling even in the wicked and the blasé Christian, the Holy Land swarmed with men of his own sort, not necessarily speaking his language,* but all serving the same cause. He was reassured by familiar organization. He came as a conqueror, in the wake of conquest. And knowing that if he died here, it would be in a state of grace, he swiftly assimilated the widespread notion that one might as well be saved for a sheep as for a lamb.

As for the politics of the country, it would be some time till he could see the wood for trees, discern the main trends in the medley of their interaction. It would take time so much as to get the leading names straight, let alone the shades of difference between the factions and their objectives.

One Baldwin was King of Jerusalem, another Count of Edessa, the Archbishop of Caesarea was called Baldwin, and the same name

* In the armies of the First Crusade nineteen languages were officially recognized.

cropped up again and again, among barons, soldiers and clerics; nor was it lacking in men who had no title to distinguish it and had to fall back on epithets. There were Stephens: of Blois, of Boulogne, of Burgundy, of St. Pol; notable Raymonds and Adhemars abounded; many, too, shared the name of Hugh. To make matters worse, any one of these might own half a dozen different sobriquets, connected with personal characteristics or feat of arms.

Admittedly, the man who could neither read nor write had the advantage there, with a more serviceable memory, expert in reeling off genealogies and detailed territorial lore, as illiterate peoples are to this day. The layman who knew his letters was extremely rare, though the utility of the written word even in war had been convincingly demonstrated during the siege of Sidon, when an arrow shot into King Baldwin's camp with a message had defeated a plot to murder him.

That learned, saving arrow had been sent by a native Christian resident in the besieged town. The native Christians added further complexity to the situation. They were not always so friendly. Belonging to a variety of sects, in that state of brotherly hostility which is what makes civil war more savage than war between different nations, some of them had suffered cruelly at the hands of the first Crusaders. Many had preferred to emigrate with the retreating Moslems, as had the Jews. Those who stayed on had had to resign themselves to the status of fourth-class citizens, treated at best with contempt by the warriors and colonists from Western Europe — especially by the newly arrived. Since fresh manpower was the foremost requirement of Outremer, there were, for every one acclimatized and seeking to establish integral relations with the natives, a dozen newcomers to spurn them and raise an outcry against the decline of good old Frankish ways among their precursors.

Yet in order to survive here, they must learn to adapt themselves to the climate and conditions of this country, parched and fever-ridden as it was, and devastated by countless campaigns. The blame for so much ruin did not lie with them alone. The Moslems were divided among themselves still more deviously than the Christians, and by their own unceasing internal strife had contributed no small share to the Frankish victories and the impoverishment of the land.

The wonder of it was, then, not so much that the French dialects of the colonists already showed exotic deviations, nor that their physical and moral fiber was deteriorating, but that in the midst of ravage and decay they managed to live in such splendor.

Kings in Western Europe were ignorant of luxuries which the ordinary châtelain had come to take for granted here. Accustomed to slabs of timber laid on trestles for his meals at home, the newcomer for the first time sat at tables that were delicate units, carved and intricately inlaid. Exquisite napery, dinner services of gold and silver, cups of faience, finely wrought cutlery were common table furniture. Instead of straw and rushes, the floors had handsome carpets, often covering mosaics; beds were sheeted in whitest linen, sometimes in silk, which also swathed the residents on social occasions. The bath, an infrequent ceremonial amenity where they came from,* was here considered a daily necessity; there was constant washing of hands in perfumed water, and handsomely appointed baths formed an indispensable feature of every civic center. The women's quarters were delightful places which the parlors of even the wealthiest European nunneries could not equal. Unknown fruits from the tropical Jordan valley and unbelievable confections of sweetmeats were everyday side dishes. Physicians, informed with the dying echoes of Hellenic science and some heritage from the priestly anatomists of ancient Egypt, were savants here, no mere barbers and butchers or empirically practicing housewives, and really could alleviate much suffering — provided one was not too hidebound to avail oneself of them. Aqueducts and piped water were familiar means of supplying mansions that had not their own wells or storage tanks; and at Jerusalem, for all its crumbling walls, the durable sewage system built by the Romans was still in operation after well-nigh a thousand years of repeated siege and sack.

* The Knights of the Bath derived their appellation from this noteworthy feature of their order's initiation ceremony.

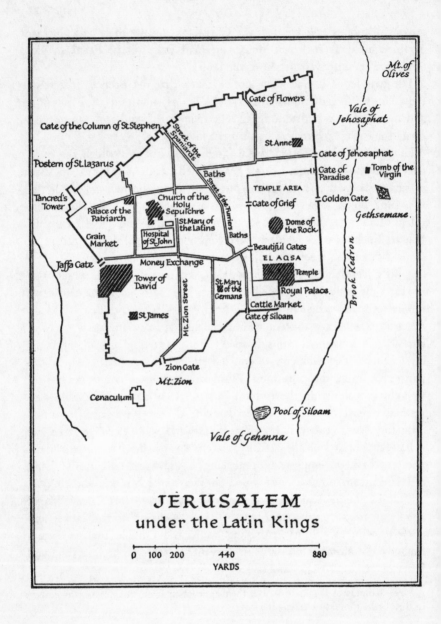

JERUSALEM
under the Latin Kings

Mt. of Olives

Gate of Flowers

Gate of the Column of St. Stephen

Street of the Spaniards

Vale of Jehosaphat

St. Anne

Postern of St. Lazarus

Gate of Jehosaphat

Baths

Gate of Paradise

Tomb of the Virgin

Tancred's Tower

Street of the Furriers

TEMPLE AREA

Golden Gate

Gethsemane

Palace of the Patriarch

Church of the Holy Sepulchre

Gate of Grief

Dome of the Rock

Grain Market

Hospital of St. John

St. Mary of the Latins

Baths

Brook Kedron

Jaffa Gate

Money Exchange

Beautiful Gates

EL AQSA

Tower of David

Temple

St. Mary of the Germans

Royal Palace

St. James

Cattle Market

Gate of Siloam

Mt. Zion Street

Zion Gate

Mt. Zion

Cenaculum

Pool of Siloam

Vale of Gehenna

0   100   200   440   880

YARDS

The city of Jerusalem embodied every inspiration and every incongruity of the kingdom which bore her name. Here were the very streets Jesus had trodden, the very stones had known Him, even though the fabric they made up had been several times destroyed and rebuilt. Here was the site of the Holy Sepulchre, whose aid the Crusader invoked with his famous war cry, *Sepulchrum adjuva!* The Royal Palace stood where Solomon had erected his Temple, and the great sanctuary there, the Dome of the Rock, was a mosque — topped now by the cross, to be sure. The moneychangers had come back in force and occupied not only booths and stalls in the shadows of holy places, but entire streets reserved to the merchant embassies of several nations. The banners and liveries of Frankish magnates, inextricably mixed with the whole crowded oriental scene, made it a home from home: the more so as the concentration of (it is reckoned) at no time more than ten thousand fighting forces in the Holy Land lent the whole set-up, as it were, compact proportions. It was at least possible for everyone to know of everybody else; in principle no one, however eminent, was inaccessible. The Franks were as one huge if infinitely subdivided family — as the German pilgrim John of Würzburg was duly to note, more in indignation than in sorrow.*

In the streets soldiers robustly jostled pilgrims wan and radiant with awe; imperious hoofbeat raised the dust where the devout retracted hallowed tracks on their knees, kissing the ground and watering it with tears of contrition. Litters passed, bearing ladies like stiff idols with their carefully painted faces and jeweled robes; religious processions interrupted other traffic with their hieratic rhythm; signal calls were forever sounding through the hubbub of commerce, litany and chanting of beggars and vendors.

Jerusalem was the center of government as well as the center of three major faiths. Here every faction had its camp and latent warhead, every power its spies. This was the goal of the pious and the springboard of Holy War.

There were new lessons to learn in strategy and fighting tactics. The

---

* For the Crusades, he claimed, were really a German enterprise, likewise the Burgundian Godfrey de Bouillon and all his illustrious kin were Germans really.

fervors of religious hatred, the knowledge of assured heavenly reward produced on both sides capacities one would have thought superhuman. The Saracen had for his allies forces which the Frank must painfully experience before ever he could hope to exploit them for his part: the desert and the sun, the hot khamsin wind stirring up the sands so as to blind and choke and utterly demoralize troops that had been maneuvered to receive it in their faces. The Saracen tactic of keeping a calculated distance from the formations under attack, so as to maintain a rain of arrows shot high into the air and in their descent disabling horses rather than men, foreshadowed Agincourt and thus, already, another age. Trumpets and kettledrums, both Saracen inventions, infused an added potency into their war cries. Indiscipline and greed, however, impartially did fifth-column work for each of the opponents, since a sudden chance of plunder might, even in the midst of fighting, completely disrupt unity of command; while wallowing in the tangible fruits of victory had frequently rendered a victory nought by subsequent failure to press its advantage.

In general, prisoners were taken only when their apparent wealth and standing made it worth while to hold them for ransom or as hostages, though sometimes the young, handsome and strong would be sold in the slave market and others publicly tortured to death.

For the wounded whom it had been possible to rescue from the field of battle and take back to base, the provisions were few and haphazard. The charity of private households or a convent here and there would be their best hope. To us, who know sepsis and shock as most serious agents of fatality, it seems miraculous that the wounded recovered as often as they did, so that the crippled ex-soldier was a common sight.

However, in the last fifty years or so something of a hospital service had begun to evolve. Early in the preceding century, a group of merchants of Amalfi had clubbed together to provide at Jerusalem a hostel for pilgrims of their own nationality, gradually extended to take in others also. With St. John the Almsgiver, a one-time Patriarch of Jerusalem, for patron, the charity had grown until its hostelry could house as many as one thousand pilgrims, and its ministrants ranged far afield, even serving the armies as an occasional ambulance corps, and more and more appropriating the task of caring for the sick and wounded who had no establishments of their own to look after them. The Knights of St. John, as they called themselves, had lately begun to wear a distinctive uniform, abandoning gaudy secular colors for a monklike sobriety of garb: black, with an eight-pointed cross of white, which recently had been honored with formal sanction by the Pope.

But although they thus combined professional acts of mercy with a growing military trend, it had not occurred to the Knights of St. John to beome associated under vow as a regular order.

It was left to the handful of plain knights under the leadership of Hugh de Payens to conceive this brilliant synthesis and so, incidentally, to set off a neck-to-neck race of rivalry between the two groups. Thus was started a movement which in its rise, apex and decline, its enthusiastic drive, its triumphant sway and later its débâcle, reflected the pattern of the entire Crusades within which it occurred. The seed of success must carry also the germ of ultimate downfall; the effects of the former must be numbered among the causes of the latter. It is this process which we want to trace.

As for the originator, very little is known about Hugh de Payens. We do not know the date of his birth, what he looked like, nor his precise personal circumstances. We do know that he was a veteran of Outremer, we know the background and influences that went to shape him, we know of his achievement. We can deduce with some assurance the type of character and intelligence which had assimilated his world to such effect. Since during his lifetime he acted throughout as the representative and ambassador of his order, extremely successfully, he must have managed to make himself acceptable to an infinite range of interests. Since, however, his personality does not emerge built up in detail, the hypnotic, overbearing species of magnetism, which takes care that there shall be monumental portraits of its possessor, would seem to be ruled out. There is one other kind of universal appeal, compounded of sincerity, confidence and unfailing natural resource.

2 The Founding

EVERY AGE HAS ITS OWN IDEALS OF BEAUTY, GOODNESS AND PERSONALITY, but the practical joke is universal and timeless. It had all started almost as a boyish prank one day. Hugh de Payens and a friend decided to hide by a watering place on the open road where the pilgrim transports were wont to stop for refreshment and which consequently was a favorite Saracen ambush. Imagine — as they might have told their cronies afterwards — the consternation of the Infidel marauders when they found the tables turned on them! No doubt it tickled the audience no end and helped to swell the band.

Like the First Crusade and like Christianity itself, the movement found its first followers among the humbler sort. The element of humor faded as their exploits grew in effectiveness and regularity, but instead there came an influx of more and more exalted members and benefactors. As the brotherhood rose in the world, new adherents further raised their social level, and as their reputation grew they attracted more recruits enabling them to earn still greater repute, in an endless cycle of mutually enhancing action and reaction. The same applied to the charitable gifts on which they had pledged themselves to subsist. A few deniers, a handful of dates, an old shirt, a mantle past its best, a night's lodging in some orchard or stable were recognizable as alms; when it came to lump sums, a promise to supply so many loaves of bread per week, so many lengths of stuff per annum, and when the King of Jerusalem provided permanent house-room in his own quarters on Mount Moriah, site of the celebrated temple built by Solomon, charity began to lose its edge and merge insensibly with acquisition.

So when after nearly ten years of it, towards autumn 1127, Hugh de Payens made ready to take leave of absence from the Holy Land for the first time since he had come, that was no simple matter. He must put his house in order, and there was a great deal to it. Although he and those of his knights chosen to go with him left at the onset of the peaceful season — from autumn until spring, when the rains and the cold and the lack of pasturage tended to act as natural truce-makers — there was no telling precisely when he would return. He must install a capable deputy and make all arrangements for the continuance of the good work of what was now an institution, on which King, country and pilgrims had come to depend.

He was going to attend a synod convoked for January· 14, 1128, at Troyes, capital of his native country of Champagne, with the chief purpose of conferring official status, with international effect, on his Brotherhood. He also carried letters, from Hugh, formerly Count of Champagne, from the Patriarch of Jerusalem and from King Baldwin II himself, empowering him to collect money and men for Outremer, and highly commending to whom it might concern *Pauperes commilitones Christi templique Salomonis,* the Poor Fellow-Soldiers of Christ and the Temple of Solomon. That was the name they had chosen for themselves.

Officially the president of the Council of Troyes was the Cardinal-Legate to France, Matthew of Albano. The true presiding spirit, however, was the Abbot Bernard of Clairvaux, known and revered throughout the Christian world as the absolute image of the contemporary ideal of goodness.

Illness delayed the saintly Bernard's appearance at the council, but he scarcely needed to be present in the flesh to dominate the gathering. St. Bernard's magnetic vitality was such that even after his death he managed to take a decisive if deleterious hand in crusading affairs,* not to mention our indebtedness to him for shepherding Dante through the zones of purgatory.

St. Bernard never did anything by halves. When in his early twenties he first received the call to the monastic life, he took with him into the celibate service of God all the males of his immediate family: his father, four brothers and an uncle, besides thirty friends. Where he came to preach, it was said in after days, mothers would hide their sons, wives lock up their husbands, young men snatch their fellows out of the way of hearing Bernard. For to hear was to follow him. He entered the

---

* He persuaded King Amalric of Jerusalem in a dream to precipitate a disastrous battle the next morning.

famous House of Citeaux, but deemed its austerities insufficient, so that at the age of twenty-five he set up his own abbey in the most forbidding countryside he could discover, which was Clairvaux.

Count Hugh of Champagne had donated the land for the new foundation, and even after his departure to the Holy Land his friendship with the founder was warmly maintained. Hugh of Champagne had joined the brotherhood of Hugh de Payens in 1126, whereupon St. Bernard in a most loving letter congratulated him upon "his *promotion* from the position of wealthy lord to that of a poor knight," deploring only that his friend had not chosen a religious retirement nearer home, "where we would still have had the pleasure of seeing something of you!"

But Bernard's imagination had been touched, in its most sensitive area as it happened, that of creative vision, by the account his former patron gave of the Poor Knights of the Temple as a kind of household posse to the Patriarchate of Jerusalem, a fighting arm uniquely attached to a spiritual body. The fate of Christianity in the East had long been among St. Bernard's chief concerns, rivaling his preoccupation with the worldly knighthood of his day, which he held in extreme abhorrence. Here at one stroke was the perfect opportunity of implementing both, and his nature responded with all the ardor of the man sincerely convinced he must see to everything himself to get it done. All his life he avoided sleep like a sin and only gave in to it to keep from fainting.

The assembly foregathered at Troyes was a distinguished mixture of secular and ecclesiastic forces. There were present the Cardinal-Legate, two archbishops, ten bishops and seven eminent abbots, all friends and admirers of St. Bernard, with the exception of the Bishop of Orleans, *"un succube et un sodomite,"* sometimes nicknamed "Flora": but he was a protégé of the King of France, which made him valuable. Count Tibald of Champagne and Brie and the Count of Nevers headed a brilliant concourse of nobles, with a nebula of savants, scholars, learned masters of canon law, monks and scribes and appropriately resplendent lay entourage. The leading members sat on benches, the lesser as was usual on the floor, in all splendor and holiness.

The dual composition of the council corresponded to the dual purpose it was intended to serve. Formal recognition outside Palestine for the Poor Knights of the Temple was in the hands of the Church, promoting extensive concrete support for them depended on the laity.

The need of Outremer for help was constant, but had entered another phase of particular acuteness. As always the foremost requirement was for men. The West, on the other hand, was perennially troubled by a surplus of unruly younger sons and discontented, brutalized commons. Recruitment into the ranks of the Poor Knights was an ideal means of solving both problems. St. Bernard put his finger on it when ebulliently he pointed out that a brotherhood of fighting monks would attract and regenerate all manner of able-bodied but hitherto vicious persons — *"Sceleratos et impios, raptores et homicidas, adulteros,"* he enumerated eagerly — in whose departure their own country would rejoice while the Holy Land would benefit by their assistance.

Having thus amended his previous postulate that the activities of all worldly knights were sinful, their evil varying only in degree, by isolating moral aimlessness as the germ of evil in the warrior character, St. Bernard hastened to show that as it stood, the brotherhood was far from being a horde of blasphemers, rapists, murderers and fornicators.

Here was their leader in person, together with Godfrey de Saint-Omer, Andrew de Montbard, Gondemare, Godefroi Rossal, Payen de Montdidier, Geoffrey Bisot, and Archambaud de Saint-Agnan.* An uncle of St. Bernard, Andrew de Montbard had already joined up, and there, Hugh's right-hand man, stood a scion of the substantial lords of Saint-Omer, of Flanders. One of the greatest magnates in French lands, Fulk of Anjou, had lately served under Hugh in Palestine. Respectability was leavened by their appearance: starkly bearded and unkempt, their arms and accoutrements stout but unadorned — here and there shield or dagger might show traces of gilding and inlay rigorously painted black — and, perhaps the most astounding trait, acting in all things as one man.

Like an inspired showman, St. Bernard underlined it all with glowing commentary. Aware that praise cannot attain the highest luster save by

* The list and the spelling vary.

some denigration to give it scale, he contrasted "the new chivalry" with the old. Behold, he said, this amazing phenomenon, knights dwelling together in brotherly love, meekness and frugality, eating abstemiously, touching intoxicating liquors not at all, abominating chess and dice, avoiding all theatrical performances, and having forsworn the pleasures of venery, the vanity of falconry, the vainglory of pointed shoes and all contact, even the most harmless, with woman.

In their rough and simple hall at Jerusalem (having no decorations save some war gear hung up about the walls) you will encounter no levity of any sort, no pointless activity, laughter, whispering or muttering whatsoever. The Ideal Knight of Christ's Militia has his hair cropped that it may not interfere with sight and respiration in battle, but he lets his beard grow as it will. He does not comb himself, he does not wash, much less perfume his body, he welcomes vermin as a penance, and eschews the luxury of an extensive wardrobe, wearing his garments till they fall off him. ("Ye others: are ye knights or prinking ladies?") Prayer, drill and fighting are the sole business of his life, worthy champion of the King of Kings, bearing not peace, but the sword.

To forestall a smile at the formidable description, it is well to remember that equating cleanliness with godliness in everyday life was an essentially Protestant formula of the future. On the contrary, since bodily filth on the whole is scarcely less uncomfortable than an iron girdle or hair shirt, saints and hermits deliberately adopted all three. The standard of personal hygiene among even the highest in the land was such that the King of France and his family changed their clothes three times a year, while, on state visits to Italy, his courtiers had to be officially requested not to blow their noses into the sumptuous bed curtains of the palaces where they were lodged, though nobody seems to have balked especially at the use of the marble staircases for urinals. Neither were sense of humor, understatement, and short-windedness reckoned qualities of oratorial virtue. No, the one would have come under the head of levity, the second and third definable as awkwardness and want of fervor. St. Bernard's praise was taken in the spirit in which it was offered, and with a pinch of salt automatically allowing for the distinction between art and life, between the shining portrait limned of rhetoric and the actual, breathing delegation for whom it spoke.

The next step was to record the Rule of the Brotherhood and submit it for approval by the council, whereafter it would be sent to Pope Honorius II who alone could give it final sanction. This rule was an elaborated version, owing not a little to St. Bernard's editorship, of the regulations Hugh de Payens and his comrades had worked out between them, and which derived partly from the canons of the Holy Sepulchre, partly from St. Bernard's own Cistercians, and partly from the nature of the task and the territory of operations.

The first eight of sixty-two articles laid down the knights' religious duties, the next eleven their daily routine. Subsequent statutes dealt with the subject of obedience from every aspect, and the remainder with miscellaneous matters, such as property, care in sickness and old age, and the knotty problem of relations with the excommunicate.

This last was of the greatest importance. Normally, anyone having any commerce with persons or communities under the interdict thereby placed himself under the ban of the Church. If the new order was to incorporate those godless brigands, perjurers and adulterers, who were *ipso facto* excommunicate, some form must be found which would exempt the blameless receivers, since they would have to negotiate such persons' admission *before* upon admission the ban was lifted. Furthermore, it was the heyday of schisms, with rival popes appointing rival bishops on occasion. A whole village might find itself outlawed according as its parish priest took sides in some ecclesiastical dispute — or even if the parish priest happened to have been ordained by what later turned out to have been the wrong side. Thus Hugh de Payens' forthcoming campaign of recruitment would be gravely hampered without explicit permission to enter such communities.

Both this and the next most significant amendment were to have consequences of a magnitude not then foreseeable. Herewith the Knights of the Temple were granted the keys to unprecedented power, the keys, at the same time, that would eventually close the door of history upon their exit. The benefits which the council recommended should accrue to excommunicated knights desirous of entering the ranks of the Templars, and the exemptions to protect the latter, though small as yet, in effect altered a fundamental ecclesiastical precept and opened the way for the future independence of the order — which it was the present objective of all concrned to bind most securely to the Church. And the modification which followed, regarding the vow of poverty, might as well have been designed to reinforce that thin end of the wedge, since without wealth there is no independence.

It was decided to make provisions for the endowment of the order, that it might have footholds in Europe for recruiting stations. Henceforth the vow of poverty was to apply to personal property only. The order should accept, even appeal for gifts of every kind; everything owned by the individual knight fell to the order; postulants should bring a dowry, and even those entering in a serving capacity were to deposit something of material value in pledge of their serious intentions.

For now three new categories of brother were recognized: squires and servants, equivalent to the secular groups of serjeants-at-arms and foot soldiers, and associates. A host of different ordinances was devised governing the respective duties and privileges of all categories, from their hours of worship down to their diet and the number of paternosters to be said for them on their decease. Other clauses took care of points arising from the military character of the Brotherhood, such as regular spells of recuperation for men and horses, avoidance of excessive asceticism which weakened the body and maintenance of morale. There were severe penalties for grumbling and boasting. This included inverted boasting; any talk of past sins was forbidden, especially with regard to carnal transgressions.

The chastity of military monks, who had not the refuge from temptation of conventual confinement, needed to be guarded with peculiar strictness. Knights were forbidden so much as to enter a house where a woman lay in childbed, or to attend her churching, lest a longing for family ties be revived in them. Likewise were they forbidden to stand godfather. They were to sleep fully dressed in lighted dormitories.

Unlike most religious societies, the Temple might not admit children, even as associate members, and certainly not women. No brother might allow himself to be ransomed, dissipating the goods of the order. None might peruse a private letter privately, but had to have it read out in the presence of the master.

In future the soldiers of Christ should wear the livery of their Lord, as did the vassals of lesser lords. Here was an end to the assorted reach-me-downs which had proclaimed their humility in visible shape. White was to be their color, hue of purity; plain, white wool, with linen undershirts permitted in the hot season, and jerkins and drawers of sheepskin for undress.

Every contingency was minutely covered. Yet the concluding article of the rule expressly stated that the master stood above it and had power to make any changes at his discretion — a measure of the impression Hugh de Payens had made. For even though it is known that men are mortal, the figurehead who first presents himself as representative of a cause stamps his own image on the office he occupies, in terms of which others will visualize its future continuity. Thus in effect the rule was left flexible, to say the least — almost as if all the time and breath expended by the council had gone, not so much towards fixing a constitution, as into safeguarding its margin of development.

The concrete support which it had been hoped to rouse proved overwhelming. Donations began to pour in from the nobles, and the prelates formulated a circular letter to the entire lay chivalry, announcing "the rebirth of knighthood," in lyrical cadences — even though the rule, and the order as such for that matter, had yet to be confirmed by the Holy See.

Perhaps St. Bernard's friendship was sufficient guarantee of papal ratification — as well it might be. St. Bernard's standing in the world might be compared to that of a Schweitzer, a Churchill and an Einstein rolled into one, moreover without a single ideological enclave in Christendom dissenting from the consensus of homage. He not only answered an ideal such as men scarcely expect to find embodied, but also had unparalleled command of the language of his era, not less in respect of sentiments than of eloquence. In time he was to set the Second Crusade in motion, single-handed, single-tongued, insofar as it is possible to credit one man with such tremendous authorship. Only two years hence, Christendom would look to him for a decision between two Popes, each formally elected of a faction of cardinals. He would accompany the Pope of his choice on progress all over Western Europe, thus personally ensuring recognition for him, and finally push the German Emperor into routing out the Antipope by force of arms — all without flagging in his other activities, which ranged from the affairs of his abbey to the first project for a translation of the Koran. He was a diligent letter writer, too, and in this capacity would vouchsafe touches of geniality for which otherwise he had perhaps little scope.

"Once, twice, and now for the third time, my dearest Hugh [de Payens], you have asked me to write a homily on your behalf: to brandish my pen at the foe in place of the lance I may not wield. . . . I am so sorry not to have answered sooner. . . ." His enclosed epistle on behalf of the Poor Knights of the Temple, *"Laus novae militiae,"* traveled all over the Western world and popularized such happy sobriquets as "Athletes of God," "New Maccabees," and the like.

Meanwhile Hugh de Payens traveled also, first of all with Godfrey to St.-Omer, the fief of Godfrey's father, who welcomed them with liberal gifts of land, rights, and revenues. His suzerain the Count of Flanders overtopped him with a truly princely oblation, ceding to the Knights of the Temple the *"Relief des Flandres,"* the dues payable to the overlord throughout his domain on every feudal benefice changing hands by probate. In the general enthusiasm the lord of St.-Omer lost another son to the new order. The young man's name was Odo, and should be noted.

Everywhere men flocked craving admission into the order or to make what offerings they could. One gave a village, one a house, another so many villein families, a perpetual percentage of tithe or tax receipts or pasturage; some pledged all first fruit, part of their incomes in fines and toll, exemption from mill dues and parish payments; others made testamentary bequests. Legacies are recorded, of one book, of two books, of a suit of armor, somebody's best gown, another's second-best cloak; a horse, a sword, a saddle, a horse with saddle and full complement of arms, a sum of ready cash, an annual supply of one shirt and one pair of drawers, in infinite and revealing variety.

No less revealing, sometimes, are the lists of novices, with their bald statements of antecedents. The delinquents whose passions it was hoped to canalize into pious channels as yet were scarcely in evidence. One knight had lost wife and children in swift succession, the wife of another, having borne him three daughters, had been stricken with leprosy after only a few years of marriage, and was condemned to live apart from him and the world for the rest of her natural existence. Some had lost all they possessed through imprudence, misfortune or feud — though no one was accepted unless free of debt. Others had been disappointed in love, or at all events done out of a good marriage on which they had staked much — though none was accepted unless he could swear that he harbored no grudge. (This theme of aborted prospects recurs so often in the life-histories of crusaders, that one might be tempted to essay an outline of the Crusades in a linked sequence of such stories.) Accidie, the soul-disease of monks and nuns, claimed victims also among those who led far other lives; for self-indulgence in its sameness is no antidote to sloth, boredom and depression. Many sought a revivifaction of the spirit, an aim in this life as well as salvation in the next, without having to forswear the energies on which they ran or the skills for which they had been bred. The Templars' uniform might be pure white, but their gonfalon was parti-colored, black as well as white: white for Christian gentleness, but black for ferocity in war — and Beauséant the Piebald was, after all, a battle standard.

Just as for all their successes in Palestine the Knights of the Temple achieved their supreme synthesis only in and by the West, so also many men ripe and ready to go on Crusade had, as it were, awaited just such inspiration as the Templars provided to give themselves up at last.

Everywhere in the wake of Hugh de Payens branch preceptories of the Brotherhood sprang up, each requiring its deputy commander and its system of administration, as well as ways and means of keeping all the new knights in good order until they should be sent overseas. He himself crossed the Channel, having met King Henry I of England in his dukedom of Normandy—a meeting with the no longer remarkable result of royal largesse and letters of recommendation.

In England a great religious revival was on the way. A long, embittered quarrel between Crown and Church had been very recently concluded, so far only by provisional compromise, which did not suffice to re-establish that atmosphere of moral serenity which men and nations need to live by. King Henry would be glad of any intimation that the attention of the Holy See was shifting to the East again, away from Britain, and glad to make a friendly gesture in return that cost him nothing but a little money; his subjects longed to salve the collective conscience.

Hugh de Payens was no politician, he was no thinker either, but a man of action who happened to have a knack of organizing—unaware of the interlinked complexities of the field into which he had ventured. The issue for which he was canvassing would have seemed simple and straightforward to him. His cause was good, that was why people were supporting it, and that was why whoever was next in line of attack certainly ought to support it too. Thus he swept all before him, a moral bulldozer, and the grass did not grow beneath his feet.

Temple nuclei firmly implanted in London, Essex, Buckinghamshire, Lincolnshire and Hertfordshire, also in Scotland, he reappears betimes touring the Southern provinces of France.

Here a new quality came with the ardors which he kindled. The North, home of feudalism, monastic development, burgeoning national self-consciousness and of incipient central monarchy, was staid by comparison with Provence and Languedoc, home of the troubadour, of romantic individualism and speculative enquiry, with sympathies attuned to Romanesque Spain rather than Frankish Gaul, and natural resources both more abundant and more cultivated. Though Hugh's triumph was if anything even more rapid and lucrative in these richer latitudes, their outstanding contribution was the sense of poetry informing the Southern brand of verve. This set to work at once, to lend the Templar movement the heroic proportions and the glamour usually reserved for legendary figures and bygone events. Humanity has always sighed for the past, from which one may pick and choose whatever elements most felicitously mirror the contemporary scene to its detriment. Whilst thus endowing the New Chivalry with the priceless asset of unreasoning nostalgia, the men of the South at the same time knew war against the Infidel as a thing far more real and nearer home than the happenings in a distant Holy Land. In neighboring Aragon, Castile and Portugal the Moorish flood was yet at high tide and Holy War was a struggle for survival.

So, in the Spanish peninsula Hugh met with a reception that was warmer still. Land, castles, forests were bestowed on the Temple in a veritable shower, whose golden luster was not essentially dulled by the fact that some of the gifts had yet to be redeemed, that is, to be wrested out of Saracen hands. The lure of pioneering always has been fully as strong as the pilgrim instinct, although answering an opposite incentive: blazing trails rather than retracing them. In one way such conditional donations were better, just as they were bigger, than the unearned income of pure alms. They bespoke the confidence of the giver and augmented that of the recipient. Moreover, for the Spanish recruits war began at once, their warlike spirit did not have to be elaborately stored for shipment overseas.

Hugh de Payens did not tarry a day longer than needful. Back to France he went, for renewed conferences of nobles and clergy at Toulouse and at Troyes, assemblies which, now attended also by ladies, soon acquired the character of festivities, not unlike the charity balls of a later day. Invariably there was a fruitful harvest. Hugh's son had become Abbot of St. Colomb at Sens, and so the estate of Payens itself was now made over to the Temple.

In so short a space of time as had elapsed since the promulgation of its statutes, the order had already changed again. Hitherto there had been only one fixed office, that of the master. Now there were many provincial masters, each with other officials grouped below him, such as marshal, seneschal and drapier, having charge of personnel, horses and arms, food stores, clothing and other effects.

No longer were decisions made as and when they came up; lasting machinery had to take the place of the leader, now styled grand master, who needs must reside at the Chief House, *the* Temple of Jerusalem. Regular chapter meetings had been instituted, ordinary and extraordinary, the former held once a week to conduct routine business, the latter to settle special questions. That was the way most religious orders were run, with one important difference: the Temple, a military organization, adopted the security measure of absolute secrecy, to cover all internal activities.

It was time for Hugh to return to Palestine, but he would continue to exercise some direct control over the many European houses: as laid down, the office of grand master was elective, but the grand master alone had power to make all other appointments.

It was high time to return.

The death had occurred at Damascus of its ruler, the Atabeg Toghtekin, with the usual consequence of dynastic struggles for the succession.

The deaths of princes, often heralded by comets and eclipse as the catastrophes they were for the common people, almost invariably opened such periods of internal insecurity, inviting attack from outside. King Baldwin of Jerusalem was gathering all his forces for a concerted onslaught on Damsacus, the garden city of the Syrian desert, which combined golden lure with constant menace to the Christians.

Conquest of Damascus would not only enlarge and enrich Christian territory, but also serve to stabilize tenure, provide a link between the Christian colonies, and terminate the scissors-like co-operation of Moslem Damascus and Moslem Cairo. At the same time King Baldwin II desired to make provision against the day when his own demise would place his own realm in the same vulnerable position.

His predecessor and cousin, the first Baldwin, brother to Godfrey de Bouillon, had died without a designated heir. But for good fortune and prompt action on the part of Baldwin of le Bourg, then Count of Edessa, the throne would have gone to another brother of Godfrey de Bouillon, who, however, had no crusading experience and not much interest in the condition of Outremer.

Baldwin I had died childless; Baldwin II had no male heir. While his daughter Melisende could inherit from him, the barons would never submit to a woman's rule. It was imperative for Melisende to marry while her father was alive and able to exercise his judgment with regard to the future regent. The candidate proposed by the King of France and seconded by the Pope was the Count Fulk of Anjou, who had served in Palestine as an associate Templar a few years before. Fulk therefore was no stranger. His prowess had won him no small renown. And he came of so great a family in France, that he could not but be acceptable to the Frankish warrior nobles who would have to swear fealty to him. Fulk himself was willing, although a widower with grown children and well off enough where he was: the royal title of Jerusalem seemed worth any amount of wealth and power at home. With a man of his repute for second in command, the expedition against Damascus looked auspicious indeed.

Fulk was to arrive in style. Having equably handed over the enormous family possessions to his eldest son, he arranged a rendezvous at Tours with Hugh de Payens, that they might travel together at the head of the handsome reinforcements which attested the success of Hugh's mission.

So in the spring of 1129 they sailed to the great wedding overseas, in ships beflagged and garlanded, bright with the blazons of many hundreds of shields studding the sides, and reverberating with the chant of pilgrim hymns which, already familiar throughout Europe as the music of the Crusades, were the popular songs by whose strains survivors would in after days recapture the mood, the feel, the smell of that brave time.

For the first time a future King of the realm landed in Outremer under the Piebald standard and conducted by a Grand Master of the Temple.

3 The Flaw

COUNT FULK WAS A MIDDLE-AGED WIDOWER, SHORT AND PHYSICALLY UNDIS-
tinguished but for his red hair. The Princess Melisende had all the
loveliness of youth and royal nurture, and she did not find him at
all a husband after her dreams, for which she had had a model close
at hand during all her adolescence. For the present that was neither
here nor there. Fulk, at all events, was inordinately pleased with his
bride; more to the point, the barons of the kingdom were pleased with
him. The marriage was celebrated amid popular rejoicing, and high
confidence prospered the congress of nobles thronging to discuss details of the expedition against Damascus. The details were settled.

This was in May, 1129. Everything was prepared. When summer came,
they were still getting ready. The transitory weakness of Damascus
passed. The heat reached its peak, prohibitive of movement. There
was much to be said for reconsidering the expedition. Damascus in
the past had more than once formed alliances with the Christians,
and might well be prevailed upon to do so again. A far more serious
threat to the kingdom was materializing from the direction of Mosul
and Baghdad, and, next door to Frankish Antioch, the city of Aleppo
was in a state of civil disorder which made it at least as feasible a
target as the city of Damascus. But Aleppo was twice the distance from
Jerusalem, Damascus was the pearl of the desert, where the fountains
spouted milk and honey and the wares of three continents came to
market, and the newcomers from the West clamored for the prize.
Apart from those enrolled by Hugh de Payens, the envoys of King
Baldwin's bridal embassy had collected some contingents of worldly
knighthood.

The situation was typical of the everlasting clash of interests and
opinions between the Palestinian Franks and those fresh from Europe,
whose boisterous unruliness lent them excessive impetus. Again and
again this had prompted disaster. Here was another sphere in which
the Order of the Temple would, with luck, act as a counterweight,

with its strict discipline under experienced leadership. Meanwhile, however, the noisy amateurs tipped the balance once more. It was decided to go through with the attack on Damascus and await the next favorable opportunity, though the upkeep of so heavy a concentration of troops threatened Jerusalem with famine. The opportunity came in September. By the time the army set out, it was November. Damascus had had ample warning, almost her scouts were weary of looking out for the Franks. In all, King Baldwin had been planning this campaign since 1127. It was a typical situation.

A flaw went right through the fabric of Outremer, and from it sprang many tributary defects, cumulatively rendering the whole structure unsound.

It began with the nature, the special and dual nature of this realm. A Holy Land should not be ruled by ordinary flesh and blood, not in worldly fashion, but in sacerdotal, by the priesthood. The Pope should be sovereign and the local Patriarchs his proconsuls.

But, Holy or no, the commonwealth of Outremer was a mere archipelago wrested from a hostile sea, and hardly held. Under these conditions only military experts could govern it effectively.

Godfrey de Bouillon, elected chief of the Christian armies that took Jerusalem, had declined to don a crown of gold in a place where Jesus Christ had worn the crown of thorns, and accepted only the honorific of Advocate to the Holy Sepulchre. The pious quibble was abandoned after his death, and Godfrey's successor as head of the state assumed the logical title. Jerusalem had got its keystone of fealty and commander-in-chief, but he was king in the most archaic feudal sense, and his powers were limited — yet the form of monarchy had been adopted expressly as an instrument of comprehensive power which the Vicar of Christ could not himself wield.

The Vicar of Christ was still the liege lord of the King of Jerusalem, who in principle was still elected of his peers even though in practice the throne became heritable. The King as seigneur distributed land but depended for his own income on toll and fines, and although justice was administered in his name, the state was no party to it but acted merely as an umpire. The magnates' right to private war stood uncurtailed; the concept of high treason was not yet among the King's resources. Indeed, *gager le roi,* a kind of temporal excommunication, one may call it, of a minority of one by the rest of the nobility, who had but chosen him to be their leader and, given the circumstances, chose to suspend their fealty, continued in usage. Here was one secondary flaw — an anachronistic diffusion of authority.

In the West this ancient form of kingship was well on the way out, as nations were emerging from the chaos of tribal warfare, as the captain-cum-totem changed into the monarch proper, having brought more and more land into his private possession and acquiring personal control of law and mint. In the Frankish East the feudal system had had no natural evolution, but had been imposed fully grown as it were, and artificially, upon a transplanted society which was already a stage beyond it. The system therefore lacked any flexibility which might have helped to modify its artificial, pure form — a form so pure as had never actually existed in the countries which had supplied the pattern. Insubordination, rivalry and breach of trust — not merely incidental as they will be anywhere, at any time, but prominent, distinguishing factors — were the offshoots branching from this flaw. And these were absent in the Templar Order, which swiftly became the hard core of feudal reaction on the one hand and of national stability on the other, while developing its own flaw — inherent in its very expansion. Returning to the point of departure, the Temple mirrored, more or less faithfully, the dual nature of the land which had given birth to the fighting monk — a contradiction in terms, to the poor Templar Knight, fast becoming a symbol of wealth.

But Christianity as a whole was split in two.

In the fourth century A.D. the ancient empire of the Romans had divided into an Eastern and a Western section, later known as the Byzantine and the Holy Roman Empires. Regional and dogmatic fission went hand in hand: Greek Orthodoxy became the established religion of the Eastern Empire, Latin Catholicism ruled in the West. The

Byzantine Emperors at Constantinople claimed temporal authority over all Eastern Christians, which they interpreted as signifying all Christians in the East — two very different things once Western colonies had been set up in Palestine by Christians of the Latin Catholic persuasion, who acknowledged the suzerainty of the Western Emperors and denied the Eastern. The Papacy, on the other hand, resident in the city which had been heart and name of the classical empire, declared itself the spiritual head of Christendom in its entirety, whether errant or submissive. It stood in unrelieved conflict — now fulminant, now merely smoldering — with both halves.

Since the day of Charlemagne, the West Roman Imperial Crown had been the perquisite of Frankish and German kings, for the most part bent on reducing the territorial power of the Holy See, at whose hands they were anointed. Until the great Moslem inundation under the successors of the Prophet Mohammed, Asia Minor, Syria and the Levant had been part of the Eastern Empire, and for centuries it was the principal political aim of the Eastern Emperors to recover these lost provinces. On the spiritual side, the Greek Church and the Latin each believed itself the exclusive proprietor of doctrinal truth. Each, therefore, saw itself as the sole rightful steward of the cradle of the faith and the sacred monuments of the Saviour's passion.

The First Crusade owed its inception in no small measure to the efforts of the Papacy to heal the rift of the Empires and reunite Christendom. In the event, however, the fissure had been widened. So far from restoring to Byzantium its former possessions in Asia Minor and the Middle East, the Crusaders had there set up independent kingdoms. Furthermore, the Greek churches, tolerated by the Moslem conquerors, had been forcibly latinized by the Christian.

Nor had the Papacy profited appreciably. Although now the Holy Land belonged fitly to the Holy See, the Latin-Palestinian ruling class looked to temporal Europe, to the mother country rather than to Mother Church, for political alignment. Leaving aside the incessant changes in the balance of power, the very balance of good feeling was at all times in dizzy oscillation.

The Moslems were in scarcely better case, although to begin with, there was no separation of religious and military leadership under Islam, a fighting faith if ever there was one and lacking a professional priesthood. Technically the Islamic Empire was such a theocracy as the Christians had once envisaged for themselves. Nevertheless, to all pratical purposes the same separation had been effected by degrees. As conquest came to a standstill and its gains became consolidated, the head of a nomadic warrior people settled down. He exchanged his mobile tent for a static urban palace, and delegated the command of his roving armies to his warlords. Before long he had delegated almost all executive power. It is not easy to define his position by analogy. The caliph, that is, the successor to Mohammed, was neither high priest, patron saint, nor king, though having something of all three; he embodied leadership and suzerainty far more than he exercised them.

Where there is a faith, there is schism, heresy the natural child of doctrine. The inevitable happened. Less than fifty years after his death, the true succession to Mohammed was called in dispute. The Prophet had died without male issue and that before the theory of legitimism had been enunciated. From 680 onwards, two rival caliphs split Islam, the Sunnite or orthodox, who held the Prophet's mantle as of apostolic right, and the Shia or Fatimite, descended from Mohammed's daughter Fatima and her husband Ali, who asserted the right of heredity. The Sunnite caliphs reigned from Baghdad, the Fatimite from Cairo, sessile heads of the two main sects which were widely dispersed, cutting across each other everywhere in Moslem territory, each with its warrior caste hierarchy of sultans, emirs and atabegs, besides numbers of semi-independent princes and the chieftains of a host of mercenary tribes fluctuating in allegiance. Untroubled by religious and ethnic distinctions, the Christians lumped them all together as Saracens, just as they — French, Italian, Spanish, German, Slav, English, Gael and Scandinavian, Catholic, Orthodox, or dissenting — perforce bore the generic label of Frank.

The greater part of Asia Minor was under the sway of two peoples of Turcoman origin, called Seljuk and Danishmend Turks, after their respective dynasties. The rule of the Seljuk sultans extended as far as Aleppo and Baghdad. The Danishmends controlled Northeast Anatolia. Between their dominions and Frankish Syria lay a group of Armenian states, Greek Orthodox by religion like Byzantium but outside the Eastern Empire and not often in political harmony with Constantinople. (They might therefore have acted as the most effective allies of Outremer had it not been for the sectarian intolerance which characterized the Latin-Frankish magnates.) South of these states, in the extreme North of Syria, was the Frankish principality of Antioch, the Frankish county of Edessa adjoining. The Kingdom of Jerusalem stretched from Beirut to Gaza with a few remaining Moslem pockets of which Ascalon was one, comprising Palestine and the lands of Oultrejourdain bounded by the Dead Sea on the western side and the Arabian Desert to the east of it.

The strategic importance of the city of Damascus, apart from its geographical position, lay in its mercantile prosperity, which was also the source of its comparative independence and eclecticism. The opportunity which the Christians hoped to turn to advantage had arisen in the following way.

The late Atabeg Toghtekin of Damascus, himself of the orthodox Sunnite persuasion, had entered into alliance with a certain formidable Shia subsect, much to the disgust of his subjects. For these heretic sectaries were the Assassins, who took their name (really "Hashishiyun") from the drug of which they ritually partook, and in turn passed it on to the world at large as a synonym for murder. Hashish and murder their chief weapons — the one for domestic use, the other in promotion of their political ends — the Assassins in their way formed a military order of the Moslems. Their transcendent aim, however, was the destruction, not of the Infidel invader, but of the orthodox caliphate of Baghdad.*

As soon as he was fully established, Toghtekin's son and successor,

* The birthplace of the sect was Persia, and their founder is said to have been a bosom friend of Omar Khayyam.

Buri, took steps to disembarrass himself of the uncomfortable legacy. Toghtekin had given the Assassins his frontier fortress of Banyas, which the Franks forever harried — a gift bestowed in much the same spirit as were the gifts of the Spanish potentates to the Templars — and they had done their bit to earn it. Now Buri took a leaf out of their book and assassinated his pro-Assassin vizier as a signal for organized riots in which the entire local branch of the sect was exterminated. However, he could not touch the garrison at Banyas, and the commandant of the fortress immediately offered it to the King of Jerusalem. Frankish troops took over the fortress, and the Assassin survivors were granted refuge in Outremer. Thus the Christians had already a base on Damascene soil.

In November, then, the armies of the kingdom moved north at last, across a hundred miles of sands and stony hills and withered grass, skirting the jungle scrub of the lowest valley in the world along the river bed of Jordan, to encamp at Banyas.

Exactly how many there were of them it is hard to say. The chroniclers deal lavishly in round figures and noughts as a sort of code denoting large, very large and enormous quantities. Every vassal, every community, every institution — latterly including the patriarchate, under protest — was obliged to furnish the King with a fixed number of horse and foot, but the levies were augmented by volunteers and irregulars. Auxiliary and noncombatant forces in any case formed the majority, in a land where neither the civil population nor natural supplies were to be relied on. The army had to carry all its stores, from biscuit, salt-pork, fodder and water, to materials for repairs and, since wood was very scarce, timber for siege engines which it might become necessary to construct. Although the war formations of the Franks yet owed a distant debt to the Roman legion, infantry had lost its importance, under the influence of the tactics of Turk and Arab, relying at all times on speed, mobility, surprise, and thus, the horse. In close combat and in charging the advantage was with the Franks, having heavier horses and heavier and longer weapons; but the Moslems were swifter and more accurate bowmen, and preferred to wear the enemy out before giving him the chance of employing his superior weight.

The Franks had four types of cavalry: the first, *chevaliers en harnas,* who needed each three horses, one for travel, one for combat and the third to carry the load of armor, packed in nets of braided rawhide; *chevaliers à une chevauchure,* more lightly armed so that one horse could carry them with their equipment and serve them in battle as well; third, serjeants-at-horse, having fewer arms and hardly any armor; and Turcopoles, mounted troops of mixed native and Frank parentage, armed only with sword and bow, to act as scouts or decoys. The last two were mercenaries, paid by whichever lord furnished their services to the King. The knight, however, provided all equipment and maintenance for himself and his men out of his own pocket. Military rank was determined by a man's fortune, though without considerable physical strength he could not occupy it.

Theoretically the infantry consisted of serjeants, archers and engineers, but there were vast irregular bodies, diversely armed so that one might have a dagger, one a mace or cudgel or cooking spit, others being left to pick up what might come to hand, especially the stones that lay about in profusion everywhere — if indeed they ever participated in the battle otherwise than in plundering after victory or giving momentum to the panic after a rout. They were treated as servants rather than fighters, and consequently proved of small efficiency in either capacity. They had no tents, no cooking pots, no assured supply of clothing; they had no ransom to offer their captors and so were invariably massacred. Not unnaturally, personal safety and personal enrichment were their main concern.

But altogether disciplined co-ordination barely existed. For one thing, there was the language difficulty, affecting not only soldiers coming from every country in Europe and the Levant, but also those from different parts of France, with very different dialects.

Often the banner of the commander-in-chief supplied the only guidance as to direction and maneuver — hence the importance of keeping it flying; hence also the death of the leader was likely to decide the issue. The value of a fighting man lay in his ability to fight, whatever language he spoke. No matter where he came from, he was trained in hand-to-hand fighting; he had not been trained to function as part of one whole. For that matter, all combat was hand-to-hand, apart from the most general movements, such as attack and defense, and even these were ultimately carried by individual action, spontaneous and erratic. Confidence in one's cause, one's leader, one's self, together with ties of loyalty between lord and liege or pairs of sworn brothers-in-arms, provided the only cohesion.

The Knights of the Temple showed how war might be waged differently. Whether on the march, in camp or in face of the enemy, they operated as one body impelled by one single will. There was no straying from the column to chase after some chance quarry or in sheer high spirits — a commonplace cause of unnecessary loss of life and self-betrayal of troop movements. There was for them no dicing and betting, a notorious mania with the bulk of Crusaders, which could result in a knight's rising after a gambling session denuded of all he had — horse and saddle, arms and armor — so that at one stroke he was worse than useless. The Templars had been stripped of vanity; deprived even of the incentive of boasting. Yet, without any hope of glory save the heavenly crown of martyrdom, though fighting always in concert and wholly under control, they excelled in feat of arms.

The armies of Jerusalem marched on towards Damascus. They halted a few miles southwest of the city, to rest, revictual and reconnoiter, and to construct the battering rams, siege towers and ballistae for the forthcoming assault.

Thus far they had seen little of the enemy and encountered no more serious challenge than, now and again, a galloping raider squadron discharging its arrows and vanishing as quickly as it had come. This served to inflate the valor of the secular newcomers exceedingly. When sizable detachments of them were sent out on forage, they disobeyed orders, to enjoy their first taste of what, after all, they had come for. They roamed about the countryside, their appetite whetted even as they slaked it, for killing, rape and pillage, until they had propelled themselves so far afield that the Atabeg's cavalry was able to close in on them. Cut off and cornered, they fought well indeed, but that was hardly the point. The point was that only forty-five escaped alive to tell their sorry tale. It was, alas, a typical misadventure.

King Baldwin was a man of untypical character. He had weathered not a few reverses in his time, and would not be wasteful with bootless recriminations. Although a large part of the precious new blood had been squandered, it might be possible to save the day. The enemy was human too, and certain to be celebrating. Surprise attack would find him wallowing unprepared.

The King quickly marshaled his remaining forces and ordered instant advance. Then there occurred what would have been acclaimed a miracle, had it but worked for the right side. The heavens opened and the winter rains chose this moment to set in. The arid plain was transformed into a morass; the war was over for this year.

They all — good kings and quarrelsome nobles, votive pilgrims and deported sinners, intending martyrs and fortune hunters — all alike believed from their hearts that defeat in Holy War was caused solely by the volume of their sins. To keep up morale in retreat is never easy, and all the harder of accomplishment if besides the enemy God Himself be sensed in pursuit. The Crusader could be as extravagant in contrition and despair as in overconfidence. Achieving an orderly withdrawal was no mean task, in the pouring rain, through mud and cataracts where there had been not a rivulet before and across country already razed of everything edible, depleted and laden with shame in place of booty.

Achieved it was. The King paid tribute of high praise to the Templars. The only positive result of the campaign, on which such hopes had been built, was that the army had acquired a proven constant of adamantine integrity, whose example the most virile would not be too proud to follow. And the standards of prowess and fortitude were as high as those of discipline were low.

Headache and costiveness then were not sedentary maladies, but rather, the occupational affliction of the knight on active service. Casques of great weight and weird shape encased his skull, chafed his face and cramped his neck. He could not wipe his nose nor dry his perspiration when the fight was on, while the heat of action would make a veritable sweatbox of his armor, even in a cold climate, let alone the Middle Eastern summer. On the march he could not relieve his bowels, for this would have meant cumbersome disarmament, which took time and could not be accomplished without help. Galled in every joint by iron and leather impregnated with the harsh effusions of his body, he had to manipulate a large shield in one hand, with the other wield a heavy sword — or, more exacting still, the eight-foot-long lance — and not only keep in the saddle but maneuver his mount. When one thinks of engagements lasting several hours, imagination is scarcely equal to interpreting this in terms of human endurance and adaptability. A retreat over a hundred miles might take weeks.

This was King Baldwin II's last big aggressive expedition. It was not the last calamity of his reign.

The galloping consumption of disunity in the Moslem organism was suddenly halted. A new vital factor had arisen in the shape of the Turk Zenghi, Atabeg of Mosul, who was making great strides toward mastery of the whole of Moslem Syria and, cyclone-wise, absorbing all the available floating particles of potential alliance, irrespective of their precise religious denominations. The husband of King Baldwin's second daughter Alice, Bohemond II, Prince of Antioch, attempted a thrust into Armenian territory at a moment of Turco-Armenian alliance. His army was massacred to a man and Bohemond's embalmed head sent as a gift to the Caliph of Baghdad. The only child of Bohemond and Alice was a two-year-old daughter, for whom a male regent would be procured in due course. But the widowed mother's desire to retain the regency in her own hands was strong — so strong that she sent messengers to Zenghi with an offer of homage if he would guarantee her tenure. Baldwin was compelled to rush an army to Antioch. The immediate danger was averted; he subdued his daughter and forgave her, but it was the last time he took the field. He was an old man, though a fine upstanding one, and had led a very arduous life. In late summer, 1131, he died, and left Fulk and Melisende King and Queen.

The coronation was overshadowed by the obsequies. Even the Saracens praised the memory of Jerusalem's second King, a chivalrous opponent, and one who always kept his word. The Franks caressed their grief with other recollections of the departed: how he had tricked his Armenian father-in-law, how he had made a blessed incongruous end as a monk of the Holy Sepulchre; how there had now passed a living legend, the last of the paladins of Godfrey de Bouillon.

That story about Baldwin and his father-in-law was cherished particularly; it had always served him as excellent publicity. As already indicated, the late King had been exceptional in a number of ways, not least in marital fidelity and the fact that (like the Templars) he wore a beard. Now, in the East the beard was considered an indispensable attribute of militant manhood, the clean-shaven faces of the Franks one obstacle among many to harmonious co-operation with the native Christians. Again exceptional, Baldwin as Count of Edessa had married an Armenian princess. In one respect, however, he was just like everybody else, always short of money. So, years ago, he had once demanded a present of 30,000 besants from his wife's father, saying that this sum was owing to his vassals and that he had pledged his beard to them for payment. As Baldwin's vassals backed him up and swore by everything holy that their lord was obliged to cut off his fine beard unless he paid them, the father-in-law had hastened to pay up, in return for Baldwin's solemn oath never under any circumstances whatsoever to jeopardize that beard again. . . . Ah, and we shall not see his like again.

There was more than the endearing-heroic apotheosis of the old King to hamper the new one. The barons of the Kingdom of Jerusalem had accepted Fulk at the dying Baldwin's behest. But the lords of those parts of Outremer which were not strictly of the kingdom, the Counts of Edessa, Tripoli, Sahyun, the Princess of Antioch and the Prince of Galilee, saw their chance to break away from the Crown of Jerusalem and reassert a debatable independence which it had formerly suited them to surrender to Baldwin's strength of guardianship. Fulk was forced to begin his reign, even as the last one had concluded, with a march on Antioch where Alice had emerged buoyant as the center of rebellion. He had the barons of the kingdom with him, and the Templars of all Outremer held fast to their whilom brother-in-arms, even to the point of drawing swords against fellow-Christians. That this marked a novel departure went unnoticed; though vexatious and bloody, the incident was soon over. Only its upshot seemed important, in that the hand of the new King had been strengthened. Fulk won apologies all around and peace for the time being, at home and abroad. Zenghi's hopes — so well founded since the Franks were acting as though ignorant alike of his existence and intentions — were balked once more, decisive contest once more delayed.

Through war and peace, the pilgrim transports came and went. Twice a year, about spring and autumn, the convoys sailed from the ports of Italy and Southern France, and again from Acre, Jaffa, Haifa, whence the returning would go with palm leaves hung around their necks in token of vows fulfilled, and wearing the cross on the back now instead of on the shoulder.

It was not only among the great, or among the soldiery, that purity of purpose and conduct failed to prove indivisible. Whether caught up in power politics, in the clash of ends and means, or simply in the toils of trite temptation, the contradictions of human nature and human ideals flourished. The fetid overcrowded pilgrim ships were hotbeds of crime and immorality of every kind. The Holy Places swarmed with relic mongers, until one would have thought the Seamless Garment several miles square and every martyr possessed of many times the customary number of bones. The portals of the Church of the Holy Sepulchre, most sacrosanct spot in the Christian world, were becoming covered with the signatures of worshipers who evidently did not trust immortality hereafter to preserve their identities.

The Poor Knights of the Temple were not immune. Insensibly the balance of their corporate life had shifted until its fulcrum rested on soldiering rather than benevolent police activity. Although King Fulk's reign saw great progress in the control of the roads, it was beginning to be said that the dangers of pilgrimage in these days were greater than before the Latin conquests.

That was not all. While the Templars flaunted poverty in their very name, their wealth was much in evidence. The constantly growing needs of administration opened their ranks to all manner of people qualified to cope with this, but not necessarily possessed of the stringent qualifications of religious knighthood previously imposed — *sceleratos, impios* etc. notwithstanding. If wealth be the root of all evil, this is not because wealth is evil as such, but because in the pursuit and conservation of it men are willy-nilly committed to step after step, decision after decision, in which moral evaluation can have no intrinsic part but only, at best, a fortuitous one. In wealth lay the seed of the Temple's destruction; its flaw came in the guise of efflorescence.

To Hugh de Payens, first Grand Master of the Temple, the phenomenon was not apparent. He was too close to it; it grew upon him unawares. Nor did he live to see the most ominously brilliant intimation of it yet. He might die happy indeed, his life marvelously fulfilled, his eyes dazzled by the panorama of achievement that lay spreading about him, and assured of deep mourning throughout Christendom.

Hugh de Payens died in 1136, on May 24.

His successor was Robert de Craon, one of his earliest disciples, and incidentally another of those who took the cross and forswore the world when his love was blighted. But no shimmer of moping pallor, no sentimental excursions blur the impress of his mastership.* Under Robert de Craon the order received its final stamp, and its final brief of power unequaled, before or since, in the history of the Christian Church.

* There is a legend that he was related to the great Anselm of Aosta, Archbishop of Canterbury.

Hugh de Payens' gift of natural aptitudes in happy combination was superseded by a more aware intelligence, operating with calculated consistency and timing. Luck, of course, as well as a good grasp of the forces at work in his world, helped to make his breadth of vision practicable. At the same time, it must be borne in mind, a grand master had to prove over and over again the military abilities on the strength of which he had been elected, no less than for sagacity. He must lead in war as in organization, and all contemporary writers couple gallantry with Robert's name.

Robert de Craon extended eligibility for affiliate membership as well as the benefits allowed to associate brothers — yes, and sisters. Women lay pensioners, with dreams of proxy knighthood enlivening the dreary round of penitence, came to be admitted, upon cession of their fortunes. At first, however, these feminine Templars had to be certified as of an age where they could give rise neither to temptation nor to evil gossip.

It is easier to rouse enthusiasm than to keep it going. Robert succeeded even in improving on the gains in men and property Hugh had obtained in the first flush of novelty. The greatest haul was the King of Aragon's bequest to the Temple of one-third of his whole kingdom on his death. In this matter Robert displayed an almost unlikely degree of good sense. When the King died, his heirs contested the will. The Grand Master of the Temple gracefully waived his share, thus in the long run strengthening the position of the order in Spain, instead of involving it in a struggle costly to both sides and withal uncertain of issue. He would never know how well he had served the order here. Two hundred years hence it would reap the full profit of this inverted investment.

For the present, the loss of the royal legacy was more than made up for, in that same year, 1139, by an epoch-making papal charter, the bull known by its opening phrase, *Omne datum optimum*, published by Innocent II and reissued time and again, wholly or in part, during the next hundred years.

Exhaustively detailed, now poetic and now hortatory, this document covered much ground. But its essential significance was the emancipation of the Templars from all authority, temporal and ecclesiastical, save that of the Vicar of Christ.

It was laid down that in respect of internal government the Temple administration should be responsible only to the order itself, in spiritual matters answerable to none but the Pope. The order was granted tithe exemption such as hitherto only St. Bernard's monastery had enjoyed. At the same time it was to have full and exclusive rights over all tithes transferred to it by deed of gift.

... And so that nothing shall be wanting for the welfare of your souls, you shall have your own clerks and chaplains, to keep in your House and under its jurisdiction, without reference to the Diocesan Bishop, by direct authority of the Holy Church of Rome. These chaplains shall undergo a novitiate of one year, and should they turn out troublesome or simply useless to the House, you shall be at liberty to send them away and appoint better priests. And these chaplains shall not meddle in the government of the Order. . . . It shall be their duty to obey you, my dear son Robert, as their master and prelate. . . .

... Further do we grant you the right to set up sanctuaries in the precincts of any Temple domain, that you may there attend divine service undisturbed, and also be interred. For it is indecent and dangerous for the souls of the professed Brethren of the Temple, that they should rub shoulders with sinful persons and frequenters of women. . . .

Again that gratuitous insistence on antifeminism, which in a celibate order might have been taken for granted by this time. The continual protestation was to bear unexpected dire fruit in times to come, and it was not the only element inherent in the grand patent of autonomy which would eventually prove fatal. The unique and sweeping exemption from rendering accounts to any authority save the highest, which authority obviously would never trouble itself about anything but fundamentals, besides being flagrantly disposed in the Templars' favor, implicitly approved both arbitrariness and secrecy. In particular secrecy, like many a means, became an end in itself. The chapter meetings which no outsider might attend became a manifestation as well as a symbol of arrogance. And since so much was made of it, the world in pique and thwarted curiosity began to seek nefarious reasons for an exclusiveness so jealously guarded.

The Knights Templars stood together, and stood fast; words and envy could not hurt them. They were the New Chivalry, a byword for strength and intransigence. They might shun the female principle, that peril to salvation, incarnated in the daughters of Eve, but as the worldly knight had each his lady, so, too, must they have theirs. The churches they had been empowered to build for their own use were for the most part dedicated to the Virgin Mary, the gentle Queen of Heaven, Mercy personified. At her feet they laid the trophies of their victories, and decorated the walls of her dwellings with instruments of bloodshed.

4 The Enemy

WITHOUT A WORTHY ADVERSARY, THE KNIGHT CANNOT DEMONSTRATE HIS mettle. An exterminator of vermin does a necessary job, but does not occupy a particularly honorable position.

On the wedding night of the father and mother of Mahomet, two hundred virgins died of chagrin. The fruit of the invidious union, however, grew up to be only a filthy, ignorant driver of camels and asses, beasts fitly noted for their respective lewdness and vicious stupidity. One day in the Arabian desert he met a renegade Christian priest. This servant of the devil proposed that Mahomet set himself up as God, to which end the priest offered to hide in a deserted well and act as a miraculous Voice before an invited audience. Mahomet collected his audience; the Voice spoke; the hearers fell on their faces and worshiped; whereafter the newly accredited divinity ordered them to block up the well with stones, as too holy ever to be used again. Thus the priest perished and deservedly went straight to Hell.

Mahomet went on performing spurious miracles. He filled some pits in the wilderness with milk and honey, and then took a company of his disciples to find them, as though by accident. He secretly wrote the Koran, and caused a camel (or a cow) to bring the book to him as a gift from heaven, held in its mouth. He filled his ear with grain and trained a dove to sit on his shoulder and seemingly whisper divine messages into his ear.

Mahomet's chief teaching was the practice of sexual excesses. He soon commanded a large following. So the Jews thought he must be the Messiah they were still erroneously awaiting. When they noticed their mistake, they made the best of it and did everything in their power to set Mahomet against Christianity, with conspicuous success. Mahomet became the most bloodthirsty persecutor of Christians.

God afflicted this fiend in human shape with epileptic fits. Out for a stroll one fine day Mahomet fell in a faint and rolled on the ground, foaming at the mouth. A herd of swine came and ate him up alive — alternatively, he choked to death first and dogs later devoured his rotting corpse. At all events, he came to a suitably unsavory end, reflecting discredit on his persistent worshipers.

Thus, roughly, the gist of Christian belief during the Middle Ages, concerning the nature of Islam and its founder. As apocrypha go, told by one people about another, these were not uniquely insulting. The Normans said that Englishmen grew tails, the Romans that the Jews adored the head of an ass in Solomon's holy of holies. The wonder is only that such deficiency of understanding could persist after several hundred years of contact. The Saracen invasions of the seventh and eighth centuries had carried them as far as Lyons and Tours, and they were not at all exclusive with their religion. Their European empire had not crumbled until the eleventh century; in their Eastern dominions, even the native Christians spoke the language of the Moslem masters, so that more accurate information was, one would have thought, easily obtainable. It is further remarkable that the Christians, whose own faith was bound up with literal acceptance of miracles, should be so nimble in supplying rational explanations for other miracles which they would not accept, and strange that false miracles should form the main drift of detraction, when true miracles played no part in the essential dogma of the Prophet.

On the contrary, challenged to perform miracles and taunted for his inability to do so, Mohammed in his recorded sayings had deplored this lack — yet found therein but another expression of the purity of a creed that dispensed with all material manifestations whatsoever. Legends subsequently did tell of trees wandering to meet him, a shoulder of mutton warning him that it contained poison and the moon descending from the skies to pass under his shirt, in at the collar and out at the sleeve, as well as attributing to the Prophet various supernatural powers. But none of this was part of the official canon.

Neither was there any question of exacting divine honors for him. He was not even classed as a saint. He was the last of the great apostles who in a scale of rising merit and enlightenment had proclaimed the word of the true God: Adam, Noah, Abraham, Ishmael, Moses, Jesus, Mohammed — in that order; all of them venerable, but representing the stages from tyro to master. On the Day of Judgment, Mohammed would appear at the right hand of God to intercede for the faithful; that, apart from having propagated the true faith, was all his function. The Prophet did, indeed, claim to have received the divine revelation straight from the lips of the Angel Gabriel, time-honored messenger of the Jewish God. But that, in a manner of speaking, was a modest, a passive miracle, scarcely different in character from the services rendered by Mohammed's friends who noted down the gospel of the Koran, on stones and palm leaves and the scraped shoulder bones of sheep, as fast as the Prophet's mouth relayed it. Just as he himself could not write, so the rest of humanity was incapable of hearing the celestial dictate.

The Moslems accused the Christians of idolatry, and Christian theologians countered that Moslem monotheism was nothing but a snare, a delusive bait. Yet the ultimate triumph of monotheism, rescued from and purified of the accretions of past Error, was the sovereign object of Mohammed's life. The ruling tribes of his native district worshiped stones, trees, fountains, animals and a whole college of graven images, with human sacrifice and much other barbarous ritual. The Jews, of whom there were prosperous colonies in the area, grown from a handful of refugees starting from nothing, had departed from the uncompromising creed of Abraham; also they refused to allow either Ishmael or Jesus (or Mohammed) the standing of prophets. The Christians, ceding divinity to Jesus and attributing separate existence to the Holy Spirit, and venerating saints in the shape of images and relics, had fallen lower than the pagans who had never owned the word of God at all. In other words, Mohammed was primarily a reformer, and his inimical zeal against Judaism and Christianity was a brotherly one, family feeling turned bitter in the face of intractable wrongheadedness.

As for the law he laid down, nothing could have been less reprehensible on the face of it. Divine in origin, human in subject matter, its object was the welfare, through perfection, of man — where admittedly by Judaeo-Christian doctrine the whole object of man's existence and of very creation was the perpetual adoration of the Creator. The union of God and man was everything. It was to be complete and direct, without reservation or mediators. There were no priests, though there had to be teachers, who should lead the faithful in common prayer. Although there might be buildings consecrated to prayer, God did not dwell in these any more or any less than He dwelt anywhere; prayer could not be affected by the surroundings in which it was performed; everywhere was holy ground, of God's making. But the instruments of prayer, hands and mouth, should be purified by frequent laving with water or, in the absence of water, with sand. Tithe was not a tax payable to God, and charity no stepping stone to virtue: the two were combined, in that it was every man's fixed religious duty to give one-tenth of his possessions to the poor — unless he be especially troubled in his conscience, when he should make it one-fifth.

True, Mohammed scorned asceticism, as a short cut to, or rather, a substitute for daily striving after goodness of thought and conduct; but he prescribed one month's fast every year as a kind of purgative preceding spiritual regeneration. True, he painted the delights of Paradise in terms of sensual pleasure, but the same applied to the Christian Hereafter, with the one exception that the blissful were sexless, their portion of heavenly delight thereby somewhat cut down. Green pastures, flowering gardens, laden orchards, inexhaustible crystal fountains, together with leisurely enjoyment of music and other recreations, were the obvious antithesis to the hard life of the desert; equally Hell must rely on imagery of the utmost physical discomforts to give an inkling of the eternal misery of the rejected soul. And polygamy, when all is said and done, went only a step further than matrimony as such, reluctantly permitted by the fathers of the Church for purposes of procreation. The more wives, the more children, the more souls, the more worshipers, the more perfectibility.

The soul was intellect, intellect worked in this world through the soul, excepting the souls of animals, which had branched off along the wrong path into pure materialism. True, the concept of justice was not abstract and therefore not genuinely impartial: right being right only so long as it was morally good, and, the social structure being built upon blood kinship, "Help thy brother even if he is unjust," was a material axiom. Yet the converse, "Injure your enemy even if he is just," was not valid under either creed, and the Moslems did not act upon it, while the Christians did. "This people [the Franks] make truce when they are weak, and violate it directly they feel stronger," the Moslem chronicler explicates. The Christian chroniclers tacitly take it as a matter of course.

But religious concern is not with comparison of ethics. The ungraspable core of the mystique, and the monopoly of revelation are what counts. In any event, no matter how praiseworthy the tenets of a faith, men will more commonly incline towards infringement than observance of these. Human goodness or badness are not determined by the goodness or badness of a professed religion, although they will influence each other.

Ostensibly, the historian's business is to present the facts, not to pass judgment. But manner of presentation itself involves evaluation, and no one can make assessments other than in the ideological currencies of his time. With regard to the Crusades, whatever the conclusions that have been drawn in the past and those at which the future may arrive, whatever the individual exceptions from the general rule in each camp — according to our present standard of ethics the facts on the whole favor the Moslem, once we dismiss the insoluble question as to the rights and wrongs of initial aggression on either side.

Without a crippling background consciousness of inconsistency in serving their God with the sword, the Moslems may have found it easier than the Christians to live up to their religious precepts. Without any hierarchy of priests, the ideal of a classless theocracy remained viable. Where even the lowest of the low was not debarred from the highest office, perhaps men more diligently cultivated virtue, the only recognized qualification. Granted that schism and political strife rent Islam as they did Christendom, that atrocities were committed in its name also — treachery and sadism did not become integral features of Holy War until the Franks by long practice had made them commonplace. *Ze Akers sint ungetriuwe kint,* ran a pilgrim saying, which may be freely translated as "Acre is the home of perfidy."

Originally the warriors of Islam were expressly directed to fight clean. There was to be no mutilation of prisoners, no hamstringing of beasts, no destruction of fruit trees and crops; women and children and the aged were always to be spared; with the sole exception of tonsured priests, objects of the Prophet's particular detestation.

Among the Christians many held that if it were pleasing to God to kill an infidel, it should be still more pleasing to kill him slowly and horribly. There is no need to go into the cruelties habitually perpetrated nor to repeat the statistics of their incidence. We have too recent data to need such recital, though it may be soothing to reflect that in wholesale frightfulness our own age has not stood alone.

When in A.D. 638 the Caliph Omar entered Jerusalem as a conqueror, after a siege lasting more than a year, he reverently said his prayers in the porch of the Church of the Holy Sepulchre, and, apart from certain civic disabilities, granted life, liberty and freedom of worship to the

Christian and Jewish population — inasmuch as they, too, were "People of the Book." When in 1099 Jerusalem was taken by the Franks, Godfrey de Bouillon also went to render thanks to God in the same church. But the while he knelt there, his Crusaders rushed through the town, into houses and mosques, massacring men, women and children, no questions asked until by next morning the streets were knee-deep in dismembered corpses and jelled blood, as the chroniclers relate with satisfaction. Many native Christians survived, although every man with a beard stood to be slain on suspicion; but of Moslems and Jews not one remained alive, and their sanctuaries were systematically desecrated, so far as they were not burnt to the ground with the congregations inside.

In fairness it must be said that while the Orthodox Caliph Harun-al-Rashid (786–809) had made the Emperor Charlemagne an outright present of the Holy Sepulchre, the Fatimite Caliph Hakim had profaned it in 1009 and initiated a term of anti-Christian persecution which in turn gave rise to the crusading idea. But only a decade later his policy was reversed, and in 1023 the first Christian hospice for pilgrims — the Hospital of St. John, forerunner and subsequent rival of the Temple — was founded at Jerusalem under the patronage of the next caliph. Once the Christians were settled in possession of Jerusalem, Moslems ever found short shrift.

To be sure, when the heat of war settled down to a steady simmer, chivalrous gestures were from time to time exchanged. Baldwin I as he raided a passing caravan extended his personal protection to an Emir's wife in childbirth, and was repaid not long after when the Emir brought him stealthy warning of a planned Egyptian assault.

The Emperor Manuel of Byzantium besieged Konya, seat of the Seljuk-Turkish Sultan and defended in her husband's absence by the Sultana. On hearing that a false rumor of the Sultan's death had reached the valiant lady, the Emperor sent at once to reassure her. He also tried, albeit unsuccessfully, to save the Moslem graves on the outskirts of the town from desecration.

When in the days of the Third Crusade, Richard Coeur de Lion lay sick before Acre, his opponent Saladin sent him fruits cooled with snow

from Mount Hermon, and his own physician. In the surprise attack at
Jaffa, Richard had no time to find his horse and rushed into the fray on
foot. Observing this from a hillside vantage, Saladin's brother sent into
the thick of battle a warhorse for the English King.

Then there is the incident of the marriage of Kerak. Kerak was one
of the greatest of the Frankish castles and a standing menace to the
Moslem communications between Syria and Egypt. Saladin laid siege to
it while a great wedding was in progress. Gallantly the festivities were
continued as the enemy battered at the walls, and the bridegroom's
mother with her own hands prepared dishes of titbits from the feast
which were sent out to Saladin. Saladin retaliated with a courteous
enquiry as to the whereabouts of the bridal chamber, and gave orders
to cease bombardment of the tower that housed it.

Franks and Saracens would drive their horses out to graze after the
rigors and enforced idleness of winter and hold joint picnics and tournaments in a pastoral no-man's-land graced with profusion of flowers
and feminine spectators. The written correspondence between Moslem
and Christian lords often was extremely cordial, and distinguished prisoners on their release from enemy captivity would scatter largesse among
the jailers and take home thoughtfully chosen presents for themselves.

In course of time a King of Jerusalem, Henry of Champagne and
Navarre, paid a friendly visit to the Assassins at their Persian headquarters. For the benefit of the guest, the Old Man of the Mountains, as the
head of the sect was styled, gave a spectacular display of the devotion
of his subjects. As the Sheik beckoned, man after man jumped off the
parapet of the fortress into the sheer abyss below, until the visitor (no
milksop, either) could bear no more and cried a halt. The Old Man of
the Mountains did not hold it against him, and upon their parting
effusively begged the King to call upon the Assassins' services any time
he might wish to have anybody put out of the way.

On another occasion, the same King Henry wrote to thank the Sultan
for the gift of a turban, saying how much he enjoyed wearing it.
Tancred of Antioch went so far as to have himself depicted in a turban
on an issue of gold coin — which, however, public outcry soon forced

him to withdraw from circulation and remint in more conventional form.

Duality of feeling developed strongly in the forcing atmosphere of chronic hostilities, the more as expediency came to inure both parties to once unthinkable alliances with each other. For the duration of such alliances, at any rate, soldiers must be weaned of looking on the Infidel as subhumans against whom no holds were barred. The Turks especially, as the long-standing foes of Greek-Orthodox Byzantium, recommended themselves to the Roman Catholic Franks, who declared them the finest of races but for their religion. Franks and Turks, they said, enjoyed a common descent from the Trojans — which would explain and hallow their common loathing of the Greeks. (The Trojans were popular as ancestors — the Counts of Flanders claimed Priam as their progenitor.)

A species of respectful affection, possessiveness even, grew up towards an enemy who, requiring to be fought over and over again, must be acknowledged heroic in his fashion, if only for the sake of Christian amour propre. There was one other way of rendering this palatable, through that romantic appeal of the Noble Nomad which has immemorially worked its spell upon the Western mind, with the lure of the harem on the one hand and that of clean-limbed masculine brotherhood without frills or burdens, on the other. The most admirable of Moslem leaders without a doubt must be sons of Christian captives. Thousands of Christian women indeed were carried off as slaves and presumably bore children to their Infidel masters. But the truth of the story that the Dowager Margravine Ida of Austria, a famous beauty in her day, became the mother of none less than Zenghi, is doubtful to say the least. Legend similarly averred that the sister of Bertrand of Toulouse became the wife of Nur ed-Din (son of Zenghi) and mother of his heir as-Salih. One marriage of this kind, which certainly would have had interesting consequences, and which was seriously contemplated at least by its royal promoter, never went beyond the stage of negotiation: the union of Joanna, sister to Coeur de Lion, with Saladin's brother al-Adil. As Joanna was horrified and the Pope unlikely to give dispensation — not to mention al-Adil's polite evasiveness — Richard next toyed with the idea of marrying a niece, of whom he had the sole disposition, to another kinsman of Saladin's; but nothing came of this either.

In Saladin, most famous Saracen warlord of the Crusades, Moslem chivalry had its apotheosis. It was impossible to call his pure Kurdish descent in question; but since as a young man he had taken part in a prolonged Franco-Moslem parley, it was told of him that he had then been initiated into Western knighthood and received shield and dubbing at the hands of the Constable of Jerusalem.

Fond appreciation of the foe had its stimulus in propinquity. It infuriated the Western newcomers and furnished them with an additional bone of contention — except when they came over as recruits of the Temple or the hospital, which latter had meanwhile attained an equal status. For the military orders, as the most permanent force in the land, rightly prided themselves on their insight into everything pertaining to Outremer. Possibly they paraded their expert handling of the Moslem, in peace as in war — something like the lion tamer disdainfully exhibiting his intimacy with the jaws of death.

One Usama of Shaizar, prince of a petty state constantly maneuvering to evade absorption by the greater Moslem powers, and acting Damascene ambassador, stayed frequently with the Templars of Jerusalem. He gives the following account. . . .

. . . Adjoining the Mosque of al-Aqsa [the Dome of the Rock] was a smaller mosque which the Franks had converted into a church. When I came to al-Aqsa, which was occupied by my friends the Templars, they assigned this little mosque to me for my devotions. One day I went in and glorified Allah. I was immersed in prayer, when suddenly a Frank pounced on me, seized hold of me, and roughly turned my face to the East, saying, *"That's* the way to pray!" A group of Templars hurled themselves upon him and threw him out. I resumed my prayers. Presently, having evaded the vigilance of my friends, the same man returned, pounced on me anew, again turned my face East, and reiterated, *"That's* the way to pray!" The Templars ejected him for the second time, after which they told me in excuse, "That man is a foreigner, who has been in this country only a few days. He has never seen anybody pray without facing the East [i.e. facing in the direction of Jerusalem]." I replied, "I have prayed enough for today," and took my leave. . . .

When Templars joined with Saracens in calling any Frank a *foreigner,* when they expelled a fellow-Christian from a Christian sanctuary for having disturbed a Moslem at his prayers, matters had come to a pretty pass. One can imagine the Frank in question indignantly holding forth to a receptive audience at the tavern, about his experience. As it was, independent newcomers hoping to fulfill their vow in one swift campaign and go home again as soon as practicable, were wont to blame the machinations of the Templars for their disappointment, if they happened to arrive during a period of truce. Spleen wants to be vented, and the Templars' right to conclude treaties on their own account made them an easy mark.

In wartime, treachery always is the handiest accusation. Why would the Templars go to the lengths of stopping up every crack and keyhole before their chapter meetings, why would they rudely hunt down the curious who sneaked up on to the Temple roof to see what might be seen — why, unless they had something to hide? Were they not in touch with the Assassins, who supplied them with medicinal drugs, and whose strictly guarded mysteries were echoed in the haughty reticence of the Temple? They employed large bodies of Pullani and Turcopoles — those half-caste soldiers who, like mule and hinny, were named according as their mothers or their sires were of native origin, and whose firmness in the Christian faith was ever problematical.

One of the many new offices in the Temple's increasingly ramified administration was that of the turcopolier, in charge of the mercenary cavalry as well as slaves, Arab clerks, interpreters and native craftsmen whom the order employed in great numbers.

But any reproach based on this ventured on uncertain ground. Popes and cardinals were crying out for Saracen labor: "They lack our faith: we lack their works." Saracen carving, metalwork, textiles, were far in advance of Western skill, and in great demand. On the state robes of German Emperors, as ornamental motifs in paintings of the Madonna, and circling the coins of Christian potentates, the intricate patterns of Arabic calligraphy were copied, in blithe ignorance that this was script, let alone that the text might announce Allah was great and Mohammed his Prophet.

European knowledge of geography, mathematics, physics, chemistry, astronomy, mechanics and medicine was practically nil; whereas, west of Constantinople, the Moorish city of Cordoba was unique in the possession of seventy great libraries, attracting students from all over the world — in an age when every book, laboriously handwritten, was a treasure. The first university of Baghdad had been founded as early as A.D. 1065. The first Moslem hospital was created earlier still, in 872, at Cairo. And those were hospitals quite in the modern sense, not merely places for the sick and dying to lie with a roof over their heads, but having resident physicians, medical stores and ambulance units, also medical schools with their own libraries of tracts and cram-books, examinations and diplomas.

In architecture it would seem that the Saracen influence was not as strong as has sometimes been made out, nor can the reverse proposition be upheld, that the West exercised a dominant influence on the East. The evidence even of equal give-and-take is befogged by the varying dictates of necessity: the presence or absence of types of material; the climate; or functional differences, as between shrines built on top of a tomb or other sacred spot (like the Church of the Holy Sepulchre and the Dome of the Rock) and structures designed for prayer meetings, between palaces built for show (like the fairytale residence of the caliphs at Cairo) and for fastness (that of the Kings of Jerusalem), and between fortresses serving defensive or offensive strategy. Furthermore, one side often inherited such buildings from the other; and both would quarry from, repair, or adapt to their own requirements what Greeks and Persians had constructed in their time of supremacy. The Franks brought with them their own architects, and these eventually took home the lessons of the East, after having themselves worked to Western specifications as modified by local conditions, of which the Eastern craft in turn incorporated a share, and so on.

The languages borrowed from each other where they had no words for things unknown or known but vaguely until the enemy introduced them. Thus in Arabic *comte* or *comes* (count) became kumes; *prince,* al-brinz; *imperator,* inbirû; *hospitaler,* arbitâri; *castellum,* kustul and *burgum,* bord attached themselves to many place names. Our own vocabulary is indebted to the Arabic for such words as traffic, tariff, risk, tare, quire, caliber, magazine and check; azure and gules, alcove, talisman, amulet, elixir, sofa, mattress, rebeck — and of course assassin; also dysentery, and sterling, derived from the Greek *stater* by an Arabian detour; it appears that in Spanish the technical terms of the carpenter's trade are mostly of Moorish origin.

Regarding literature, there seems to have been little cross-fertilization. For one thing, the nature of Arabic was too different from that of the Western European languages to make it at all easily assimilable, its extreme flexibility and a literally infinite vocabulary too taxing for the type of memory trained in putting a limited verbal raw material with a comparatively rigid grammer through every permutation of concept and expression. Further, since to the Christian layman perusal of his Holy Scriptures was forbidden, he felt no urge to study those of the Moslem; while Islamic poesy and prose drew inspiration from the Koran to which, in final antithesis, it was a prescribed religious duty to have daily recourse.

This also constituted a unifying factor which the Christians lacked. The Koran must be read in Arabic only, so that proficiency in this language became incumbent on every convert to Islam, and that Babel confusion, which aggravated all differences in the Christian camp, did not arise. One standard language acted as a powerful civilizing agent, lending momentum to the cultural advances of the East. At what point, by what specific cause this momentum was spent and standstill turned into retrogression, is a question which has tempted much investigation, as yet indecisively. But that the ravages of the Crusades, which sank blooming centers of agriculture and industry in dust and dereliction, which contaminated piety and science alike with every evil of intolerance — that the two hundred years of these wars have at least a bearing on the subject seems a reasonable conclusion.

At the time with which we are concerned it was small wonder that Arab chroniclers spoke of the Franks as savages, now with indulgent contempt, now in fastidious revulsion. One thing they singled out for admiration was Frankish civil justice, to which they held up their own in most unfavorable contrast. In truth the "Assizes of Jerusalem" were a model of their kind and an example also to the West. We are reminded that every world is made up of all sorts, and that between any two worlds no demarcation line exists in absolute division of good from evil, civilization from barbarism.

The Infidel vermin had become human. At the same time, the soldier's trade had lost much of its old opprobrium, if not all. The distinction between paid and unpaid professional had ceased to count in Heaven. Previously the mercenary *routier,* who plied his sword for hire, had been automatically excommunicate, despised as much as hated, and entirely without legal rights even in the country which he served; anyone might slay him without incurring either sin or judicial enquiry. Naturally his answering brutality had grown until he was truly as a ravening beast. By virtue of the loathing with which he was regarded, in him the essential pacifism of Christianity had, paradoxically, continued to live. Once even he was able to attain salvation provided he sold his services on Crusade, the last lingering stigma upon living by the sword had been removed. He and the Templar linked hands. With the appearance of the fighting monk, the warrior rose to positive sanctity. With opponents creditably matched, and without that nasty lurking shadow of doubt to temper righteousness, Holy War entered a new phase.

On Christmas Eve, 1144, the city of Edessa fell to the Sunnite Moslems under Zenghi. What had been the first Frankish colony wrung from the Infidel was the first to be destroyed, and with it the initiative went over to the other side. At one stroke Outremer was reduced to a coastal strip, deprived of inland purchase. A dam, which had at once held off and isolated several Moslem powers, was annihilated, and upon the flood of their reunion rode a tidal swell of Moslem hope. Moslem hope spelled

Christian dismay. The shock was the more appalling as no one in the West had appreciated the gravity of the situation in Palestine. For that matter, very few among the Eastern Franks themselves had clearly foreseen the disaster in their preoccupation with internecine frivolities.

A trickle of reinforcements, however constant, would no longer answer. Another Grand Pilgrimage was called for, a Second Crusade on the lines of the first huge expedition of 1096. The Pope in the West and in the East the King of Jerusalem raised their voices to conjure it into being.

5 The Two Faces of Homage

ONE SINGLE HOUR OF HISTORY THAT SHALL COVER ALL CONJUNCTIONS WOULD be hard to confine within the covers of one book. The attempt to arrest a moment in the incessant shifting of historic constellations, to flatten teeming superabundance into a pattern of diagrammatic clarity, cannot but result in some distortion, just as happens in purely geographical cartography.

Briefly, the particular viewfinder here employed shows the positions from which the Second Crusade was launched, as follows.

One Antipope had died in 1138, but another had been put up in his place against Innocent II, rightful pontiff by St. Bernard's backing. *Omne datum optimum,* dated 1139, therefore was published in a year of very serious crisis for the Holy See — which casts some light on a significant aspect of that bull. Innocent himself died four years later, and his short-lived successors Celestine II and Lucius II, harassed as he, both heaped further favors on the Templars. Every reissue of *Omne datum optimum* will be found to coincide with times of trouble for the Papacy, which had no other working champions than the military orders.

The Templars were no longer unique. The companion Order of the Hospital had appeared for the first time marching under arms, on Baldwin II's expedition against his daughter Alice of Antioch. Although the Hospital of St. John of Jerusalem had been founded long years before the Crusades — indeed by Moslem charter — its Brethren of Mercy had not turned themselves into a fighting fellowship until Hugh de Payens set the example. They were formally incorporated some years after the Council of Troyes. Originally their patron saint had been St. John the Almsgiver, an early patriarch of Jerusalem; but as they uncovered their light from the bushel and struck out along more egregious paths, he was replaced by one higher up in the heavenly hierarchy, St. John the Evangelist.

That there was room for two such organizations is shown by the fact that for the Hospitalers the snowball of wealth and power fairly gathered avalanche proportions precisely as it had in the case of the Templars. Yet inevitably this meant that the two competed, for endowments and recruits and for renown, and there was perpetual muffled bickering as to which order was the truly first-born. First-come, at all events, the Temple still held the ascendancy.

Robert de Craon was dead, the Grand Master-elect Everard des Barres, formerly of Clairvaux, who had made his name in the ranks of the Templars in Spain, prominent in a new successful offensive against the Moors. Until he should be able to take up his appointment, the Temple at Jerusalem was governed by the seneschal, St. Bernard's kinsman Andrew de Montbard. "I am surprised not to have heard from you for so long," St. Bernard writes to Queen Melisende with barbed mildness, "though happy in receipt of good news of you from my dear Uncle Andrew."

Queen Melisende was much occupied. Her consort Fulk had also quitted this life, in consequence of a hunting accident, like so many medieval princes. The widow, whose extramarital friendships had brought the kingdom to the verge of civil war in the latter years of Fulk's reign, now ruled jointly with her thirteen-year-old son, another Baldwin, at the hub of all the consultations and wide-flung embassies concerning a new crusade.

Pope Eugene III banked heavily on France. King Louis VI, surnamed "the Bruiser," "the Wide-awake," and more commonly still "the Fat," had sloughed off the mortal bulk which towards the end of his life had rendered him incapable of mounting a horse — thus, however, leaving him the more time and capacity for tightening up the government. His son and heir — crowned co-King in his father's lifetime as was still the custom in France — was Louis VII, a "very Christian King though somewhat simple-minded," in contemporary judgment. His Christian outlook was directed, his simplicity stayed, by his father's old friend and adviser, the Abbot Suger; and both these qualities were sorely tried in his marriage with the beautiful, discomforting Eleanor of Aquitaine.

In England civil war and feudal anarchy were making havoc of the conqueror's work, under his grandson, Stephen. The Church and the Church-minded pinned their hopes of order and pacification on the Holy See, lodestar of permanency even though for the time being it had been evicted from Rome.

At Constantinople, Manual Comnenus, grandson of another great monarch, the highly civilized Emperor Alexius, occupied the throne and stood in negotiation with the Danishmend Turks. In Spain the Christian states were engrossed in their Moorish wars; in Sicily, the halfway house of West and East, a Norman adventure had once again ended in triumph, and the self-crowned King was busy playing off against each other all the powers of the Mediterranean, feared and distrusted by every one.

The Pope saw virtue in necessity. The First Crusade had succeeded, yes, but against heavy odds in the shape of dissension, cross-purposes and jealousies with enormous attendant losses and unconscionable delays. The ruling class of Outremer was French-speaking and French-thinking; a Crusade drawn entirely from the countries of France under one single command, was the most desirable.

Who should set it in motion, who but the one man with power to sway every heart, who but Bernard of Clairvaux?

St. Bernard with a will took the scheme in hand.

At Easter, 1146, visitors from all over France flocked to Vézélay where he was to preach his first crusading sermon. Church and town were far too small to hold them, and they, the greatest in the land, assembled in a field outside to hear him. He began by reading out the papal bull promising total absolution to all who would take the cross. Then he spoke. The speech is not recorded, only its effect. So violent was the responsive outcry for crosses, that soon the material prepared for making them ran out. St. Bernard doffed his robes and cut them up, and, in his undergarments, himself helped with the feverish work of stitching crosses to all the proffered cloaks, well into the night.

Where the preachers of the First Crusade had hauled in the lowly first and foremost, St. Bernard concentrated on the nobility, who had shown small eagerness to heed the previous appeal of their King. Having duly swept them off their feet, the sublime recruiting officer proceeded in his usual methodical resistless manner. He went on, through Burgundy, Lorraine and Flanders, on, without consulting Pope Eugene, to Germany. Although, so far afield, the impact of his eloquence was dulled by having to be translated word for word, everywhere it was the same story, and men streamed by the hundred to succor the Holy Land. Only the German King and uncrowned Emperor, the Hohenstaufen Conrad III, held out against him. This was no arbitrary recalcitrance, but in St. Bernard's view no reasons of state could offset the demands of the paramount cause.

It is no exaggeration to say that in the end Conrad was bullied into taking the cross. Among St. Bernard's innumerable accomplishments was an unselfconscious histrionic gift. As a last resort he thundered at the King-Emperor in the voice of Christ: "Man, what have *I* not done for *you* — what ought *I* to have done for *you* that *I* have left undone?" Conrad the politician broke down, and Conrad the Christian vowed to do everything Christ's impersonator asked of him.

Jubilantly St. Bernard wrote to the Pope: "You ordered, I obeyed . . . I opened my mouth; I spoke; and at once the Crusaders have multiplied to infinity. Villages and towns are now deserted. You will scarcely find one man for every seven women. Everywhere you see widows whose husbands are still alive. . . ."

Alas, St. Bernard had exceeded his duty. Pope Eugene had counted on King Conrad's intervention to re-establish him in Rome. The last thing he had wanted was to see the German armies vanish across the sea.

However, there was nothing he could do about it now. At Easter, 1147, exactly one year after Bernard had first "opened his mouth" in the matter, the Pope went to Paris, there himself to hand the Oriflamme, the battle standard of St. Denis, to King Louis. There also he attended a General Chapter of the Temple, in company with the King and many prelates. Three hundred white-robed knights were assembled for departure: Everard des Barres had recalled the élite of the order in Spain for service in the Holy Land. They made a noble showing, and the Pope honored the occasion by granting the Templars exclusive right to the blazon of an eight-pointed cross in red, being the color of martyrdom.

Meanwhile Queen Eleanor was doing war-work on the secular front. She formed a corps of amazons for whom remarkable breastplates were constructed, and who made it their first task to present any remaining masculine laggards with distaffs, an early parallel to the campaign of the white feather.

Pope Eugene's misgivings as to the international character of the expedition were justified. From the outset the same antagonisms which had hampered the First Crusade made themselves felt again, between Germans, Slavs and the various French-speaking nationals. A contingent made up of English, Frisians and some Flemings seceded on the way to the Mediterranean as bad weather forced their ships to seek shelter on the Portuguese coast, where they were persuaded to stay and help with the Moorish wars. All the rest went overland, which prolonged and thus exacerbated mutual ill-feeling — this route having been decided on largely because the King of Sicily had offered marine transport to both Louis and Conrad and everyone from St. Bernard downwards suspected his motives. This meant abandoning St. Bernard's pet scheme of launching the great counteroffensive on Islam as a whole simultaneously on three fronts: in Spain, Syria and by way of Egypt.

Even on a less ambitious scale, co-ordination of the two main armies proved next to impossible. Conrad's forces preceded the French through the Balkans, and everywhere behaved as though in conquered territory, so that the French, counting on the co-operation of benevolent neutrals, instead met with costly hostility all along the way. The same had happened at Constantinople, where King Louis found the quarters assigned to his army an uninhabitable shambles, and the population anything but friendly.

The Emperor Manuel, forewarned by the depredations the First Crusade had wrought on his country in the reign of his grandfather, and vigilant as ever in regard to former Byzantine provinces which it was hoped to reconquer, demanded as a condition of free passage that the Crusaders take an oath of allegiance to him. This was not at all in the program of the Western princes. But the formula, cast as an oath of non-injury, had been so cunningly worded that, if they refused to swear, they would appear to be withholding a plain decent assurance of their honorable intentions.

Germans, Flemish, Slavs and French were united in one sentiment. With one voice they railed against their Byzantine hosts, whom they accused of niggardliness, blackmail, swindling, extortion and downright treachery in view of the Byzantine-Turkish alliance. Continual clashes occurred, increasing in proportion and severity, and more than once imperiling the whole venture while yet close on a thousand miles from Outremer. Relations between the principals, however, were improved when King Conrad fell ill and allowed himself to be doctored by the Byzantine Emperor, a keen amateur physician, who could not but grow to love whom he had tended.

At last the Crusaders, already not a little depleted, moved on. Above, a distance of a thousand miles is mentioned. As the crow flies, that would be true. As the road dips over hill and dale, as through bog and woods it is attenuated, looping round insuperable obstacles, as the horse stumbles and the footsore infantry falls back, distance becomes incalculable. Add to this complete ignorance of the lie of the land and of the geographical relationships involved, coupled with mistrust and obstinacy; add recklessly provocative conduct in transit and unnecessary battles, add sickness, famine, squabbles; add also in this instance the perilous romantic fancies of a headstrong Queen — and distance in terms of time, effort and expenditure ceases to have any meaning. One can only marvel that even the remnants of any Western army going by land ever reached Palestine at all.

Of Conrad's troops, by far the greater part was lost. The French fared slightly better.

The new Grand Master of the Temple represented a new type developing among the officials of the order, namely, the knight diplomat. Hitherto diplomacy had been a sideline of the ecclesiastic with his command of letters and an international language. Now the Temple stocked a class of envoy equally free of national bias and at the same time carrying expert authority in matters military.

King Louis had come to rely on Everard des Barres during the devious negotiations with the Emperor Manuel. Now, as in late autumn of all seasons the French forces found themselves meandering in hostile mountainous terrain, it was all too obvious that the Templar Knights alone had experience of weathering such hardships, rehearsed in the Pyrenees. Louis called on the grand master to take command and reorganize the whole army on the Templar model.

Even so it was by the skin of their teeth that they gained the coastal plain at Attalia. Here the royal family, together with as many cavalry as could be crammed into inadequate shipping space, completed the journey by sea. The rest of the army was left to make its own way as best it could, and less than half eventually arrived.

The King landed at Antioch after three weeks of storm at sea, penniless. Immediately he was inundated with messages from all the princes of Outremer, each importuning him for aid in precedence of the others. Bewildered by a surfeit of plausible plans, Louis accordingly was undecided to whom to apply for financial assistance himself. Again the Temple solved his difficulty. Everard des Barres hurried on to Acre to produce funds from the order's treasury. King Louis in his letters home to Suger could not say enough about the Templar's speedy and generous help, and asked that they be reimbursed in like manner at Paris. He was in a quandary, although he might not yet realize it.

The French Crown had already passed legislation narrowing down the kind of donations its feudatories might make over to the military orders, so that gifts which involved seignorial rights were henceforth excluded. Yet, as if to show that nothing personal was intended, that royal ordinance had been followed up almost at once with another royal gift to the Temple, in the shape of some mills near La Rochelle. And the control which mills and milling rights gave to the owner as good as equaled the power of, say, a castle.

Again and again the Crown took steps to brake the progress of Templar autonomy within the state, which went contrary to the direction in which that state itself was growing; again and again it proved to be a case of one step forward and two steps back, over the decades. Again and again, too, it would be a case of not letting the right hand know about the doings of the left. Edicts designed to check an organization potentially hurtful to the health of the monarchy appeared simultaneously with fresh demonstrations of gratitude to the same organization in its capacity of indispensable military aide; censorious addresses to the order as a whole left royal friendships with individuals unimpaired. King Louis VII was shortly to endorse his thanks, over and above repayment of his actual debt with the promptitude that increases liberality, in just the manner which his own law had forbidden. He gave to the Temple, outright, a piece of marshland on the outskirts of his capital, where presently the cystic state-within-the-state would be flagrantly exemplified.

Meanwhile, King Louis at last made his decision, in favor of Jerusalem — it is thought because his wife tried to persuade him to stay at Antioch and he had reason to believe her military acumen smaller than her adulterous affection for the Prince of Antioch, who was her uncle and a man of great fascination.

The King-Emperor Conrad had arrived at Jerusalem a month before. His army was diminished and chastened, and sedated by its unexceptional welcome here. No untoward incidents marred the general amity, although Conrad had already occupied the best lodgings — at the Temple on Mount Moriah, where a round of festivities was inaugurated, and plans for another attempt upon Damascus were hammered out.

Whatever his relations with Queen Eleanor, the plan of Raymond of

Antioch, to attack Aleppo and strike at Nur ed-Din's power before it might wax insuperable, was more sensible by far. But once again the irrelevant dazzle of Damascus blinded common sense. To begin with, the campaign went well. The largest Christian army ever assembled in these parts made excellent speed and occupied the famous outer gardens of the coveted city within not much over a week of setting out. The Damascene army was driven back behind the walls, on both sides of which it was thought that Christian victory was only a question of days. The Franks already talked of investing Ascalon next; the Moslem townsmen already barricaded the streets. But while desperation brought to the defenders their access of second wind, the attackers began prematurely to quarrel about which of them should hold Damascus after it was taken.

The defenders returned to the attack; exactly what happened in the Christian camp is not at all clear. There is no uncertainty as to the actual motions. But why the Palestinian barons and the military orders insisted on the Christians' evacuating their orchard encampment in favor of a new position which had neither shelter from the sun nor cover against the enemy, no food and no water, and how they succeeded in persuading the Franco-German allies, remains matter for conjecture. In the heated post-mortem, accusations of jealousy, of cutting off the nose to spite the face and of betrayal were freely bandied about. But nothing was brought home to any quarter and no one save the Damascenes themselves made any gain. Far from it: for months afterwards the route of the Franks' harried flight was pestilential with the wreckage of men and beasts.

That was the end of the Second Crusade, over as soon as it had rightly begun, with Frankish prestige not the least of its casualties. It was the beginning of recriminations which would never again cease. Everyone looked for a scapegoat. Western apologists on the whole fancied the Emperor Manuel in this post, since he ought to have marched with the Franks in the first place, they considered. King Louis roundly charged defeat to Byzantine treachery, no less — with the naïvely honorable addendum that "our own fault" might have had something to do with it too. The European contingents and the Palestinian barons indulged in vigorous backbiting; Conrad blamed them both (and accepted a pressing invitation to spend Christmas at Constantinople); and for the first time, Europe hummed with rumors of disloyalty on the part of the military orders. In particular the Templars were credited with having sold themselves to the enemy, for many barrels of gold pieces; but when they came to open the barrels, God turned all the coins therein to copper — one cannot help feeling He might have gone the whole way and made it scorpions and tarantulas.

Its prosperity had simultaneously created enemies to the Temple and furnished them with a weapon, the edge of which was never blunted.

The riches bestowed on the Temple had not been conjured up from a void; they had been carved out of other estates. It was not only the Crown, in labor of the centralized state, which had come to view Templar aggrandizement with alarm. Humbler voices, faint and scattered to begin with, were raised in complaint — as we see by episcopal letters to damp the murmuring of parish priests whose incomes had been cut and of monasteries seeing their rights reduced to a minimum, by encyclicals threatening with excommunication any person who pulled a Templar off his horse and threw stones or used insulting language against Templars. (It must, then, have happened quite often.)

In Champagne the vintners protested piteously that the Templars undersold them, being able to market wine tax free. In Provins the cloth merchants applied for redress to the government, as the Templars had appropriated the public scales and were strangling the industry by exorbitant levies.

Among the most interesting internal evidence of *Omne datum optimum* is the evidence of antagonism to the Templars. Many passages *confirm* the Templars in the enjoyment of privileges which others evidently wished to see rescinded.

Besides the little parish priests and rustic monks and common burgesses, the higher clergy and nobility were awakening to their grievances.

The bishops who had once decreed special ecclesiastical advantages for persons willing to join the Templars, who had been the first to recommend that in districts under the ban church services be permitted once a year for the benefit of Templars passing through with their collecting sacks, realized what they had started. People were joining the White Knights in order to claim those advantages; and as the Temple's huge apparatus could absorb all classes of men, not only fighting personnel, the numbers of the privileged were growing out of hand. The dispensation for opening churches closed by interdict soon made nonsense of the ban altogether, as the Templars gradually stretched associate membership until anyone contributing to their collections might consider himself a lay brother and attend divine service with them. Deathbed initiations were common, in which wealthy excommunicates assumed the white mantle as they were about to breathe their last and thus departed with full ghostly comfort to burial in consecrated ground, against appropriate testamentary bounty.

The nobles not only feared the encroachments of a feudal interloper, but found also that many of the landless men who used to swell the supply of mercenaries available to any lord who could pay them, passed out of their reach under contract to the Temple.

The catastrophe before Damascus provided a release of feeling. Yet in the eyes of all who had been there with them, the Templars' stock had risen still, for they had fought like lions, the white mantles showing up in the thickest mêlée, before greater numbers than ever of eyewitnesses to their valor.

Ambivalence may be a term of comparatively new-fashioned coinage; that love and hate are but the obverse and reverse of one and the same medal is knowledge of ancient currency.

The Templars were loved, and they were hated. They were admired, therefore begrudged and feared, and therefore vilified. The failure of antipathy to make any impression on a wealthy, powerful, secretive minority has never yet caused such a feeling to weaken, nor can men easily forgive their creditors. The Second Crusade failed and dispersed, and Outremer was left more than ever dependent on warriors whose vow to fight for Christ neither defeat nor victory could conclude.

Everard des Barres was the exception to that rule. He returned to France with Louis and resigned the grand mastership with its statutory residence at Jerusalem. Whether disgust or disappointment set his course, or whether he felt himself too much a European to remain, all entreaties were in vain, and he ended his life as a monk of Clairvaux.

Louis VII on his way back paused to make friends with the King of Sicily, and the two monarchs began to plot another Crusade — a punitive one, against Byzantium. St. Bernard, who keenly felt the débâcle and welcomed the explanation that the Emperor Manuel was responsible for it, took fire again and embarked on a fresh propaganda tour to preach vengeance on perfidious Constantinople. But Conrad of Germany had had enough; he was not to be overborne a second time, and without his co-operation, there was nothing further to be done.

St. Bernard had been ailing most of his life, sustained like many another invalid of genius by his own creative propulsion. This first failure of his life could not have been a more resounding one. With it his influence was broken and so, as men say, also his heart. The fuel gave out, the body crashed. He died in 1153, and among the last letters he dictated on his deathbed two were concerned with and one addressed to the Templars, asking them to pray for their old sponsor.

His other correspondent, Queen Melisende in Jerusalem, also had suffered a decline in fortune. Her son, King Baldwin III, aged twenty-two, felt himself old enough to throw off her leading strings and have himself crowned again, as a ruler in his own right and without her. But she tenaciously arranged to share his coronation for the second time. So Baldwin, to forestall her, burst into the Church of the Holy Sepulchre with a troop of armed knights, and at the sword's point forced the Patriarch to crown him, and him only, as Protector of the Saviour's Tomb.

The reign which began with so determined an affirmation of the conflict inherent in the union of Cross and sword, was to end ineffectually. Though full of military exploits, it would show considerable territorial losses, in spite of collaboration now with Damascus, now with Cairo, now even with the House of Zenghi — or possibly in part because of the erratic making and breaking of these treaties with the Infidel.

If the history of the Crusades could be outlined by a tale of lovers frustrated or ill-matched, or fitted into a thesis on the inexorable rot of rivalries, certainly it would be possible to make out a case for faithlessness as the direct cause of final disaster. Yet faithlessness, for all the common, often cynical indulgence in it, remained the cardinal sin of the chivalric code. Whatever sticks might be on hand to belabor an object of dislike, that of faithlessness would be snatched up in preference. It was so used against the impervious Templars.

Towards the end of June, 1153, the siege of Ascalon, Palestinian seaport fortress of the Egyptian caliphs, had been in progress for six months. For months, until now the worst of summer was upon them, the armies of the Kingdom of Jerusalem had sealed off the spreading inland circle of mighty walls from all relief, and bombarded the city with everything from blocks of stone and flaming brands to battering rams and arrows. They had built the largest movable tower ever to have been trundled against enemy bastion, and its timbers were seasoned with the blood of crew after crew of crack volunteers who had manned it, and whose grappling hooks, axes and bolts had not availed. They used up gallons of vinegar and urine to lubricate the hide roofs under which they would approach the scaling ladders, as a protection against missiles and unquenchable "Greek fire" * from above. The heat was daunting, their horses pined and sickened, their tents were falling into tatters; food gave out, so that perhaps it was as well that the pervasive stench of refuse, excrement and carrion, and huge swarms of flies, diminished appetite. Somehow Moslem agents must have managed to get out and poison the water supply, else dysentery and typhoid would not be attacking the attackers.

King Baldwin II, young, handsome, a pattern of knighthood for all that he could read and write, and fresh from his domestic coup de main, was in command. With him were all his vassals, great and small, also the archbishops of Tyre, Caesarea and Nazareth, the bishops of Bethlehem and Acre, and the Patriarch of Jerusalem leading into battle the most

---

* An incendiary mixture, the chief ingredients of which were pitch and naphtha, originally invented by Arabian alchemists, but for a time monopolized by the Byzantines — hence its name.

sacrosanct relic of the True Cross, promise of victory and safeguard of retreat, for God would never suffer this spar of the world's salvation to fall into the clutches of Antichrist. The Knights of the Temple had charge of the main assault area round about the siege tower. Their new grand master was Bertrand de Trémélai, from Toulouse, commandant of the fortress of Gaza which was the hinterland base of the campaign.

The defense also was in a bad way. But, in that month of June, the Egyptian fleet broke through the Christians' naval patrols and replenished Ascalon with men and arms and fresh provisions. Six months of blockade were set at nought. The Frankish barons were for cutting their losses and calling off the siege. But the military orders of the Temple and St. John's Hospital for once joined forces in vehement opposition, and after much bitter debate they carried the day together. The siege went on.

One night in July the garrison made a surprise sortie and succeeded in setting fire to the prodigious siege tower. But as the irreplaceable machine became a furnace, self-consuming, a wind sprang up and threw the roaring flames against the wall of Ascalon. It was indeed a very big tower, there was a very great deal of wood to it, all sun-dried; it burnt well and long.

Bertrand de Trémélai, rushing with the rest half-armed from his pallet, was quick to realize what was happening and marshaled his men from their despairing attempts at putting out the fire, to assist it. By morning there was a breach in the wall of Ascalon, at last.

By the rules of war, first come was first served in a conquered city, and whatsoever he could lay his hands on, movable or immovable, was his. But for the Templars' pertinacity, the whole siege would have been discontinued altogether and the wooden tower, perhaps, might have burned to no advantage: thus they will have reasoned. Bertrand de Trémélai set a detachment of his knights to guard the breach, that nobody else might get in, while forty Templars fought their way through to take possession. Thinking them the vanguard of the entire army, the defenders were about to capitulate. But as no other forces followed, they took heart. Every one of the forty was killed, makeshift repairs closed the breach; the forty corpses were hung out over the walls, and the siege was prolonged by three more weeks.

The grand master himself had been among the forty and could not defend his decision — perhaps luckily for him. The explanations given by the chroniclers vary according to each writer's bias. Some suggest the Templars were greedy only for the *honor* of taking Ascalon by themselves, and some do not mention the incident at all. However, no one ever contradicted those who did.

The Franks often had to hear it said that they were great fighters, but foolish in strategy and politics, and quite likely reckoned this what is called a "good fault." How often has not the bluff, forthright warrior basked in favorable comparison with the strategist and the politician, whose avocations are fraught with guile and ambiguity? The case of the breach at Ascalon was straightforward and venial; whereas some seventy years hence the Emperor Frederick II was to be pelted with offal in the streets of Acre and with blasts of anathema from Rome, because he had recovered Jerusalem by diplomacy and not by force of arms. Indubitably force of arms and nothing else in the end took Ascalon, "the Bride of Syria," and the Templars had paid with their blood for that lucky breeze and themselves canceled out its fortuitous effect.

There was no falling off in the applications for membership to the order. But henceforth every act of the Templars became subject to dual interpretation.

In the year following the capture of Ascalon, the feckless young Fatimite Caliph al-Zafir of Cairo and two of his brothers were murdered by his favorite, Nasr ibn Abbas, son of the Grand Vizier, who, however, failed to establish himself in power. He was forced to flee, together with his father and Usama of Shaizar (the Templars' friend once disturbed in his prayers in Jerusalem) who had had a hand in the affair. They were accompanied by a brother of Usama, a large train of horsemen and slaves, and a cargo of gold stolen from the Treasury of Cairo. While they were crossing the Sinai desert, the Caliph's sister, having three brothers to avenge, sent information to the Templars at Montferrat and offered a large reward for the extradition of the culprits. The Templars ambushed the caravan; Nasr's father was killed, and Nasr and Usama's brother were taken prisoner. Only Usama himself escaped.

Nasr at once declared his intense desire to become a Christian and asked to be instructed in the language and the faith. Four days later his instruction was terminated by the arrival of emissaries from Cairo with the promised 60,000 gold pieces. Nasr was handed over to them and transported in chains to Cairo, where the late Caliph's four widows took their personal revenge on him.

Usama, having been able to redeem his brother in exchange for a Templar officer held in Damascus, later wrote of these events without rancor or complaint. But the contemporary historian of the Kingdom of Jerusalem, William of Tyre, tells the story differently. His prejudice against the Templars was not without reason, as will become apparent — but to make out that the Templars in their ungovernable greed betrayed the trust of a sincere convert who (in the space of all of four days) had already become proficient in the Latin language and the Christian dogma, remains disingenuous.

Other writers of the time, compilers like Matthew Paris and learned moralists like John of Salisbury, though less tendentious than the Archbishop of Tyre, evince kindred leanings. Even scandal that is patently absurd was grist to Matthew Paris' mill; even though he speaks of the Templars as "the only men waging a just war," John of Salisbury takes categorical exception to their control over their own clergy, which in effect had created a church within the Church — exactly what some temporal rulers were trying to prevent on the secular side.

Yet John of Salisbury was a close friend of Pope Alexander III (1159-1181), who gave so much publicity to a new edition of *Omne datum optimum* that for centuries it was thought to have been the original bull. Its dispensations were even enlarged. Not only were all Temple possessions exempted from tithe payments, but the Holy See now actually taxed itself in support of the order. Bishops and parish incumbents were commanded to give every assistance to the Temple in its alms collections. Any who persisted in interfering, or who sought to extort a percentage of legacies bequeathed to the Temple, were threatened with severe disciplinary action. The Poor Knights were not to be molested with visitations even by the papal legates, which involved expensive hospitality. Any Abbot who connived at a Templar's transferring to another order would be suspended. The Temple's right to grant asylum was inalienably confirmed.

Confirmed, too, were the Templars' special powers with regard to the excommunicate, in the teeth of increasingly outspoken representations and increasingly insolent abuse of those powers.

For the Templars were God's own soldiers and the guardsmen of the Pope. Alexander III was hard-pressed in a fresh outbreak of schism, with Antipopes springing up as fast as they were put down, and both sides appealing for the support of the Templars. The Templars had at first declared for Octavian, the Antipope sponsored by the Emperor Frederick Barbarossa — but then they had changed their minds, as who should not, in view of Alexander's lavish extension of their grand charter. The Pope was inclined to change his mind too as soon as the Great Schism ended in 1177, when suddenly he began to attack the Templars' misuse of their privileges. However, as abruptly the attacks ceased again and everything stayed unchanged — as was bound to be the case unless the disputed privileges had been in fact repealed. Even without other pretenders to the tiara, the position of the Holy See was none too happy. The Patriarchs of the Church in Outremer were continually trying to shake off papal suzerainty — almost the only issue in which for their part they were at one.

They were united also in quarreling with the military orders, which once upon a time had been sworn to the service of the Patriarchate of Jerusalem, not to the Holy See, and which in latter-day practice strengthened the hand of the King of Jerusalem against the Patriarch and not the other way about. The feud between Patriarch and military orders attained such venom that the Hospitalers built tall towers, equipped with large bells, directly opposite the Church of the Holy Sepulchre. Whenever the Patriarch wished to address the people, these bells would be rung until they drowned his voice. The Templars amused themselves more thriftily, merely shooting arrows at the door of that holiest sanctuary in

Christendom so as to cause disturbance in the Patriarch's congregation while service was in progress. The canons of the Church gathered the arrows and hung them up in bundles on the site of Calvary in silent suit before the Almighty, whose mills for the nonce lived up to their repute of grinding slow.

Perhaps meantime He was gathering other silent testimony, which went unremarked on earth — such as the Temple's directives to the Western authorities to restrain pilgrims who were poor, or old, or sickly, and who only became a charge and hindrance on the military orders; such as the changing bill of fare at the hospital, where once upon a time the poor, and elderly, and sick had been regaled with white bread and wine as against the brethren's sustenance of coarse rations and plain water. On the other hand, perhaps He too found such defections amply balanced by the glory of the orders' deeds in war.

6 The Promised Land

IF ALL ROADS LEAD TO ROME, NO SUCH COMFORTING INEVITABILITY ATTACHED to the roads by which Zion might be attained; for all one knew, the most round-about might in the long run be the shortest and the surest, and what appeared as the back door might be really the main portals. One things was plain: the Holy Fortress would never rear foursquare unless the whole of Syria with its approaches was in Christian hands. The same in reverse applied from the viewpoint of the Moslems, to whom also this land was holy ground, contaminated by the presence of the unbeliever. Strategic thought on both sides was shifting to Egypt as the true key of empire.

Egypt at that time was the most thickly populated country in the known world and far the most developed industrially. The lure of Damascus, which had exercised so strong a pull on the Christians, paled beside the very much more cogent one of golden Egypt, the Orient's bursting treasure house, with infinite resources of manpower as well as all the fruits of the earth. So long as the forces of Islam could always be replenished as if by magic from the valley of the Nile, no Christian victory would be final. Until the potency of Egypt was harnessed to the service of Islam as a whole, that is, until Fatimite Cairo was reunited to Sunnite Baghdad, there would be no ejecting the alien intruders. But the very might of Egypt offered equal resistance to Frankish aggression and Moslem unity. For the impulsion of Moslem unity emanated from the Sunnite conquerors of the North who would, if they could, make an end of the Fatimite caliphate. The Fatimite viziers could afford to employ the largest armies and buy up the most able vassal generals. The ablest generals, whose command of the largest armies rendered them also the strongest, thus became the most resolute, independent and unscrupulous, and guarded their territory as they saw fit.

This was how, soon after the collapse of the Second Crusade, the Franks came as close as they ever would to seductive Damascus, and how Damascus, satellite of Cairo, finally fell to the Sunnite usurper instead. So close came the Franks that, in alliance with the Mameluke general who held the city, they practically took up residence there, encamped in the suburban orchards and cemeteries, and forever in and out of the palace. They omitted nothing from their conduct that could earn them the loathing of the Moslem population, which had been ready to hold out against the heretic unionists. As a result the latter had to do little more than accept the town's surrender, and the Franks were driven off. The strange fact was that the grain of Damascus, which for the Franks would have been in the nature of an agreeable but inessential luxury, for the Moslems more than balanced the fall of Ascalon.

King Baldwin's retreat was guarded by the Templar brigade, under the command of the new grand master, Bertrand de Blanquefort, who together with eighty-eight of his knights was captured, and thus for a crucial period of three years left the order without its proper head. He had only recently taken over the leadership from Andrew de Montbard, St. Bernard's uncle. The latter after three decades of devoted service had been raised at last to the highest office, which he lived to enjoy for only three years. The year of his death, 1156, was rendered portentous by a series of terrible earthquakes throughout Syria which caused more damage than a hundred battles.* Indeed if we wish we may take it that these great impersonal convulsions ushered in an epoch of Gadarene self-destructiveness in Palestine, by the agency of personalities and personal relations. From then on everything conspired to bring to the fore precisely the wrong type of Crusader in the Christian camp, and clear the road for precisely the best-fitted among the Saracens to advance Moslem supremacy.

There is always a skeleton at the feast of dialectics, a spoke to balk the smooth course of analysis, a point where the orderly stream of prognosis is suddenly deflected. This is where a flea, by irritating somebody perhaps quite unimportant at a fateful juncture, can alter the progress of history, where defeat and victory may change places at the spur of a malarial mosquito.

Thus the dread Imad ed-Din Zenghi of Mosul died because he broke the Prophet's prohibition of wine, because he could not fathom the rankling resentment of which castration would be ill-designed to purge a Frankish captive, because his dignity had not waxed sufficiently with his power to overlook a slight. He furiously rebuked a eunuch of Western origin whom he caught drinking wine from his own glass. The eunuch thereupon murdered Zenghi in his sleep.

Zenghi was no longer young, his powers were at waning point. But his sons were young and strong and trained in his formidable school. There were four of them; however, any hopes that their father's empire would now accordingly break into four pieces were disappointed. They shared out his realm between them in brotherly amity, thus relieving the one who emerged as Zenghi's true successor of much responsibility which might have been ballast to his drive. This man was Nur ed-Din; it was against his leadership that Frankish efforts at recuperation foundered after the Second Crusade, and to him that Damascus surrendered with open arms. Nur ed-Din's senior warlord was a Kurd named Shirkuh, who had a brother, Ayub, also a warrior of great distinction. Yet

---

* From the citadel of Shaizar, one of many devastated, the reigning Princess and the indestructible Usama were the only human beings to escape.

the greatest distinction of Ayub, the greatest act he ever performed for his faith, was no feat of arms. It was siring Salah ed-Din Yusuf, known to generations of Christians as Saladin, who began his career modestly enough on the staff of his uncle Shirkuh and ended by reconquering Palestine.

On the side of the Franks, among those who, without prospects in their own countries, had stayed behind in Outremer after the Second Crusade, was a scion of the French petty nobility, named Reynald de Châtillon. He was attractive to women, and very attractive to men of his kidney, the least responsible and temperamentally most unstable Western adventurers, who were to find in him a rallying point, example and apogee. At home in France, he could never have furthered his career by a good marriage, nor risen in the world by banditry. St. Bernard verily might have had him in mind when long ago he listed the kinds of sinner who could be useful to the Holy Land: Reynald de Châtillon embodied them all; and overseas his fortunes prospered. The widowed Princess of Antioch gave him her hand and with it her great possessions, and although the barons eyed him with disdain and dislike, he was able to win the friendship of King Baldwin and the Templars as a man of verve.

Position and respectable connections had no mellowing effect on him, perhaps because their most stabilizing adjunct, financial solvency, was lacking: like most of the Frankish princes, he was never out of pecuniary difficulties. These, in fact, were what continued to feed his reckless aggression until it became habitual, seeking an outlet first and reason after. When he needed funds, Reynald allowed nothing to stand in his way, not humanity, piety, public opinion, not alienation of his friends, nor policy and least of all the common weal. All the time he went to work with more brutality than was ever called for, unrelenting even after he had got what he wanted. A deeply unhappy person was Reynard, no doubt, but in default of data concerning his infancy, one is more impressed by the sum of suffering he caused to others. He thought nothing of torturing the Patriarch of Antioch to obtain a large sum of money — the less as the profound indignation of all Outremer was vented only in words. He thought nothing of truce treaties, if a tempting caravan appeared on his horizon; and he was no more afraid of injuring the mighty than of despoiling the helpless.

The most far-reaching of his earlier misdeeds was an attack on Cyprus — an attack unprovoked save by the island's succulence — which was Byzantine territory, governed by a nephew of the Emperor at Constantinople. King Baldwin learned of Reynald's plan, but his warning came too late to save the Cypriots, who fell victim to the most appalling horrors yet inflicted by one Christian nation upon another. King Baldwin could do nothing more concrete than threaten to withdraw his friendship; the Temple held its peace, and thus tacticly prevented effective sanctions on Reynald.

But Reynald had chosen the wrong time to aggravate the rift between himself and the King of Jerusalem. Nur ed-Din was at the gates. No relief was forthcoming from any of the monarchs of the West despite all Baldwin's urgent distress signals. There was only one great power left to canvass, the Eastern Empire. King Baldwin opened negotiations for a Byzantine bride. The Emperor Manuel granted the request and promised immediate military aid; breaking Reynald de Châtillon was part of the price.

The Emperor came, and the price was paid in full. Even Reynald realized that he could not hope to hold out against the huge imperial army that marched on Antioch, with or without Baldwin's sympathy, which he had utterly turned against himself. He surrendered his citadel unconditionally and submitted to a ceremony of public humiliation.

Few scenes were better designed to convey an authentic flavor across the ages, than that of Reynald's petition for the Emperor's pardon. The Emperor's camp outside Antioch was thronged with lordly visitors, and Reynald, barefoot, bareheaded and in penitential garb, had to make his way through the lines of the entire host, up to the tent of state before which the Emperor sat enthroned, holding court. Manuel left him to wait prostrate in the dust for some time before so much as appearing to notice his presence; for many more minutes Reynald and his men were left crying aloud for pardon, with uplifted hands. In this way Reynald not only saved his life, but was even allowed to retain Antioch — as the Emperor's liege, however. At long last, Byzantium regained a lost possession.

On Easter Sunday, 1159, Manuel, swathed in purple, wreathed in pearls, made his ceremonial entry into Antioch, with Reynald holding his bridle and the Frankish magnates who had come to the meeting all walking on foot. Baldwin III alone was mounted, but rode behind the Emperor, wearing no crown and bearing no arms. The streets were covered with carpets and with flowers, and rang with acclaim and tolling of bells; the celebrations went on for a week without pause.

Baldwin was overjoyed at his new bride, the Emperor's lovely thirteen-year-old-niece Theodora; and alliance waxed unto warmest friendship when he broke his arm and let the Emperor doctor him — always the infallible way to Manuel's heart. In deference to Manuel's other hobby, of theological debate, public disputations were arranged, besides tournaments in the Western manner and Oriental sports like polo — favorite recreation, as it happened, of the opponent Nur ed-Din.

All this, and not least the resolute manner in which Manuel had dealt with the unpopular malefactor, Reynald, had won a novel esteem for the Eastern Empire in Outremer. But as the Emperor's intervention ended in truce with Nur ed-Din, the Franks relapsed into their traditional outlook of hatred and contempt for all things Byzantine — even though the King of Jerusalem had previously come to a similar agreement with the foe (but then, he had broken it very soon after), and even though under the new treaty six thousand Christians obtained release. Most of these prisoners were of little account, more liability than asset; only the reappearance of Bertrand de Blanquefort, Grand Master of the Temple, received a genuine welcome. He began immediately to act upon the special information gleaned during his enforced sojourn among the Saracens and imparted it to the crowned heads of Europe in letter after letter, trying to revive some wholesome measure of alarm and get help.

Although at present Nur ed-Din seemed content to fray the realm of Outremer about the edges, wearing down its manpower and encircling its weak spots, he was inexorably extending his command and concentrating his forces in Syria, obviously in prelude to another major onslaught.

"Send help," wrote Bertrand de Blanquefort to Louis VII, *"seigneur et cher ami,"* whom he bombarded with mounting entreaties, "Send help . . . let everyone who calls himself Christian take arms . . . lest the land the fathers won be shamefully lost by the sons. . . . Take no notice of any contrary reports. . . . None knows the position so well as I; trust my words and heed them. . . ."

Nur ed-Din saw to it that the military orders had to be everywhere at once, and of all the Frankish losses theirs were the heaviest. By dint of the constant minor operations they became so reduced in knights, serjeants, affiliates and Turcopoles, that in recruiting new members Templars and Hospitalers came to grips in open conflict on European soil. Standards were lowered, they now took whom they could get.

There was one man removed from the fray, however, whose disappearance was greeted with a general sigh of relief. Reynard de Châtillon considered himself yet far from finished; the lesson could not be devised by which he would learn. Once more he could not resist raiding Moslem territory as droves of cattle, camels and horses passed his citadel in seasonal migration; but this time he ventured in the midst of unsuspected superior forces and, after a brave fight, was overcome and captured, together with all his surviving troops. Neither the Emperor Manuel, whose peace with Nur ed-Din Reynald had strained to all but breaking point, nor King Baldwin, neither Bertrand de Blanquefort nor the citizens of Antioch, made any serious attempt to ransom him. For the next sixteen years he remained a prisoner at Aleppo — sixteen years which wrought many changes, but not a whit of change in Reynald de Châtillon.

A change occurred in the tenancy of the throne of Jerusalem. Early in 1162, Baldwin III died at the age of thirty-two, childless. Nur ed-Din's preparations were far advanced, and it was suggested to him that now was an excellent time to attack Jerusalem, but Nur ed-Din declined to "disturb a people mourning the loss of so noble a king." Eight days after Baldwin's death his brother Amalric received the crown — on condition that he consented to the annulment of his marriage, contracted within the forbidden degrees of consanguinity. Amalric made no difficulties about this: his wife was older than himself and her morals were not above reproach. The only thing he in turn stipulated was that the legitimacy of their two children, Baldwin and Sibylla, be recognized beyond contesting and their inheritance guaranteed.

Amalric is described as tall and handsome like his brother, if something too plump in the chest. Apparently he stammered slightly, and was given to sudden bursts of laughter which were considered to impair his dignity. Be that as it may, his dignity otherwise rests secure. The civil justice of Outremer, which compelled the admiration of the Saracen, owed much to Amalric's reign, and his prompt and diligent efforts to strengthen the law throughout the land did not flag as the new broom's novelty abated, though it had hard work to sweep clean in sundry other directions as well. Systematic in all his dealings, Amalric saw to it that the authority of government stood firm at home, before resuming prosecution of the war. Upon his accession the idea of achieving the Promised Land through conquest of Egypt first began to crystallize into a concrete proposition, which would be the basis of all future Frankish endeavor in Outremer.

The Fatimite régime in Cairo was patently in decline; if the Franks did not take over Egypt, Nur ed-Din surely would. Towards the close of the preceding reign, Baldwin III had brought off a rare démarche by which the mere threat of invasion had extorted a promise of yearly tribute from Egypt — which, however, had never been paid. This default gave Amalric all the excuse he needed for an invasion. The armies of Jerusalem got as far as crossing the isthmus of Suez; but the Nile was in flood and the defenders destroyed the dams, and at the same time Nur ed-Din took the opportunity to attack in Tripoli and invest the Hospitalers' gigantic castle, Krak des Chevaliers, which dominated the narrow plain between the hills of Tripoli and Margat. Amalric was forced to turn back. Six months later he was unexpectedly recalled to Egypt by desperate invitation from Cairo. The reigning Egyptian Grand Vizier had installed himself in office by a palace revolution, in the aftermath of which he had rid himself of all potential rivals — unfortunately they comprised almost the entire general staff of the army. Now the previous governor whom he had displaced had made common cause with Nur ed-Din, and Nur ed-Din's chief warlord, Shirkuh, was on his way to Egypt. (With Shirkuh was his nephew Saladin who, unconscious of the nudge of destiny, would have preferred to stay in Iraq.) The leaderless Egyptian army was no match for such an enemy, and Cairo urgently besought the King of Jerusalem for help.

Shirkuh's forces moved so swiftly that the issue was decided before the Franks' arrival on the scene. But the reinstated governor in the fullness of complacency went back on the bargain he had struck with Shirkuh, who topped this surprise turn with one still more astonishing and immediately made a pact with the King of Jerusalem. The extraordinary alliance flourished, until events in the North once more obliged Amalric to withdraw his troops: Nur ed-Din was attacking Antioch the while his second-in-command dallied (speaking figuratively) in Egypt.

Although Antioch, a sovereign principality until Reynald de Châtillon had lost it, was now held by grace of the Byzantine Emperor, it remained an essential part of Outremer. Nur ed-Din acted as if Shirkuh's treaties were nothing to do with him, as if he were ignorant of them, or pretending ignorance, or dissociating himself. Liaison between two forces so far apart as those of Nur ed-Din and Shirkuh might well be fitful and faulty, so that no treachery was necessarily involved. Nonetheless it looked as if the chance of annexing Egypt was about to set back that triumphal progress of Moslem unity — even as it enticed the Christian defenders of Palestine away from the very corner of the realm which was truly threatened.

For the next few years the approaches to Egypt became the stage for a veritable ballet of troop movements and alliances, now advancing, now retreating, changing partners, crossing over, and altogether describing the most tortuous of interweaving figures. Nur ed-Din, Shirkuh and Amalric were the principals, supporting roles filled by the Emperor Manuel, the Princes of Armenia, Antioch and Tripoli, and the lords of Damascus and Cairo, with an infinite corps of barons and petty chieftains executing their background maneuvers. Almost the spectacle has an air of engaging absurdity, at so distant a remove in time.

In space, the spectacle was kept within certain bounds, in the North by Nur ed-Din's healthy respect for the imperial Byzantine armies, and in the South by fear of Shirkuh. Time and again one of these factors or the other saved the Franks, without their doing.

By 1167, however, King Amalric was in a position to pursue simultaneous alliances with Constantinople and with Cairo. He despatched two pairs of ambassadors in opposite directions. To Constantinople went the Archbishop of Caesarea and his butler, the Templar Odo de Saint-Amand (or Saint-Omer) — that younger brother of Hugh de Payens' right-hand-man Godfrey, who was one day to do as much as any single person in digging the grave of Outremer. These two bore proposals for a joint conquest of Egypt and a proposal of marriage between King Amalric and any Byzantine princess the Emperor might care to select for him; and they were held in suspense at Constantinople for no less than two years. The second embassy was entrusted to the Temple treasurer and vice-master, Geoffrey Foucher, nominally under the Count of Caesarea as the King's deputy. Foucher was another specimen of the Templar politician par excellence, on terms of intimacy and trust with the King of France, and fully in accord with Bertrand de Blanquefort, whose realistic foresight he endorsed with vigorous correspondence on his own part. He and the young count were treated to a breathtaking exhibition of the fantastic pomp and ceremonial at the Caliph's court; meanwhile their business was transacted with despatch. They were able to return betimes with 200,000 gold pieces and the promise of another 200,000 on receipt of Amalric's oath that he would not withdraw his support from the Caliph so long as a single soldier of Shirkuh remained on Egyptian soil.

The combined Franco-Egyptian armies now outnumbered Shirkuh's, which in addition had been weakened by a sand storm. The opponents occupied opposite banks of the Nile. Amalric effected a surprise crossing, but was inclined to leave it at that for the moment. Shirkuh's emirs were equally for caution: their forces, though very numerous, were composed entirely of infantry. Shirkuh decided to disregard advice, and there was one on the Christian side as impetuous as he. St. Bernard, dead these fourteen years, came to King Amalric in a dream and browbeat him even as he had Conrad of Germany in days gone by. The King of Jerusalem could not withstand St. Bernard either, and next morning led the attack. Shirkuh's expertise was more pertinent than that of the dead monk. His center, under the command of Saladin, pretended to yield, and when King Amalric and his knights charged in pursuit, they found themselves surrounded — a time-honored Turkish device which, for all that, succeeded once again. The King and what was left of the allied armies barely got away to Cairo.

Within a month or two the situation was altered again. Shirkuh and Saladin had gone on to Alexandria and had taken that important city. The allies besieged it, with sufficient effect for a compromise to resolve impending deadlock: both Shirkuh and Amalric agreed to evacuate Egyptian territory. Saladin had been in command of the occupying garrison of Alexandria, and it was during this siege that he first made a name for himself among the Christians. During the negotiations which ensued, and which were conducted with flawless chivalry by both parties, he made not a few personal friends in the enemy camp.

Thus ended King Amalric's second Egyptian campaign. By launching a third, he threw away every Christian gain of the last decade.

In 1168 the Caliph's tribute was again late, and rumors reached Jerusalem that the governor of Cairo had reopened negotiations with Shirkuh and was doing his best to marry his son to Saladin's sister. The barons of Outremer pressed for war. They had the Grand Master of the Hospital on their side, but the Grand Master of the Temple energetically opposed such a breach of yet another pact: wise enough to advance the most weighty practical reasons in favor of honorable proceeding.

The defenders of the realm were so reduced by death and capture that the King had given away fortresses and land wholesale to the military orders which alone had the means of protecting what they held. Thus in effect the argument for and against war on Egypt was fought out between those two, Hospital and Temple. The King, who needed to have both of them behind him, tried to temporize: if they would but wait a little longer, the Emperor Manuel was sure to come to their assistance. The passage of time, however, had made this hope appear more tenuous rather than less so, and in any event the war party were so confident of success that the last thing they wished was to share the spoils of Egypt with Byzantium.

A council of the Frankish chivalry met in stormy session. Bertrand de Blanquefort and Geoffrey Foucher were shouted down. What if they had seen with their own eyes evidence of Moslem war preparations on a far larger scale than ever before? Had not the Christians in the Holy Land fought, and won, against superior numbers from the beginning? What if the King had given his word: the Patriarch would absolve him from keeping it. Preposterous to suggest that they, the Christians, were spoiling to serve the ultimate triumph of Islam. To believe in the possibility of Moslem triumph was blasphemy; and even if God were to permit the Moslems to become united, this would be only His stratagem the better to confound Islam, that the whole brood might be wiped out at one blow. The climax was reached when the barons accused the Templars of opposing the project purely from spiteful contrariness, for no other reason than that the Hospitalers were advocating it.

Bertrand de Blanquefort stood up, announced that the Knights Templars would not participate in any campaign against allied Egypt, and left the meeting. The decision in favor of war was carried unanimously.

The wheel had come full circle. The Athletes of Christ, the New Maccabees, the special Instrument of Holy War, had dissociated themselves from an expedition headed by the True Cross. The favorites of Popes, beloved of kings, the admiration of Christendom, the association to which everyone desired to belong, had had it thrown in their faces that they were held no better than jealous rogues. Their policy was correct, their advice sound, and both were scouted.

It was only the first revolution of the wheel, which would describe many more cycles yet. Next time it was going to be the Templars' bad advice, forcing through an indefensible policy, which swept all before it — into the abyss.

Intermediate disaster, in Egypt, was soon encompassed. That the Templars had avoided having any part in the campaign could not ameliorate the result. A strapping contingent of secular knights had just arrived from France and, King Amalric deemed, made good the loss of the Templars to his army. But before ever the expedition started, the leader of these reinforcements died of fever, and it proved impossible for anybody else to control them. So History repeated itself over again, and the atrocities committed by the irrepressible newcomers changed any Egyptian neutrals and collaborators into implacable enemies, doubling, trebling resistance everywhere.

The enduring nightmare of the Templar chiefs became fact: the union of all Islam was accomplished.

The Fatimite Caliph of Cairo had no choice but to call on the Sunnite Nur ed-Din for help. Shirkuh anticipated orders and was already on his way to Egypt when Nur ed-Din's directions reached him; the army of Damascus under Saladin was commanded to join up with his uncle. Together they circumvented every Frankish attempt to stop them, and, acclaimed as a savior, soon to be called King, Shirkuh entered Cairo on January 8, 1169. The rest was a foregone conclusion, a question only of time. In a matter of days the Caliph was persuaded to throw in his lot with Shirkuh and cast his governor to the wolves of Saladin — and that, in a matter of months, spelled the end of the Fatimites, the restoration of one single caliphate and, again, in time yet remote but inexorably approaching, the end of Outremer.

Geoffrey Foucher had already left the Holy Land, to become Commander of the Temple in France, where perhaps distance softened the impact of the calamity he had bootlessly foretold. Bertrand de Blanquefort was spared any further torments of prescience. He died six days before Shirkuh's entry into Cairo, and was succeeded by Philip de

Milly, of Nablus, one-time lord of Oultrejourdain — the first Grand Master of the Temple to have been born in Palestine. As a native and former peer he was well-known to King Amalric and extremely useful to him.

There had been no outright break between Crown and Temple. For one thing, in the absence of the army of Jerusalem on its Egyptian campaign, the task of guarding the Kingdom had fallen to the Templars, and they had discharged it with their usual self-sacrificing vigor. Also, on the surface at least, the Crown and the person of the King, the Temple and individual Templars, had retained their separate identities through all the conflict of policy. Before very long Philip of Nablus went so far as to resign the grand mastership in order to serve King Amalric's interests as a full-time ambassador to Constantinople. In the interests of King and country, he could hardly have done worse, as it turned out, for the man who became the next Grand Master of the Temple was Odo de Saint-Amand.

The prospect appeared to have brightened again. Amalric's Byzantine marriage had been arranged at last and Byzantine armies were arriving. Moreover, the menace of Moslem unity fell somewhat into abeyance. Shirkuh had not long survived his triumph; only two months after becoming master of Egypt he was dead (of a too-rich meal). His nephew Saladin stepped into his shoes, and Nur ed-Din rightly felt him to be less dependable than the old warlord. There ensued another bout of quasi-choreographic maneuvering, of the utmost complexity, as Nur ed-Din distrusted Saladin's ambition, while Amalric tried to trade on that very thing; with Saladin executing the most precarious paces to hold them both at bay: since he wished neither to destroy the Frankish state, so conveniently interposed between himself and his titular overlord, nor to commit himself to treason.

The Fatimite caliphate might have passed away, but the Shia sect of which it had been the head was not in the least ready to lie down. Its most militant branch, the Assassins, expressed their resentment in no uncertain terms, and as their striking power was out of all proportion to their actual numbers, they were proving themselves no mean thorn in the Sunnite side. With it all, they exhaled an aura of super-stitious dread, which caused Nur ed-Din himself to quail when he received their messages of doom, inexplicably delivered — like a dagger bearing the Assassin emblem which he awoke one morning to find on his pillow. Their present machinations against Saladin were rather less occult; King Amalric was in conference with an Assassin em-bassy, which came to propose an alliance and holding out strong hopes that the whole sect might go over to Christianity. However seriously one might take this particular blandishment — and the Assassins were fanatics enough to be quite capable of such paradoxical renegadism — it showed undeniable goodwill. The only favor they asked in return for putting themselves at the disposal of the Franks was that the tribute imposed on some Assassin villages by the Templar lords of Tortosa should be lifted. Amalric promised to see what he could do, and ar-ranged for a return embassy to the Old Man of the Mountains at his Persian headquarters, the fortress of Alamut.*

The Assassins' request was modest enough, and King Amalric never doubted that it would be met. It did not occur to him that the Temple would let so small a loss in revenue stand in the way of so promising an alliance. However, the Assassin ambassadors had hardly set out on their homeward journey when they were ambushed and cut down by a one-eyed Templar knight named Walter de Mesnil. The Temple would not let go any particle of its income, not, at least, without a struggle.

The King was beside himself with rage. Whatever had possessed the Grand Master Odo de Saint-Amand to order, or at best counte-nance, this unjustifiable act — he stood by it and refused to hand over Walter de Mesnil to the King for punishment. Nor did he improve matters by explaining to the King — patiently, as it were, we would

---

* The fortress was said to contain a sort of rest center, stocked with every amenity of the Arabian Nights, from sweet-scented shrubs to musical houris, for the delectation of the sectaries between assignments. It is uncertain whether these Gardens of Alamut were real, or a mirage of the hashish on which the Sheik fed his obedient servants.

say in words of one syllable — that of course the order recognized no superior authority except the Pope's.

It was too much. The Templars had already shown that they were not to be coerced into any military action that was not to their liking. Now on the top of that they had set a precedent for positive interference with the government of the country. The King must act, and at once. Amalric in person led a posse to Sidon, where Odo de Saint-Amand and the grand chapter sat ensconced, swooped down on them and bore one-eyed Walter off to justice. He then reported accordingly to the Old Man of the Mountains, who declared himself willing to forgive and forget.

Amalric was willing to do neither. He took counsel with his Chancellor William, Archbishop of Tyre, who was also tutor to the heir apparent and besides found time for writing history — with what bias in regard to the Templars we have already noted. Together they started work on a memoir to the Holy See, putting forward a reasoned demand that the Order of the Temple be dissolved.

The memoir was never completed, never sent. Amalric also made mistakes, he also could be obstinate. He fell ill of dysentery on campaign, and he had his own ideas as to the correct medical treatment. Against the remonstrances of his physicians, he forced them to bleed him, and bleed him again, till he died. He had reached the age of thirty-eight; the time was summer 1174.

Eight weeks before Amalric there had died Nur ed-Din, supreme sultan of Islam, suddenly, of a quinsy. He had been on the point of dealing with Saladin, much as the King of Jerusalem had intended to do by the Templars. Each left a son and heir who had scarcely entered puberty — that is to say, each left a throne in need of every prop and in no state for immediate aggressive action. Just at the seeming ebb tide of Saladin's fortunes, he was thus doubly saved, and his road lay clear.

The crown of Jerusalem reposed in the treasure vault of the Church of the Holy Sepulchre, under triple lock, to which there were three keys. A King could be crowned only with the consent of the three key holders, and these were the Patriarch of Jerusalem, the Grand Master of the Hospital, and the Grand Master of the Temple. There was no change. The coronation took place, and by symbolic act the throne was resting on the same three pillars as ever.

But its occupant, the keystone symbol of the whole structure, the young King Baldwin IV, was a leper.

Part Two

Domus Templum

7 The Knights Seigneurs

THE WORD "FEUDALISM" DERIVES FROM A GERMANIC ROOT WHENCE SPRING also *Vieh* (cattle) and *Fehde* (feud, war, enmity) — illustrating in a nutshell the fundamental connection between those two, and showing tangible wealth, *real* estate, at the bottom of the whole heraldic code. Money as yet had only secondary significance, particularly in a land like Syria, where possession of coin was not always tantamount to owning what the metal counters could buy. The objects of purchase were not always available; among the desert nomads the man with an empty purse but owning horses, camels, sheep, was still incomparably greater than the owner of one ass loaded with sacks of gold.

Long before the end of the twelfth century, the military orders were far and away the largest property owners in Outremer. The land was a string of oases, and the Franks were never sufficiently numerous to man extensive walls encircling large areas. A sprinkling of fortresses and watch towers enabled them to make the most of the forces they had.

The Hospitalers had become all but extinct on the ill-advised Egyptian expedition of 1168 and had hard work building up their membership anew. The Templars, left to bear the brunt of Nur ed-Din's attacks on Palestine meanwhile, also were cruelly depleted — but without disgrace; and they had the best of it in respect of recruitment. As regards castles and building sites, the honors were fairly even. Parallel with the ascent of Nur ed-Din and Saladin, the Templars of Jerusalem got Gaza in protection of the South and Safed for the control of the Northern routes; the Hospitalers got Belvoir, which commanded the several fords across the Jordan. In Tripoli, whose lord was a prisoner of the Moslems, the Templars were given Tortosa and almost every important strongpoint in the northern parts of the county, the Hospitalers received Krak and Buqaia — enormous fastnesses by contemporary standards: Krak and Tortosa especially were at least twice the size of the largest castles in medieval France. In Antioch the Hospital had yet to wrest its chartered territories from the enemy, but on the parchment they were large; in

Acre it would shortly hold so much that the town acquired the suffix
"of St. John"; in and around Baghras, Temple suzerainty was steadily
spreading.

While the fortresses of the military orders cost the Frankish rulers
nothing in construction and upkeep, they were not bound to furnish
the sovereign with troops or other dues. They acted as voluntary allies
rather than vassals, which helped to conserve their resources.

Knights entering the order brought with them all they had. Those
who came as temporary members paid down a heavy premium, and if
they were killed on active service or died in captivity, such belongings
as they had left behind at the Temple became its property. Married
knights were not accepted as full members; on their death only half
their estates fell to the order — only half. Men do not value what they
get for nothing; the honor of canonical knighthood was valued very
highly.

The proud word *knight* also is humble in origin, denoting *Knecht,*
or servant.

The aspirant Templar went to his examination in the darkness of
night. In Jerusalem, the nocturnal skyline, serrated with towers and
belfries, was charted for him by the two great cupolas that marked the
east and the west of the city: the Church of the Holy Sepulchre, and
Templum Domini, the Dome of the Rock on Mount Moriah, site of
King Solomon's Temple and of the Prophet Mohammed's Ascension,
in the shadow of which the White Knights had their headquarters. Many
and palatial as were the buildings of the fortified domain, such was its
immensity that the vast stretches of open pavement between had given
their name to the whole area, known as "The Pavement."

The candidate, arriving in his best clothes and fasting, had to satisfy
the white-garbed sentries as to his business; then he was escorted inside,
across the echoing stone slabs, through colonnades and vaulted passages
dimly lit by votive lamps. At last another guarded door was thrown
open and barred again behind him, and he was in the presence of the
chapter, all in their white mantles and white skullcaps, the red cross

on their shoulders, and standing with swords drawn. The illuminations of an altar shed the only light.

First he had to testify under oath that he was of knightly caste, of legitimate birth, unmarried, in good health and free of debt, that he professed the Catholic faith according to the Latin Church of Rome, that he was not under ban, and had no commitments to any other religious fraternity. Each question was asked thrice, with triple response.

The whole ceremony was conducted with antiphonal repetition. Three times the candidate was asked whether he wished to enter the order, thrice he affirmed his wish and thrice begged humbly for bread and water. Three times he was warned what he would be letting himself in for, in a two-part choral address:

> *You must entirely renounce your own will —*
> *And entirely submit to that of another —*
> *You must fast when you are hungry —*
> *Keep watch when you are weary —*
> *Thirst when you would drink —*

If at the end of this the candidate replied that he would gladly suffer everything for God and that he wished to be the serf and slave of the order for life, he was instructed to kneel before the presiding brother and with clasped hands repeat his application.

"And he who presides over the chapter shall say, 'Dear brother, you ask a great thing, for you see only the outward trappings of the order. You see only that we have good horses and rich equipment and eat and drink well and have fine clothing, and so you may imagine that life with us will be very pleasant. But . . . you will find it very difficult . . . to be unable to follow your own will in any thing. When you wish to be in this country, you will be sent overseas, or if you wish to be in Jerusalem, you will be sent to Tripoli, or Antioch, or Armenia . . . Apulia, or Sicily, or Lombardy, or France or Burgundy or England. . . . Do you swear to God and Our Lady that you will all your days obey the Master of the Temple and all others placed in authority over you?'

"And the candidate shall say, 'Yes, sir, if God pleases.'"

In the same manner the recruit swore to fight with all his strength against the Infidel. His horse and arms should be ever beside him. He would never be the first to flee from the battlefield, never suffer any Christian to be treated unjustly or unlawfully despoiled of his heritage and possessions, nor support anyone else in doing so. He engaged himself to embrace perpetual chastity, never to sell the goods of the Temple nor allow them to be sold, never to surrender its property to the enemy, and to protect the members of all religious orders.

"Then in the name of God and Our Lady Mary and St. Peter of Rome and our father the Pope and in the name of all the brethren of the Temple, we accept you, your father, your mother and all your family whom you wish to participate therein, as sharing the good works which have been done by the order since its foundation and such as shall be done to the end; and you accept us as sharing in all the good works which you have done or shall do. And we promise you bread and water, the the poor mantle of the order and much hardship and labor."

The preceptor then vested the new knight with the white cloak and cap, while at the altar the priest intoned the psalm *Ecce quam bonum:* "Behold how good and pleasant it is for brethren to dwell together in unity," followed by the orison of the Holy Ghost; and every brother said a paternoster. The receiver raised up the recruit and kissed him on the mouth, and so also did the chaplain and each member of the chapter. He was then taken by the hand and told, *"Eas, Deus faciat te probum hominem,"* — "Go, and may God make you an honest man," meaning honesty in the widest sense of the French *"prud' homme"*: a man of parts, integrity and valor.

He had been given every opportunity to back out, and, although only such extracts from the rule as the master had decided on were imparted to him, he entered with his eyes open on a career of professional heroism and an ascetic life. Already, having held to his purpose under the almost menacing liturgy, and now cut off from all his worldly connections, he was a man of other stature.

He was taken to the drapier's office, where he handed in his clothes and received the remainder of his uniform: two shirts, two pairs of pants and two of tight-fitting breeches, a tunic, a jacket and a cape, a spare mantle and a surcoat to go over the hauberk; chain mail for the legs, iron shoes, iron shoulder pieces and an iron hat. His weapons were a sword, a lance, a mace, a dagger, a large shield, plain and undecorated. Equipment for active service included a breadknife and a small all-purpose knife, a cooking pot with a basin for measuring out barley and a pestle for crushing it, two drinking cups, two flasks, one dipper of horn and one spoon; one hatchet, one grater; two leather straps, one with and one without buckle; three wallets, one for himself and two for his servants, and a small tent, besides the customary high saddle (stirrups must not be shortened without permission, and under no circumstances cut). It was pointed out to him that he might not bathe, take medicine, bleed himself, or walk abroad without asking permission — "and," says the rule, in anticipation of sophistry, "where he is forbidden to walk, neither may he direct his horse."

The drapier decided whether the cast-off raiment was to be sold, or kept for the use of squires and servants, or to be handed out to the poor who came daily to the gates for alms. However, fur or material dyed scarlet, reserved to the nobility, must not be passed on.

The brethren slept two by two in cells bare but for the palliasses or, failing these, two little carpets. They had one sheet, two blankets and a coverlet apiece, two small chests without locks, and a lamp which must be kept alight throughout the night, just as, be it never so hot, the sleepers must keep on their shirts and breeches, with girdles well-fastened.

They were roused at midnight to hear Matins — unless excused by reason of fatigue or illness — and say thirteen paternosters, then to inspect their horses and if necessary hold speech with their squires.

After that they might go back to bed, having first said one more paternoster. They rose again for the Office of Prime, the morning prayer, which was held at four in the morning in summer, six o'clock in winter, followed by Terce, the Hour consecrated to the Holy Spirit. Breakfast was not until after the midday Office of Sext.

There was a great deal to be seen and done, especially by the neophyte, in between the religious duties of the morning. After Terce the knights would occupy themselves with overhauling their arms and accoutrements, see to their horses again and give instructions for the day to the squires. All conversation was to be strictly confined to business and conducted with politeness: *bellement*. However, the special injunction that those retainers who served the preceptory without wages must not be beaten suggests that gentleness was relative. Then there was drill, either on "The Pavement" or at the parade ground adjoining the Church of the Holy Sepulchre, by courtesy of its canons.

The stables on Mount Moriah were the admiration of all visitors, accommodating up to two thousand horses. Although of full knights there were only five or six hundred at a time in Outremer, the chaplains, serjeants, Turcopoles and infantry, as well as artisans and slaves of every kind, brought the number of Templars up to several thousand. They had bookkeepers and translators, carpenters, smiths, shepherds, gardeners, rope-makers, engineers, millers and cooks, dairymen, masons, tent-makers, armorers, fieldhands, laundry workers, vintners, grooms. All these were dressed in black stuff or brown, with the red cross on breast and shoulder. The Templar clergy were distinguished by shaven faces, and gloves to keep their hands clean for God's body.

The old regulation for knights to eat in pairs had lapsed, and meals were taken in three communal sittings. At the first were served the master, the chaplains, the seneschal, the treasurer-cum-commander of the kingdom, drapier and Turcopolier, with the ten custodians of the Temple's own fragment of the True Cross, who were also in charge of pilgrim welfare. Only the master had a reserved seat and a goblet of glass, a luxury appropriate to a personage who ranked with princes everywhere, but at the same time a precaution against poison. The rest of the knights ate at a second sitting; the upper strata of the serving brethren took the third. Though hunting was forbidden them — except hunting the lion, symbol of Satan — there was no dearth of dogs disputing the food of knights under disciplinary ruling condemned to go bare of crosses and eat off the floor. Silence was enjoined during the meal and any necessary communications were made in sign language, as in all other religious houses, where likewise readings were given from Holy Scripture — only that almost the entire Templar membership was ignorant of Latin and did not understand the lecture.

The weekly fast days had long been reduced to two, and the two meals per diem could be extended to three at the discretion of the master, who if he wished might even cause wine to be served, besides flesh meat twice a week and otherwise poultry, which was classed as fish since God created fish and fowl on one and the same day. Brothers were to keep a check on each other, that none might practice abstemiousness to excess, for it was their duty to keep fighting fit. Uncut loaves or dishes untasted were served up again at the next meal. All broken meats, however, went to the poor, and here we must pause for a custom of exceptional delicacy. Knights were bidden to cut their food carefully so that their leavings should come in cleanly pieces, not to offend the alms-seeker. Some food was carried to the leper colony outside the Gate of Lazarus, and the lepers received the master's outworn garments.

In the afternoon the Templars heard mass again. Permission to absent themselves was granted to the brother baker if he be kneading dough, to the brother smith if he had the fire going in the forge, to the brother farrier in the act of shoeing a horse, and also to any brother who happened to be washing his hair; but they must make up for it later. After Vespers the knights supped, and at Compline again assembled for worship. Before they retired for the night the orders for the next day were given and other domestic business transacted, which included dispensing justice at the chapter meeting once a week.

The severest penalty was expulsion, imposed for simony, treachery, cowardice in face of the enemy or charging without permission, and for breach of secrecy. Temple and Hospital had an agreement not to take in each other's expelled knights. For lesser offenses the Templar might be suspended from membership for up to one year and a day, though there are cases on record of perpetual imprisonment. Among such lesser offenses were throwing off the mantle of the order in a moment of anger, keeping undesirable company or retaining private property in any shape or form, and disposal of the order's goods outside it.

We read of one brother who was cast out for having thrown a hammer, Temple property, at a bird sitting on the river bank, so that the tool was lost in the water. We read of another who, carrying a tray of glasses, tripped and broke one. Glass was precious; the brother was greatly upset. Loudly cursing God and His Mother, he threw the whole tray on the ground with a crash. He, however, was merely suspended —it seems hard on the one who only lost a hammer. To be sure, a Templar's past conduct and achievements were taken into account when he came up for judgment.

About twenty different versions of the Temple Seal have come down to us. The best known, which passed into most general use, depicts two knights mounted on one horse, in token of poverty, humility and, last though certainly not least, brotherly love. As much care was taken to foster this as over the preservation of chastity; indeed, defections from brotherly love were punished more severely than the isolated cases of rape and sodomy which have come to our knowledge.

For the aged Templar who had outlived his usefulness, loving provision was made, of gentle mounts and delicate foods. Special houses were maintained in the West for such pensioners. Even knights stricken with leprosy were not expelled without a supply of money and clothing and an ass to bear them away. Invalids were accorded every dietary advantage, with dispensation to eat butter and eggs in Lent; they might be served with fried slices of young stag's horn, or the three kinds of soup made with wine in honor of the three persons of the Holy Trinity.

Thus were the cooks kept in practice for the superb banquets which the Temple would contribute to the congresses of native and foreign princes inaugurating successive Crusades, the coronations, royal marriages, distinguished embassies, or the state funerals of their own grand masters. Cookery was a great art, its practitioners in constant competition. Soups were the especial fancy of the glutton, the connoisseur and the culinary alchemist, as elaborately concocted as medicines or sweetmeats. The sauce, in all its variations and subcategories, also was a child of the Crusades. For spices, rare and worth their weight in gold in Europe, were easily come by in the Orient, and used in lavish and irrelevant combinations, bolstering up self-assurance and snobberies.

Another criterion of social merit was the horse, and here, too, the Templars scored, with their Spanish connections and the meticulous care of their horses. Only the hawk, indispensable adjunct of nobility — discussed, compared, collected, swallowing up fortunes — was denied them. But they could make a virtue of that necessity and look down on the fripperies of worldly knighthood, the dilettanti of Holy War. They had grown very conscious of the distinction and did not care who knew what they thought of outsiders. Their privileged place in the armies of Outremer on campaign was in the van or guarding the rear, whichever was the more perilous. By popular estimate one Templar could take on one hundred Saracens and two Templars were equal to a thousand; though the Temple itself modestly declares more than three Moslems too many for one single brother. They could not look for mercy, as no ransom was allowed, and they neither expected nor conceded it themselves. Their war cry was, *Non nobis, Dominus, non nobis, sed nomine tuo, da gloriam.* (Not unto us Lord, not unto us, but to Thy name give glory.)

In camp, the knights' tents were dressed around the blue marquee of the master and the one which served them as a chapel. The serjeants, Turcopoles and foot slept in the open air and shared a number of large caldrons. Their mobility was not hampered by camp followers, not even the washerwomen permitted by the high command for the rest of the host, provided such women were unexceptionably elderly (but the age level of laundresses fell punctually and mysteriously as campaigns progressed).

The Moslem leaders would not consider any major treaty ratified without the signatures of the grand masters of both military orders — in recognition of their importance and as a safeguard against their right of independent action. A certificate by the Templar grand master was required from every substitute pilgrim who returned home, to prove that he had really been to Jerusalem.

For a new trade had come into being, as penitents sentenced to pilgrimage were allowed to hire such substitutes, many of whom made an excellent living, taking on any number of vicarious pilgrimages in as many different districts. They would lie low for a time and reappear with the requisite palm leaves around their necks, without ever having set foot outside their native countries.

The Temple had done a great deal towards mapping out the country, which for the convenience of troop direction was measured out in traveling stages. The first ships to sail under the red cross swiftly grew into a fleet and began to appropriate much of the pilgrim traffic: transports conducted by the military orders could land men and merchandise virtually free of dues. Before long it is reckoned that between them Temple and Hospital accounted for an annual average of six thousand passengers, not to mention freights. The shipping houses of Marseilles, Messina and the Italian merchant republics soon felt the pinch, and set about investigating the chances for redress.

Temple and Hospital had become the chief builders in the Holy Land. Whether they took over existing strongpoints, reconstructed the relics of bygone colonists, converted caves into fortresses or started from scratch; whether they chose sites recommended by a junction of roads, rivers or frontiers, or tackled virgin rock in positions intended to remain difficult of access — wherever they gained a new foothold, building activities recommenced.

Timber was the only scarcity; other materials were plentiful. Plains and mountain regions alike were strewn with stones, rubble outlined the defunct water veins, and ruins abounded. From cairns and mounds to fallen fortresses still recognizable and places defined only by legends and apparitions, the land was littered with these ruins as it is to this day when they bedevil the problem of identification. In a less scientific age — the fourth century of the Christian era — their very profusion had helped the Empress Helena in her pilgrimage of divination — nearly every sacred monument in Palestine had received its particular allotment at her hands.

Labor was not lacking. Peasants, pilgrims, soldiers, prisoners of war, men, women and children, and even knights usually complacent in their mechanical incompetence — all could be employed. In the first place a ditch must be dug and hollowed out of granite, ramparts thrown up or chiseled to slippery steepness, lest the enemy harry the work and render it void. One marvels at the speed with which these primary operations must have been carried out, mainly by hands we should class as unskilled. The great Templar castle of Jacob's Ford took only five months to build.

Their Castle Pilgrim was so named by the many pilgrims who lent a hand with its construction. Yet in appearance and strength it was a thoroughly professional job. It had two frontal towers of squared and polished stone blocks so large that each required two oxen for trans-

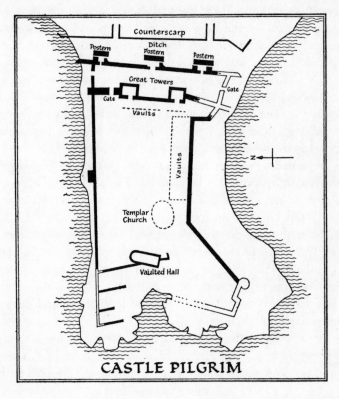

CASTLE PILGRIM

port. Each tower was a hundred feet long by seventy-four feet wide, with interior stairs; there was a double rampart, and immense battlements ornamented with colossal sculptures of Templar heads. On the north, west and south sides no ramparts were needed: the Mediterranean was their moat. Castle Pilgrim exemplified the Templar power. Nothing was wanting for its self-sufficiency; it embraced springs, pastures, orchards, vegetable gardens, fish ponds, salt mines, mills, and even some woods, a natural harbor improved by artifice, and a shipyard.

The fortifications of Safed, too, owed their existence to amateur building zeal. The Templars reconstructed this castle after it had been razed by Saladin. A standing menace to Damascus, it became invulnerable as the Maginot Line and was eventually bypassed in much the same way. But it was never again taken by assault. Here, too, the domain had everything needful for the support of fifty knights, thirty serjeants, fifty Turcopoles, three hundred arbalestiers, eight hundred and twenty squires and infantry, and forty slaves.

The only disadvantage to this way of building was that many a Crusader considered his vow fulfilled when he had done his stint. Architects and regular masons had of course to come into action and were not always lacking at the start. But they were able to make use of the unskilled hands to the end, particularly since as a rule walls were sandwiches of masonry with a filling of rubble many feet in depth. So similar were Moslem and Christian building techniques during this period that in most cases it is only by the masons' marks that their nationality can be ascertained.

The loftier the site, the weaker, relatively speaking, might the structure be. The depth of the moat usually was equal to the height of a tower; and towers, owing to shortage of beams, time, and the more sophisticated type of engineer, were still often solid up to a height of forty feet, having a vaulted upper story with loopholes and, says T. E. Lawrence, admirable latrines.

This is the only feature approved by Lawrence in his discourse on Templar architecture. Like the Archbishop of Tyre eight centuries before him, he starts out with a prejudice against the Templars, though the basis of it is less manifest than in the older writer. But his opinions always do tend to be unequivocally partisan, their roots obscure behind a smoke screen of self-revelation. In Lawrence's thesis on the Crusader castles, his adverse criticism of those erected by the Templars has a distinctly censorious note. Thus Castle Pilgrim is decried for its unsubtle reliance on brute strength and held up as a symptom of Templar arrogance.

". . . Given unlimited time and labour, anyone could make a ditch so deep and a wall so high of stones so heavy as to be impregnable, but such a place is as much a prison for its defenders as a refuge." Not at all, if such a place be surrounded by sea on three sides, having its own harbor and own navy, flanked moreover by friendly ports along the coast. With only one strip fronting land attack, subtlety would seem to be redundant.*

But it is a strange thing about the Templars that even until the present time they seem to compel partiality one way or the other, as if the frightful persecution with which their history ends depended on the character of the victims for evaluation, as if justice depended on the attractive or repellent aspect of the litigants, on the unadulterated goodness or badness of their influence and their architecture. At all events, Templar architecture varies sufficiently to make any sweeping praise or stricture rash.

It was best to build a castle on an irregular ground plan in order to frustrate enemy sappers. The Arab method was to tunnel under the moat until the central, rubble section of the wall was thought to have been reached. There a chamber would be hollowed, shored up and filled with highly inflammable material, which was then set alight insidiously to heat the masonry till it collapsed. The Arab mining engineers, particularly of Aleppo, were famous the world over, and Richard I went to some trouble to procure several of them for the siege of Daron.

Apart from practical considerations, mysticism entered into the principles of design — as it had to, where external opulence must continually

---

* In fact this castle was abandoned by the owners only after Outremer had ceased to exist.

justify itself with elaborate symbolism, forever protesting underlying intangibles. Thus, the square is the most perfect form, apprehensible by the senses, symbol of the visible world, which moves in four known directions. Next, the octagon is a square capable of moving in all directions, and thus containing the fundamental expressions of geometry. For two diagonal lines drawn between the farthest points of either side form the four-triangled cross (the cross of the Templars), which is itself the symbol of intelligence in its earthly manifestation. Completing every line of the four-triangle cross, however, will give us another octagon, which is the heavenly rose, that is, intelligence in its celestial form.

We need not here pursue a theory of which this is only an introductory sample, since one suspects it is a superstructure, rather than foundation, of the Templars' preference for octagonal or "round" churches. More likely the Church of the Holy Sepulchre and the Dome of the Rock served as prototypes, and their shape had been determined by the central shrine which each enclosed.

Nowhere did the Temple boast such sumptuous refinements as were to be found in some secular palaces, like the residence of the Ibelin lords at Beirut, with its floors of *trompe l'oeil* mosaics causing the visitor to marvel that his feet remained dry and left no prints in the realistic sand that seemed to show through gently wind-ruffled shallows. But their castles were held to epitomize safety. Popes and potentates traveling abroad would not lodge anywhere else. Henry III of England, visiting Louis IX of France, esteemed the Temple as the most secure fortress in Paris and declined with thanks an invitation to stay at the Palais de la Cité instead. Both in England and in France the crown jewels and the public moneys were frequently deposited with the Temple.

The Old Temple of Paris, dating back to 1128, was now subsidiary to the New, an autonomous township, ringed by wall and ditch, with a great tower flanked by four smaller ones, and having its own wharf, jurisdiction and police force. The privileges there obtaining attracted large numbers of immigrant citizens from other parts.

Despite the order's prominence in Spain, and its many fiefs in Germany, Hungary, Italy and Greece, the London Temple came next in importance. Hugh de Payens' original foundation in Chancery Lane had soon proved too cramped, and the New Temple of London, acquired by purchase, stretched from White Friars to the Temple Bar, with spacious grounds for exercise and recreation along the Thames. Here the order built one of its finest churches, which was consecrated in the presence of King Henry II and his court by the Patriarch Heraclius of Jerusalem in 1185, and bombed and burnt out in 1941.*

The master of the English Temple sat in Parliament as first ecclesiastic baron of the realm; and King after King of England conferred fresh benefits on the order — notably Stephen, Henry II, and John, who could all do with intercession for their souls and bulwarks for their throne. Henry III, who himself was one of the greatest benefactors of the Templars, confirmed all previous donations and privileges granted them in a charter from which extracts will give some idea as to the extent of their rights and possessions.

> . . . all reasonable donations of lands, men, and eleemosynary gifts . . .
> as well churches as worldly goods . . . with all liberties and free customs
> and immunities, in wood and plain, in meadow and pasture, in water and
> water-mills, on highways and byways, in ponds and running streams, in
> marshes and fisheries, in granges and broad acres, within burgh and
> without the burgh, with soe and sac, tol and theam, infangenethef and
> unfangenethef, and hamsoc and grithbrich, and blodwit and fictwit, and
> flictwit and ferdwite, and hengewite and lierwite, and flemenefrith, murder,
> robbery, forstall, ordel, oreste, in season and out of season, at all times and
> in all places, etc.
>
> We ordain, likewise, that the aforesaid brethren shall for ever hereafter
> be freed from royal aids, and sheriff's aids, and officer's aids, and from
> hidage and carucage, and danegeld and hornegeld, and from military
> and wapentake services, and scutages and lastages and stallages, shires

---

* It has now been restored and was rededicated by the Archbishop of Canterbury on 7 November, 1958, in the presence of Queen Elizabeth II. The effigies of Knights entombed were badly damaged and still await reconstruction.

and hundreds, pleas and quarrels, ward and wardpeny, and averpeni and hundredspeni, and borethalpeni and thethingepeni, and from the works of castles, parks, bridges, and enclosures; and from the duty of providing carriages and beasts of burden, boats, and vessels, and from the building of royal houses, and all other works. . . .

And we concede also to the aforesaid brethren the privilege of cutting down trees in all the woods they possess . . . and of clearing and bringing the land into cultivation without any licence from our bailiffs, so that they may never at any time hereafter be in any way called to account by ourselves, or our heirs, or any of our bailiffs. . . .

We ordain, moreover, that the aforesaid brethren and their men shall be quit and free from every kind of toll in all markets and fairs, and upon crossing bridges, roads, and ferries, throughout the whole of our kingdom, and throughout all lands in which we are able to grant liberties . . . also that if any of their men be condemned to lose life or limb for crime, or shall have fled from justice, or have committed any offence for which he has incurred forfeiture of his goods and chattels, the goods and chattels so forfeited shall belong to the aforesaid brethren . . . as our bailiffs would or ought to have seized them into our hands, had such goods and chattels belonged to ourselves, without the molestation or hindrance of the sheriffs or bailiffs, or any other person whatsoever. . . .

We moreover ordain, that if any of the liberties and privileges contained in this our charter shall happen to have been disused for a length of time, such disuse shall in no respect prejudice the right, but such liberty or privilege may be again exercised without contradiction, notwithstanding that it may have been discontinued and disused as aforesaid. . . . And we prohibit all persons, on pain of forfeiture, from proceeding against them or their men contrary to this charter, for we have taken the aforesaid brethren, and all their goods, and possessions, and all their men, under our especial guardianship and protection. . . .

In short, not only were the Templars freed from all the restrictions and obligations which hemmed in medieval man at every step and which make any present-day complaints of bureaucratic controls seem rather ungrateful, but their rights of jurisdiction were almost equal to, and independent of, the royal — an astounding state of affairs.

The Kings of England would often reside at the Temple for weeks at a time, and many important royal letters, treaties and publications are dated as from there. King John was staying at the Temple when forced to sign Magna Carta; Edward I was proclaimed King at the Temple; royal dowries were paid through the Temple, royal business transactions managed by the Temple.

The order's annual income in the whole of Europe has been estimated at thirty million pounds in present-day terms, its manors and fiefs throughout the world at between seven and nine thousand — leaving out of calculation the constant influx of moneys bequeathed and collected.

But it is with these figures as with those given for the armies of the period: they are impressionistic rather then exact. How could they be exact? What chroniclers were made free of the records of the Temple administration? Even had the Temple waived its autocratic secrecy, the rent rolls of each preceptory were not kept in duplicate at headquarters. What chronicler would have journeyed all over the Christian world to tot up the revenues of every outlying Templar holding? And even had this been possible, what guarantee was there that the written returns corresponded with the actual? Estimates were based on personal conceptions of wealth, not on statistics. We ourselves speak of *fabulous* wealth, and find therein a more vivid image than in astronomical figures.

Though unwaveringly conservative, the religious knighthood did its share towards the breakup of feudalism. Engendered by the rise of private as distinct from tribal property, which made of the man riding his own horse the principal military unit, the system had matured to ensure the supply of such units. In the course of the Crusades an, as it were, feudally unattached chivalry became the one dependable source of fighting strength. Also, knighthood became bestowable for valor, an honor unconnected with land tenure, as the only known form of military decoration. The individual was about to emerge into social existence.

8 The Dance of the Heiresses

KING BALDWIN IV OF JERUSALEM, A YOUTH OF PRECOCIOUS AWARENESS and probity, endowed with many gifts that should have made him an outstanding ruler, had been stricken with leprosy as a child. He came to the throne at the age of thirteen, his tutor, the historian Archbishop of Tyre, acting as his adviser, and his nearest male relative, the dour Count Raymond of Tripoli, as his regent. Count Raymond's temperament made few friends, but he was much respected. In 1173, the year before the Leper King's accession, Count Raymond had made a personal enemy, though he would hardly have been aware of the fact, or if aware, scarcely inclined to note it. The enemy was no one of any consequence — it needed the spur of affront to make him win importance. This spur Count Raymond had negligently provided. The man was a Flemish knight named Gerard de Ridefort who had taken service with him and to whom he had promised the hand of a rich young heiress. Circumstances led the count to break a promise given to one of so little account, and Gerard de Ridefort severed the connection and joined the Brotherhood of the Temple. It was an ill day for the Kingdom of Jerusalem when he did so.

The Christian conquest of Outremer had been accomplished entirely by the male element, by the agency of the spear. The distaff side, and the agency of matrimony, played a singular part in the downfall of the colony.

The Salic Law, of which later so much was to be made, at this time still slumbered well embedded in a compound of Teutonic traditions codified under Charlemagne, and entitled *leges barbarorum,* laws of the barbarians. But the barbarians, as under paragraphs 1 to 5 of Chapter 59 of this code, had not debarred women from inheritance, merely laying it down as a defense regulation that land should be handed on from man to man. In practice this meant only that an heiress's husband or other guardian became the lord of the fief in right of her possession. Not until the relevant clause was dug up for the great Anglo-French controversy of the fifteenth century was there any suggestion that it should be applicable to royal succession.

Even had it been commonly in force elsewhere, in Outremer the principle of female exclusion was impracticable. Masculine mortality was very high, masculine progenitive potency low for some reason. It is a commonplace that in human populations more boys tend to be born than girls, a greater number of the girls surviving. But it seems that among the Franks in the Holy Land the sex ratio of births was inverse, at the same time as more boys than girls continued to die in infancy.

As early as 1119, Baldwin I had to repair the gaps torn into the ranks of his vassals in the battle rightly designated "of the Field of Blood," by marrying off all the widowed ladies to replacements brought over from France.

He himself, however, put away his first Queen for adultery and, while she was still living, married the Countess-Dowager Adelaide of Sicily, for her wealth, her large Norman following and the strategic position of her island. She left behind her a grown son, that same Roger of Sicily who subsequently made himself King, greatly to the annoyance of European opinion led by St. Bernard. Adelaide sailed into the port of Acre in a galley plated with gold and silver, herself reclining on a carpet of golden thread and followed by nine other dizened ships which carried her retinue and vast treasure.

The treasure was soon spent by her new husband on overdue army pay and overdue repairs; soon, too, the fact that the marriage was a bigamous one on Baldwin's part became a politically useful lever against the unpopular Patriarch who had consecrated it. The end of it was that four years after the wedding Baldwin had his second marriage annulled and unceremoniously sent the improverished ex-Queen back to Sicily. She died one year later, but her son Roger never forgave King Baldwin, and his rancor for many years to come informed Sicilian policy towards Jerusalem.

Baldwin I died in 1188, childless, and having made no arrangements for the succession. Providentially — for he could not have heard of the

King's death in time, though possibly news of the King's illness might have reached him, and he was no fool — providentially, then, Baldwin of le Bourg, Count of Edessa, cousin to his royal namesake, happened to be in Jerusalem for the Easter celebrations. The King's funeral took place on Palm Sunday. So Baldwin of le Bourg, "of the beard," was unanimously elected by his fellow-barons and became the second King of his name on the Easter Sunday.

His unusual uxoriousness had borne fruit in the shape of four daughters, united in unusual family affection: Melisende, Alice, Hodierna and Joveta. There were no sons. Melisende, the eldest, as future Queen was provided with a consort who, while he might not be to her personal taste, filled the requirements for the next King of Jerusalem. Alice married the heir to Antioch, Hodierna and Joveta later became respectively Princess of Tripoli and Abbess of Palestine's richest convent, founded and endowed for her benefit.

Alice's husband, the Prince of Antioch, died at the age of twenty-four. The principality passed to their only child, a daughter two years old, called Constance. It was for her grandfather, the King, to appoint a regent during Constance's minority. But his daughter, Constance's mother, defied him, as outlined elsewhere. The rumor went that she intended to immure the infant Constance in a convent, which deprived her of the sympathy of the Antiochene nobles. They declined to contend for her against their King, and Alice had to ask her father's pardon on her knees. She was banished to her dower lands, and Baldwin took over the regency on behalf of his small granddaughter.

The following year, 1131, he too lay dead, and the red-haired Angevin Fulk was on the throne with Melisende. Alice immediately emerged from her exile and led a conspiracy against him. So instead of throwing all his resources into hammering the Infidel, Fulk's first campaign as King was against rebels of his own nation. He defeated them and obtained their oath of allegiance, as well as re-establishing the royal guardianship over poor disputed little Constance; but he returned to Jerusalem only to be faced with kindred trouble which concerned him more closely.

There was at his court a handsome young noble, the lord of Jaffa, named Hugh of le Puiset, who had been brought up with Melisende. Both these young people had been married to middle-aged spouses, and their friendship had continued. Hugh had grown-up stepsons, who hated him and made it their business to badger King Fulk with scandal concerning the relations of Hugh and Queen Melisende. Hugh began to gather a party of his own, and presently the nobility of the kingdom was divided into the King's friends and the friends of the friend of the Queen. Matters came to a head during a summer assembly at Jerusalem, where one of Hugh's stepsons publicly accused him of plotting against the King's life and challenged him to ordeal by combat.

This was a perfectly regular method of determining guilt or inno-cence in law; the winner was presumed vindicated, the loser, if he sur-vived the duel, would be hanged or burnt. Hugh accepted the chal-lenge, but on the day fixed did not put in an appearance. Naturally he was declared guilty by default. He fled to Ascalon, then enemy terri-tory. An Egyptian escort saw him safely home to Jaffa, whence he began incontinently to raid the plain of Sharon. His friends ceased to support him in what was open treason, and he was forced to throw himself on the King's mercy.

King Fulk dearly loved his Queen, and mercy accordingly was what Hugh received. He was sentenced to exile for three years, and given permission to come to Jerusalem to say good-by. There one evening he was stabbed in the back and head during a tavern brawl, and everyone believed the King had been behind it. The King saved his reputation by promptly having the murderer apprehended and put to death in a spectacular manner. But Queen Melisende was not appeased, and Fulk ever afterwards tried fruitlessly to regain her goodwill by giving way to her in all things. Melisende never lost the taste for power which she thus acquired.

To proceed with another strain of the family saga, Constance of Antioch was eight years old, and her vassals trusted her ambitious mother less than ever. They begged King Fulk to find a husband for the heiress with utmost despatch, in utmost secrecy. Alice and her doting elder sister, the Queen, must not learn what was afoot, or between them they would circumvent it, and the same went for King Roger of Sicily, who had designs of his own on Outremer. King Roger, however, with his extensive Norman connections, did hear, and tried to intercept Fulk's choice for Constance, Raymond of Poitiers, younger son of the Duke of Aquitaine and the fabulous Eleanor's uncle. Disguised now as a humble pilgrim, now, more humbly still, as a merchant's servant, Raymond arrived safe and sound at Antioch in the spring of 1136.

He was thirty-seven, virile and good-looking, full of charm, renowned in chivalry and untrammeled by undue learning. Alice herself was under thirty, and she was told that the interesting stranger had come to ask for her own hand. While, well-pleased, she waited in her palace to receive him, her little girl was spirited away to the cathedral and hastily married to Raymond. Having a husband to rule for her, Constance passed outside her mother's power forever. That was the end, politically, of Alice, who spent the rest of her life in retirement.

The eventful life of little Constance had only begun. While she recedes into the background for a spell and attains to years of discretion, the death of King Fulk, in 1143, refocuses attention on Queen Melisende. The lesson of Alice had not been lost on the elder sister. When she had done mourning her husband with an abandon that moved the whole court to tears, she settled the question of regency before it was mooted and had herself crowned as her young son's partner in government. In effect it was she who ruled the kingdom, which indeed had descended to her from her father. Together Melisende and the third Baldwin did the honors of Jerusalem at the brilliant assemblies for the Second Crusade and pulled their royal weight to aim it at Damascus; while Raymond of Antioch was so little abashed by his seniority to his wife as to indulge in a flirtation with his niece, Queen Eleanor of France.

He refused to join in the campaign against Damascus, which folly he had tried strenuously to expose. Neither he nor the Count of Edessa could afford to leave their lands undefended against Nur ed-Din's unremitting raids. While the Count of Edessa parleyed with the Sunnite Moslems, Raymond concluded an alliance with the Shia Assassins and went to war on his own account. In the night of June 28, 1149, he and his army, encamped in a hollow, were surrounded by Nur ed-Din's troops. When morning came and Raymond realized their plight, the attempt to charge their way out of encirclement was defeated by the upward slope and wind which blew the dust full into their eyes. The Christians were massacred; Raymond of Antioch was killed by Shirkuh's own hand. His skull was set in silver and presented to the Caliph of Baghdad, who already possessed that of his father-in-law, Bohemond of Antioch.

Constance, now the mother of four children, became a widow in her twenty-second year. Antioch was hers. She was in much the same position as Melisende on the death of Fulk, but her eldest son was only five years old and could not be invested co-regent. Her young kinsman, King Baldwin III, as an adult of nineteen, provisionally undertook the regency for her whilst looking about for eligible suitors to her hand. Not one whom he proposed found favor with her. In fact, his persistence only increased her resistance, and directly Baldwin had gone back to Jerusalem, she asked the Emperor Manuel to suggest a candidate — thus gracefully acknowledging him as her overlord. The Emperor was delighted to oblige, and, blinded by his own brand of family sentiment, sent her the Caesar John Roger, widower of Manuel's favorite sister, middle-aged like the deceased Raymond, but totally unprepossessing. Constance refused him too.

Now, in the train of Baldwin III on his visit to Antioch there had been Reynald de Châtillon. He stayed behind when Baldwin left, and within two years Constance announced their betrothal. She was, as the saying goes, infatuated with Reynald, and omitted to ask the Emperor's permission, which at best was an unwarranted discourtesy, at worst a breach of constitutional law.

The consent of King Baldwin as head of Constance's family and overlord of Reynald was asked and given. He had enough family problems on his hands without obstructing the solution, however unsatisfactory, of at least one.

It was now the turn of his aunt Hodierna, the third daughter of

Baldwin II. Hodierna was the wife of another Raymond, the Count of Tripoli, whose jealous passion drove him to keep her virtually a prisoner. Doubt had been cast on the paternity of their daughter, named Melisende after her aunt the Queen of Jerusalem. Melisende of Jerusalem persuaded her son to go with her to the deliverance of her sister; and they deemed it well to make a family party of it and summoned Constance to tell her what they thought of her behavior. Constance proved unrepentant, but Melisende and Baldwin did succeed in bringing about a reconciliation between Raymond of Tripoli and his wife. A period of amicable separation was agreed on: Hodierna should take a holiday with the Queen at Jerusalem, while Baldwin remained at Tripoli in case there were truth in the current reports of an impending Moslem offensive.

As he returned from seeing off his wife and sister-in-law, Count Raymond was set upon by a band of Assassins just inside the gates of his city and murdered in full view of his guard, who were unable to catch the killers. To make up for it every Moslem found in the streets of the town was slain; but that did not bring Raymond back to life, nor was any light shed on the motive of the murder.

Melisende and Hodierna were fetched back at once, and the countess assumed the regency for her son, twelve years old, called Raymond after his father, with King Baldwin as his guardián. Nur ed-Din was quick to see his opportunity, but the Templars rushed to the rescue, whereupon Baldwin presented them, in Hodierna's name, with the great castle of Tortosa.

The burden of so many responsibilities encouraged Baldwin to cut loose from his mother, as related earlier. There was some haggling, as she wished to retain Jerusalem, without whose military levies he would be powerless. This culminated in a measure of civil war which finally sealed the defeat of Melisende and ousted her, like Alice before her, from public life. Much valuable time, that should have been spent in hindering the growth of Nur ed-Din's strength, had been dissipated in domestic wrangles.

Constance, once herself a pathetic pawn, had reached maturity, and the conflict of mother and child was re-enacted between her and her son Bohemond. Again Baldwin' was called upon to arbitrate, and decided in favor of the son. About the same time, around 1160, the old rumor concerning Hodierna's infidelities rebounded on her daughter, young Melisende. The Emperor Manuel had lately been widowed and in courteous tit-for-tat asked the King of Jerusalem to nominate a bride for him. The two most eligible damsels were this young Melisende and a daughter of Constance, named Maria. Baldwin proposed young Melisende as he did not wish the ties between Byzantium and Antioch to become any firmer than they already were. All was made ready for the wedding, at very great expense, and the whole of Outremer saluted young Melisende as the future Empress. But along with detailed accounts of the bride's beauty, Manuel's informants had relayed the old aspersions on her legitimacy. The Emperor broke his engagement and married Maria of Antioch instead. Melisende's brother, the Count of Tripoli, furiously demanded reimbursement for Melisende's trousseau. Meeting only with rebuff, he used the twelve galleys that were to have accompanied the rejected bride to Constantinople, to harry the Emperor's coastal dominions. Young Melisende pined away and died, but she need not have envied the destiny of her cousin Maria.*

For the present it was enough that the traditional antagonism between Greeks and Latins had once more been heightened.

Baldwin III died, universally regretted, in the year 1162. His brother Amalric with alacrity put away his first and undesirable wife to get the throne, and in turn bequeathed it to his gallant young leper son in 1174.

It was believed that leprosy could be contracted in three ways: by sexual intercourse, eating ulcered sheep's tongues, and God's displeasure. In the case of Baldwin IV, the last cause was conspicuously operative, he being the fruit of an incestuous union. His father and mother had been third cousins, within the forbidden degree of consanguinity which

---

* Maria enjoyed the title of Empress for twenty years. Then, in the Byzantine upheavals of 1182, she was strangled by an order which her own young son had been forced to sign. Two months later this young Emperor himself was murdered.

was often overlooked at the outset of a marriage but furnished the grounds for a spate of princely divorces throughout the Middle Ages. Repudiating Agnes was the condition on which Amalric had got the throne, and he had not argued the point, beyond the proviso that the legitimate status of their two children, Baldwin and Sibylla, should not be affected. The difficulty here was that *divorce* did not exist; a marriage was *annulled* so that it had never taken place. Baldwin and Sibylla, therefore, were either bastards or begotten of incest inpenitent. However, Amalric by his second wife, a grandniece of the Emperor Manuel, had only one living child, another daughter. At his death there was no prince of the royal house save the young leper.

His reign began amid military confusion and dynastic free-for-all.

Exactly a fortnight after the death of Amalric and six weeks after the death of Nur ed-Din, the King of Sicily appeared with his fleet off Alexandria. He relied on land support from Jerusalem, having quarreled with the Byzantine Emperor (about a marriage proposal, be it said), and believed that Saladin was safely taken up with the Shia mutiny. But Saladin had already put down the rebellion, and in Jerusalem the new ruler had yet to find his feet. After waiting five days without results, Roger sailed home, and the first attempt on Egypt, which would have found the Egyptians unprepared, came to nothing.

At Jerusalem the question of the regency was the foremost preoccupation. Both King Amalric's wives were alive and incontestably kicking — particularly so the young King's mother, Agnes of Courtenay, who had lost two other husbands, the second by death, the third again by annulment, and now confined herself to love outside wedlock. The legitimate widow, Queen Maria Comnena, soon married again and lived happily ever after. But while her infant daughter by Amalric was too remote from the succession to be a factor in the intrigues of the moment, she took her place in the party of the house of Ibelin, to which she now belonged through her second husband.

To begin with, the regency was contested by two main parties, that of the Ibelins, who, in conjunction with most of the native barons and the Hospitalers, supported Count Raymond of Tripoli, and their opponents who strove to install none other than Reynald of Châtillon, released after sixteen years of captivity and fairly bursting with pent-up vindictiveness. Their chosen candidates indicate the respective party programs: the supporters of Raymond were for conservation and consolidation; the supporters of Reynald stood for aggression at any price.

If the majority of the native barons and the late King's lawful widow and the Hospital made up Raymond's party, one may well ask how the other was composed, and what hope had it of success? The King's mother flung herself into it heart and soul, if only to spite the Dowager Queen, and although politically she carried no weight, she came to have considerable sentimental influence on her son, who had been reared away from her and only now made her acquaintance. The Templars formed the bulk of Reynald's party: that was its strength and its promise, and they gathered behind them any independent Crusaders from the West, disproportionately vocal as always. Nevertheless, for the time being they lost out. Raymond of Tripoli obtained the regency.

This did not conclude party warfare. A few weeks after Raymond's appointment, the seneschal of the realm, who had governed it in the interim, was assassinated. No one knew who had inspired the deed, but Raymond was the inevitable guess. The seneschal's widow, lady in her own right of Oultrejourdain, married Reynald de Châtillon — Constance of Antioch having died some time before — so that once more Reynald had a rich base of operations. The struggle was envenomed by the fact that almost the entire Frankish nobility, Western and colonial, was by this time an intricate tangle of cousinships; also, within each party, feuds and wrestling for position went on as they always do.

The young Leper King tried his hardest to be fair to both sides and reconcile the two. He maintained good relations with his regent, but took for his seneschal the fiefless Count Joscelin of Edessa, who had been a fellow-prisoner of Reynald's at Aleppo and shared Reynald's sentiments. He kept on William of Tyre as his adviser, but hearkened also to his irresponsible mother. He worked in with the Hospital, but also gave the Templars their due.

Odo de Saint-Amand was then head of the order, as fierce and intractable a grand master as the Temple ever produced. The weal and power of his Brotherhood with him ranked high above all other considerations — other considerations, in fact, did not exist for him. He strained the order's privileges as far as they could humanly be made to go, and at the same time watched out hawklike against the slightest infraction. Only death had stayed King Amalric's hand against the order; Odo de Saint-Amand was not likely to forget that. Although of greater caliber than Reynald de Châtillon, and of a somewhat broader egotism, this leader of religious knighthood had much in common with the other, the robber baron. Both promulgated conquest, regardless; both despised "softness"; pride was breath of life to them and revenge as meat and drink.

In 1173, Count Raymond of Tripoli had sent them a kindred spirit in Gerard de Ridefort, that insignificant knight — Flemish of origin like Odo, intent on making his fortune in Outremer like Reynald, and hypersensitive to slights like both — whom he had so grievously disappointed. Gerard had done well in the count's service and had been promised the first heiress who should become available. A few months after this the Lord of Botrun died and his lands went to his daughter Lucia. Raymond broke his promise to the poor Flemish knight as a certain rich Pisan also desired Lucia and Botrun and offered her overlord the girl's weight in gold. It seems she weighed the equivalent of ten stone, and the Pisan got her.* Swearing vengeance, Gerard de Ridefort entered the Temple where upon entry one had to swear forgiveness to one's personal enemies. That the thirst for personal vengeance remained uppermost in his mind through thirteen years of hard work and hard fighting, thirteen years of turbulent history, events will show. Meanwhile he did well in his new calling, too, cut as he was to conform to the then ruling pattern set by the grand master.

Whatever his temperamental deficiencies, Count Raymond was a conscientious regent. As soon as his position was assured, he applied himself to placing a check on Saladin's successes. His exertions prevented the

---

* "The Italians, however rich, are not true gentlemen like the French, however poor," a Frankish chronicler improved the occasion.

entry of Aleppo (last refuge of Nud ed-Din's heir, the boy as-Salih) into the union of Damascus and Cairo, on the strength of which Saladin had now adopted the style of King of Egypt and Syria. It was no empty title.

Saladin's strength at this time is measurable by the increasing clemency and generosity of his methods.

It was as if the God whom he devoutly worshiped all his life had first endowed Saladin with the qualities he needed to get power, and then, once power was his, exchanged them for other qualities without which greatness would have passed him by. In the days of his rise Saladin showed himself cunning and ruthless — that he was courageous goes without saying. In his days of might and glory he was reserved, modest, rigidly honorable, courteous and merciful, and the greater he waxed, the more pronounced became his humanity. One may argue that he could then afford the luxury of handsome conduct; but the conquerors in history who availed themselves of this luxury are few.

Outmaneuvered by Raymond, Saladin withdrew his attentions from Aleppo and went in pursuit of his old enemies, the Shia Assassins. But in their territory he found himself assailed by the nameless influences of mysterious forces, which paralyzed his soldiers when the Old Man of the Mountains came within their grasp. Terrible dreams disturbed Saladin's sleep. One night he woke to find on his bed some cakes of a type which only the Assassins baked, still hot, and with them a poisoned dagger and a threatening letter. He sent a messenger to the Assassin Sheik and made peace.

He had concluded a truce with the Franks the previous year (1175), but Raymond had broken it in the cause of Aleppo's independence, and, with the fifteen-year-old Leper King commanding part of the army, inflicted a serious defeat on Saladin's brother and the militia of Damascus. Another unwritten truce supervened, however, while Saladin reorganized Egypt and a new crisis arose at Jerusalem.

At sixteen, King Baldwin IV came of age and Raymond's regency was ended. But the young King's disease was making rapid strides, and the succession must be provided for. An embassy sailed for Europe to find a husband for the King's sister Sibylla and at the same time try again to rouse the Christian world to action against Saladin. In the latter task the embassy was not very successful, but Sibylla was married to the son of the Marquis of Montferrat, heir to the richest principality of Northern Italy. He was attractive as well as highly connected, and acceptable to both the Princess and the barons. Unfortunately the marriage was of brief duration, as he succumbed to an attack of malaria after only a few months. His widow gave birth to a posthumous son, who would again require a regent. The search for a husband for Sibylla was resumed.

In the third week of November, 1177, news came that Saladin had crossed the Egyptian frontier. The constable of the kingdom was seriously ill, and Baldwin IV's malady now practically incapacitated him. Once more the young man's will won over his pitiable infirmity, and he acted with a speed and decision which would have done credit to a man much older and having his health. He sent out an immediate call for every man who could bear arms to join him, and hurried to Ascalon. The knightservice at his disposal numbered five hundred — no inconsiderable force if one reflects that mailed knights were the armored vehicles of the day — but Saladin's reserves were unlimited. The Temple summoned all its available knights to the defense of Gaza, to no purpose, as the Saracens marched straight on Ascalon. They intercepted the reinforcements from Jerusalem and, leaving some troops to pen Baldwin in Ascalon, continued towards the Holy City. Baldwin managed to get a message through to Gaza, asking the Templars to abandon the fortress and come to his relief — a contingency which overconfidence had led Saladin to discount. Indeed, so certain was he of victory that he relaxed discipline and allowed his troops to straggle and pillage, the while the Templars by forced marches achieved the seemingly impossible.

Directly they approached, Baldwin broke out of Ascalon and conjointly with the Templars surprised the Egyptian army at a ravine a few miles southeast of Ramleh. Many of Saladin's troops were out on forage, and he had no time to regroup the rest. Many fled at the first impact, those who held their ground were cut to pieces, and Saladin himself only just escaped from the battlefield. Foremost among the Christian warriors was the young King with his stiff limbs and bandaged hands, more than half-blind, and St. George was seen to ride beside him.

Laden with booty, the army returned to Jerusalem. It lacked the numerical strength and the means to pursue the enemy to Egypt. Thus the victory was not followed up, save in the comparatively negative way of strengthening the outer defenses of the kingdom. If only substantial aid had been forthcoming from the West! But even the offer of marriage with the heiress to the throne brought no response. Sibylla decided to act for herself. She had fallen in love with Baldwin of Ibelin, brother-in-law to her stepmother, Maria. But before a marriage could be arranged, Baldwin of Ibelin was taken prisoner in the great rout of the Christian forces at the Valley of Springs, which came about as follows.

The Templars had started on the construction of a new castle at Jacob's Ford — the place where reputedly Jacob had striven with the angel, and which by an undertaking hitherto respected on both sides was never to be fortified. The local Moslem tribesmen complained to Saladin, who offered King Baldwin 60,000 gold pieces to stop the work. But though he raised the sum to 100,000 gold pieces and the King was willing, Odo de Saint-Amand would not hear of it, and building was flamboyantly continued.

Saladin was incensed and staked everything on destroying the new castle. This time it was the Christian King who barely escaped with life and liberty, and in a second engagement soon after, Odo de Saint-Amand rashly ordered a headlong attack which proved fatal to the whole Templar battalion and ended in complete rout for the remainder of the Christian army. Among the important prisoners taken was the Grand Master of the Temple himself. Saladin was prepared to exchange him for a Moslem prisoner of equal importance, but Odo stood by his order's ancient honorable ruling against ransom (some said because he would not admit anyone to comparable importance with himself), and died imprisoned in Damascus the following year.

Nothing prevented the ransoming of Baldwin of Ibelin — except the enormous sum which Saladin demanded for him: 150,000 gold pieces. Even the Ibelins were not rich enough to raise so much. The young man was let out on parole (against the release of one thousand Moslem captives, on account, as it were) to try and find his ransom. Whilst the Princess Sibylla had been writing love letters to him in his prison, she now informed him that she could not marry a man under so heavy a debt. As a last resort her suitor went all the way to Constantinople to ask the Emperor for a loan, and Manuel magnificently made him a present of the full amount. But when Baldwin of Ibelin returned to Palestine with his money, he found his Princess about to marry someone else.

Sibylla's mother disliked all Ibelins, and she had been singing the praises of a young Frenchman, reputed to be extraordinarily good-looking, who happened to be a brother of Sibylla's mother's current lover. While Baldwin of Ibelin was out of the way on his begging errand, the well-publicized wooer was shipped across to Outremer, and Sibylla was duly dazzled. Not so the young King, her brother. Weak and ill, Baldwin IV still had his wits sufficiently about him to see that there was nothing to the said young man but his looks. Even his ancestry was nothing to write home about; and if he claimed, like the Plantagenets, to be descended from Satan through his (Satan's) daughter Melusine, that was no recommendation either. His family were the Lusignans, petty nobles of Poitou, and the dazzling young man Guy was a third son without land or reputation.

He got him land, for Sibylla and her mother overbore the sick King until he gave his consent despite the protests of the barons; and upon his marriage to Sibylla, Guy de Lusignan became Count of Jaffa and Ascalon, no less. A reputation was not slow in following, but it was a reputation for vainglory, suggestibility, and foolhardiness.

The party of Count Raymond of Tripoli had suffered its severest setback by this marriage. Only a short while before, it had looked as if the change in the leadership of the Temple would benefit them and weaken the opposing faction. The new grand master, Arnold de Torroge (*de la Tour rouge*) could hardly have been more different from the defunct Odo. He was an elderly knight and had been master in Spain for many years, sober, equable, circumspect and entirely uninvolved with any coterie. Elections were among the most secret proceedings of the Temple, and all deductions must be based on inference: it seems clear enough, however, that the electors were in reaction against the last régime. Their only chance to influence the policy of the order came with the choice of a grand master, who, once he was in power, had absolute command.

Had Sibylla married an Ibelin, party warfare must have ceased for want of balance. Guy de Lusignan, however, was a born compeer to Reynald de Châtillon. The King made one more effort to heal the rift and betrothed his half-sister Isabella (stepdaughter of the Ibelin lord by her mother's second marriage) to Reynald's latest stepson. But the next move of Reynald's party precluded reconciliation with that of all men of good sense.

The Patriarch of Jerusalem had died, and under pressure of the King's mother the chapter of the Holy Sepulchre elected one Heraclius, Archbishop of Caesarea, to the vacant office. Heraclius also was good-looking and very little else, unless one counts his amatory prowess. For he owed his position to the favor of the King's mother and was famous for his harem, at present headed by the beautiful wife of an Italian merchant, whom men dubbed Madame la Patriarchesse.

The appointment of Heraclius made a mockery of the holy office to which he had been elevated. The obvious person, and a worthy choice, would have been William of Tyre, who hurried to Jerusalem in an attempt to stop the investiture. But the King was now so much under his mother's thumb that he confirmed Heraclius out of hand. In this way Baldwin IV deprived himself of the only interested counselor remaining to him. The Patriarch took the first opportunity to excommunicate the Archbishop of Tyre, who lugged his manuscripts into exile at Rome, where he set about polishing and revising his great history, in between appeals to the Pope for redress. The work was never completed; William died, poisoned, it was said, by Heraclius's agents.

Having eliminated Baldwin IV's old tutor, the next step was to persuade the dying King that his former regent, Count Raymond, was plotting against him. It took the united efforts of his chief vassals to induce

Baldwin so much as to grant an audience to Raymond and although Raymond succeeded in establishing his innocence, Baldwin stuck fast in the bosom of his family.

He was soon made to feel what had become of the royal power.

Another truce with Saladin had been concluded in 1180, which was to have lasted for two years. The Kingdom of Jerusalem was sorely in need of such a respite. The Emperor Manuel was dead and the old story of dynastic struggles was re-enacted at Byzantium, where there was now no further interest to spare for the Holy Land. The rulers of Armenia and Antioch, released from Byzantine tutelage, felt the breath of freedom and proceeded to quarrel with each other — also to the exclusion of war against the Infidel. Saladin need have no fear of any allies coming to the aid of the Kingdom of Jerusalem, which was all he had now to reckon with.

Reynald de Châtillon, however, could see no farther than his nose, conditioned to the scent of immediate profit and easy bloodshed. By the terms of the truce, Christian and Moslem merchants were to pass freely through each other's territories. But the caravans on pilgrimage to Mecca, traversing his fief of Oultrejourdain, right under that nose of his, as if to tease him, became too much for Reynald. He swooped down upon them to kill and plunder. Saladin complained to King Baldwin, who admitted him to be in the right, but found himself unable to procure compensation, as Reynald brazenly ignored the dictate of his sovereign. So the war was resumed, at the worst possible time for the kingdom.

None of the battles, the errors in strategy, the seesaw of victory and defeat, and continual inner turmoils of the next year or so, was immediately decisive. But insensibly their cumulative effect worked for Saladin. In June, 1183, he took Aleppo. With that, his empire became the most powerful which the Moslem world had known for over two hundred years.

While Saladin was busy putting the finishing touches to this empire, King Baldwin IV, his age yet only twenty-one, completely lost the use of his limbs, which began to crumble away. He was confined to the society of his mother, his sister and the priapic Patriarch. He yielded to their combined urging and appointed Guy de Lusignan his regent, reserving only the city of Jerusalem for himself.

Reynald de Châtillon felt encouraged to improve upon his recent exploits. He built a fleet and hired every pirate he could tempt into his service with the bait of the annual Moslem pilgrim transports, and sailed down the coast of the Red Sea, raiding, pillaging, slaughtering, all the way to the ports that served Mecca and Medina, where their exuberance mounted to particularly savage outrages.

A holy zeal of indignation offset Reynald's initial advantage. The Egyptian fleet was rushed to the area and played havoc with the corsairs, whose actions had shocked Christians and Moslems alike. Reynald himself escaped; the rest were destroyed to the last man. Saladin took a ceremonious vow to hunt down Reynald wherever he might hide himself.

Guy de Lusignan, too, could not wait to overreach himself. The sick King wished to exchange Jerusalem for Tyre with its milder climate, and Guy denied the request with a contemptuous rudeness which reacted upon Baldwin as a tonic. Although he could no longer move without help, nor even sign his name, rage renewed his lease of life. He contrived to summon his chief vassals and with their enthusiastic agreement Guy was deposed. The King himself took over the government again — whatever this must have meant in terms of superhuman effort on the one hand and compassion, vigilance and loyalty on the other. Baldwin IV still had strong and faithful friends — when he cared to use them. He proclaimed as his heir Sibylla's small son by her first husband, with Guy explicitly excluded from the regency, which was once more to go to Count Raymond of Tripoli. Guy at this retired to his fief and formally threw off his allegiance to the crown, and the King sought vainly to persuade his sister to agree to an annulment of her marriage. Arnold de Torroge, Heraclius and the Grand Master of the Hospital endeavored to plead for Guy and were forbidden the palace.

Reynald de Châtillon was not in evidence at these conferences. He was busy preparing to show the world that he was undaunted by defeat and untouched by shame. News of a great feast to put all others in the shade was sure to spread farthest and widest, and he decided at this juncture the marriage of his stepson and the King's half-sister — with whose betrothal three years before Baldwin IV had vainly tried to make peace between the factions. So now there were wedding guests from both camps; and as if to do his share in disseminating peace and goodwill among Christians, Saladin advanced to besiege Reynald. For this was the marriage of Kerak,* held at that great castle which commanded the trade and pilgrim routes between Syria and Egypt.

Even Saladin could not accomplish the impossible; neither common feasting nor common danger damped the factional hatreds. However, Saladin broke off the siege at the approach of the army of Jerusalem, which was led by Count Raymond, and accompanied by a litter containing the decaying lump of flesh in which there dwelt still the King's indomitable spirit.

It was the last time King Baldwin left his bed.

He gave the grand masters of the Temple and the Hospital and the Patriarch the chance to redeem themselves in his eyes and sent them to Europe on a joint mission to impress the German Emperor, Frederick Barbarossa, King Louis of France, and King Henry II of England, with the desperate peril of the Holy Land. Arnold de Torroge died on the outward journey. At Jerusalem the grand chapter assembled for the election of the next grand master.

Raymond of Tripoli had refused the guardianship of the heir apparent, who was delicate, lest in the event of the child's death he were held responsible. He agreed, however, to undertake the regency again. If the child died before the age of ten, the Pope, the German Emperor and the Kings of France and England were to arbitrate between the claims of Sibylla and her half-sister Isabella.

It seemed as though the stable element in the realm had prevailed, and under this impression the favorite candidate for the highest office of the Temple was rumored to be Gilbert Erail, commander and treasurer of Jerusalem, confrère of Arnold de Torroge. Once again reaction super-

* Mentioned in Chapter 4.

vened. When the conclave broke up it was announced that Brother Gerard de Ridefort was the chosen one. However narrow the margin by which he had achieved it, Gerard de Ridefort, soldier of fortune, who had no cause so close at heart as the settling of old personal scores, occupied the unassailable position of Grand Master of the Temple.

Like all the barons of the kingdom, like the Grand Master of the Hospital and the Patriarch of Jerusalem who had just returned from their fruitless embassy, Gerard de Ridefort swore to carry out the wishes of King Baldwin IV, and assisted at the coronation of the small boy Baldwin V. A few weeks later the Leper King died. He had lived to the age of twenty-four. We may find it comforting to remember that the crown, thorny though it was upon his brow, had saved him from the common fate of lepers, which was complete social outlawry and complete degradation.

There was famine in the land, so that Count Raymond carried his proposal of a four years' truce with Saladin. If peace could be maintained until such time as the crusading spirit was revived in Europe, the Holy Land might yet be saved. But Raymond's fears for the boy-King's health were justified, and Baldwin V died, nine years old, in the summer of 1186, after a reign of eighteen months.

Always in that forlorn hope of peace-making, Baldwin IV had appointed to the post of the child's personal guardian Reynald de Châtillon's friend, Joscelin of Edessa. Throughout the brief reign, Joscelin had professed the warmest friendship for Raymond. It is not so wonderful as, after the event, we are inclined to think, that such pretense will commonly succeed. Even the most intelligent and cynical are apt to have sufficient liking for themselves to consider it understandable in former detractors to come around to the same sympathetic view. The stern, cold-reasoning Raymond was taken in by plausible Joscelin, who persuaded him to invite the barons to a meeting at Tiberias, out of reach of the untrustworthy Patriarch, while he, Joscelin, would sacrifice himself and take the little corpse to Jerusalem for burial. As soon as Raymond had gone Joscelin, with the connivance of the Templars and the Western independents, proclaimed Sibylla Queen. While Joscelin and the Westerners occupied Acre, Tyre, and Beirut the Templars took the body to Jerusalem, and messengers raced to summon Sibylla and Guy from Ascalon and Reynald de Châtillon from Kerak.

By the time Count Raymond discovered the trick, it was too late. Outside his own party, the only one of all those who had solemnly sworn to carry out the testament of Baldwin IV and tried to keep his oath, was the Grand Master of the Hospital. As for the new Grand Master of the Temple, he had waited thirteen years for just such a moment as this. The Church, in the person of the Patriarch Heraclius, was on Sibylla's side, and so was the majority of the population. For all that her husband was generally despised, Sibylla was daughter, sister and mother of the last three Kings, and was their heiress.

The Templars closed the gates of Jerusalem and kept them under guard. The soldiers of Joscelin and Reynald held the seaports. Still, to take the sacred crown from the treasure vault of the Holy Sepulchre, it needed three keys. Gerard de Ridefort had one key, Heraclius the second; without the consent of the Grand Master of the Hospital, the third lock could not be undone. For a time he refused; in the end, threatened with revolt in the town, he gave up and "with a gesture of disgust" threw the third key out of the window: let anyone who liked grovel to retrieve it. For himself and his knights he repudiated any part in the coronation.

The supporters of Guy de Lusignan were under no illusions as to his popularity. It would not do for the Patriarch to crown Sibylla's husband. The customary ceremony yet preserved some forms of elective Kingship; for example, the officiating Patriarch had to call thrice on the assembled people to signify their acceptance of the monarch. What if instead of Yes! Yes! Yes! the common shout were to be No?

So it was only Sibylla who had to take the oath to observe the law of the kingdom, to respect the existing allocation of fiefs, to be faithful in protecting widows and orphans, and give justice to all, only Sibylla who swore to guard the privileges of the Church and received the Patriarch's promise of assistance to the Crown, and only Sibylla whose legitimacy was affirmed by threefold acclamation, sacrament and diadem.

But, inside the Church of the Holy Sepulchre a second crown reposed in readiness beside her on a cushion.

Having solemnly consecrated her Queen, the Patriarch Heraclius asked Sibylla to bestow that second crown on the person she judged most worthy to govern on her behalf. She beckoned Guy to kneel before her, and with a kiss placed the second crown on his head. The basilica of Christ's entombment rang with cheers.

As the golden circlet came to rest on the head of Guy de Lusignan, Gerard de Ridefort, Grand Master of the Temple, exulted aloud for everyone to hear, *"Cette couronne vaut bien le mariage de Boutron!"* The slight to the impecunious Flemish knight of thirteen years before was avenged. Raymond of Tripoli had been paid back. What matter if the price was the future of the Holy Land and the lifeblood of its denizens?

9 *The Knights Financiers*

> *Li frere, li mestre du Temple*
> *Qui estoient rempli et ample*
> *D'or et d'argent et di richesse,*
> *Où sont-il? Que sont devenu?*
> *Que tant ont de plait maintenu,*
> *Que nul a-elz ne s'ozoit prendre,*
> *Tozjors achetoient sans vendre.**

THE ORDER OF THE TEMPLE CANNOT BE CONDEMNED FOR THE SHORTCOM-ings, even the crimes, of any of its leaders, any more than the pious inten-tions of its founders can excuse later malpractice. That Odo de Saint-Amand and Gerard de Ridefort were dangerous men to have at the

---

* The brethren, the masters of the Temple,/Who were well-filled and ample/ With gold and silver and with wealth,/Where are they? How have they fared?/ Who had such power that none dared/Take aught from them, no man so bold:/ Forever buying, they never sold.

head of a powerful closed organization was an unhappy accident — the type of accident, however, to which powerful closed organizations are especially prone. The flaw was there; it would be idle to attempt to fix the blame in any one quarter, just as no single conscious agency could have suppressed the symptoms.

In no way could the rank and file be held responsible for elections which were not what we should call democratic, since the grand chapter was composed of the various preceptors and other high dignitaries whom the grand master, not the general membership, had chosen — and they again could co-opt anyone they wished without reference to the groups their choice was supposed to represent. Nor is it at all certain that the winning vote obtained by virtue of numerical majority, a principle which was not then self-evident as it appears now. In the election of the Holy (West) Roman Emperor, for example, some votes counted more than others; and in view of the strict hierarchy of Templar officialdom, the same is likely to have been the case in the Temple Order.

There are other involuntary impressions to guard against. Misfortune will endear the victim to us in retrospect, where face to face it will more often repel; large faults seem more forgivable than niggling blemishes. Richard Lionheart remains romantic when he has two thousand six hundred captives beheaded in cold blood, but we must not be told of him that he picked his nose or covered his face with grease as he ate with his fingers. To break wind is only for villains or comic characters, and financial profit looks bad in print, except on commercial balance sheets.

Right up until the ultimate catastrophe, the Temple Order profited from every contingency with which it was faced.

The Christian conquests in Palestine had acted on the West much as the discovery of the West Indies and of gold in Alaska was to act on the populations of later ages; a continuous movement, eastward-bound, on the part of the enterprising, was the result. When it became apparent that the days of Outremer might be numbered, a reverse mass movement developed. The Templars profited from both. First the pilgrim rush brought them prosperity; later the many Frankish colonists who pulled up their stakes and went back to Europe while the going was yet good, enabled anyone with capital to buy up land and movable property in a cheap market.

Pilgrims liked to use the Templars' ships. On board them one might rest assured that the captain would not jettison the poorer passengers in an emergency so as to conserve stores for the safe transport of the wealthier, as happened only too often. Neither would one be held to ransom on the high seas, nor kidnaped and taken to some Moslem port for sale in the slave market — as also happened frequently. Trading with the enemy was so common, particularly among the Italian shipping companies, that papal bulls had to prohibit the practice over and over, without even putting a stop to the systematic export of ships to Egypt in the form of prefabricated timber that only wanted assembling to be launched against the Christians. The Templars traded with the Moslems too, but not in war materials, and only when they happened to be partners in a truce. They, too, used Christian slaves, but undertook to sell them only to Christian masters.

Fervent jubilation shook the ship when the coast of the Holy Land was sighted. With every flag and pennon hoisted, it made for port, and ashore every church bell tolled in welcome. The gigantic chain which protected the harbor entrance was released, and on the quayside crowds streamed together, of friends, relations and officials, the cargo owners and prospective buyers, guides and touts and navvies, and spectators with the thieves and buskers who were their parasites, and knights languishing in idleness since their horses had perished, avid for replacements.

The pilgrims who on landing had thought their troubles at an end soon discovered their misconception. Directions and instructions were issued to them, considerately in four languages; * but there was no standard table of conversion for the different currencies. There were a great many more of these than four. In France alone it was not until

* Latin, Italian, Langue d'oeil French and German.

the time of Louis IX that the mint became a royal monopoly; until then every great lord could strike his own coin, and the same held for most other nations.

Every specie of the West and the East was in circulation here. The political ups and downs of a country did not show themselves in fluctuation of its currency, which was embodied in actual metal of an actual value. But it was this actual value which was so difficult to assess in coins of varying weights and using metal with varying quantities of different alloys. Furthermore, payment in kind was everywhere acceptable, and the value of articles did fluctuate according to the state of the market. So the pilgrim's very first transactions were complicated enough — be it food they wished to buy or votive candles; and the money-changer filled a very necessary role. The Templars were considered the most trustworthy exchange brokers.

At first it was the *petits gens,* the small fry, who formed the Temple's clientèle. But the larger fry soon saw its uses too. The hazards of travel were so much the greater for the man of means, unless he wished to increase his outlay in hiring armed protection, and even then, if he was not himself a warrior, how could he hope to handle godless routiers? Also, it was inconvenient to carry large sums of money, which easily ran into wagon loads. The bank note was yet unknown.

There have been some attempts to credit the Templars with the invention of the bank note — and of the check, the safe deposit, the modern consulate, and whatwillyou, for good measure. But these attempts are bound up with the desire to prove the Templars either angels with flaming swords or villains of satanic hypocrisy. Their latter-day apologists have spared no effort to claim for the Temple a continuity posthumously confounding its persecutors, showing that Templars survive to this day, underground, that guilds, Freemasons, Rosicrucians, and indeed secret societies of every description are directly descended from them, that Vasco da Gama and Columbus were clandestine Knights Templars, and every explorer worthy of the name. So far they have stopped short only of going backwards in time and appropriating for the greater glory of the Temple the right sort of heroes who were born before it was founded.

On the other side are those who will allow the Templars no sincerity, no fortitude, no benign influence whatsoever, in the same breath minimizing Templar achievements and denouncing a black cosmopolitan conspiracy on a par with the Elders of Zion.

Most of these points must be dealt with in a different place. Regarding checks and drafts and bank notes, the latter are a development of the first, which could not evolve fully until the days of printing. As for the check, we have seen that the word comes from the Arabic; while the IOU, of which it is but an extension, is as old as what we call civilization in even its rudest forms. The Romans, with their far-flung empire, where neither great fortunes nor noble blood were derived from land tenure, dealt in bills and drafts, with promissory notes used almost as currency, and banking already a profession. Their immediate heirs were the merchant republics of the Italian seaboard; and here, as well as in the Jewish colonies of the Diaspora, were the first international banking houses. Lombards and Jews played a prominent part in the financing of the First Crusade and subsequent supporting movements; and both suffered for it — as were the Templars to suffer.

For the Templars did rise to great heights as financiers. The vaults of their fortresses were secure and neutral ground, and extremely capacious. They had to be that, since all monies collected for the Holy Land were given to the Temple for conveyance, in addition to the order's own funds, in perpetual motion through the provincial preceptories to the chief house at Jerusalem. The papal tithe was paid into safe keeping at the Temple; the kings of Western nations placed the public money there, when they had any, and employed the Temple to hold castles and whole countries in custody, pending arbitration, apart from raising loans for royal dowries and for wars.

Usury was anathematized, and so in loans between Christians the interest covering the lender's risk and trouble was calculated beforehand and included in the amount borrowed. Not that the Temple kept extensive records of such activities, which often were noted cursorily and in code — a lordly casualness that could occasionally lead to trouble. Joinville, the friend and biographer of Louis IX, relates that he deposited

400 deniers at the Temple House of Acre. When he wished to draw on his money, he was told that no such deposit could be traced and indeed "nobody had ever heard of him at all." He appealed to the grand master, without success, and sadly resigned himself to his loss. A few days later the master came to him, laughing heartily, and said the money had been located. The Temple commander to whom Joinville had entrusted it had been transferred to another preceptory; he alone had had knowledge of the matter, hence the regrettable mistake.

A mistake of this kind may not accord with our notion of a mighty company, but bookkeeping in the Middle Ages was a tenuous and confused business — sometimes items belonging on a specific roll are missing or else duplicated, while items of quite other categories make an incongruous appearance. Not for nothing are some kings and chancellors specially commended by the chroniclers for tidying up the state accounts. Many a transaction was concluded by oath and handclasp only, as a matter of honor, or else as too shady to be set down.

Most of our knowledge of the Templars' internal economy comes from the flotsam of correspondence recovered after the deluge that swept them away. Those wily politicians and redoubtable warriors who were their preceptors, show themselves to have been also the most careful of husbandmen. Subpriors are urged to make sure that a consignment of poultry shall contain males as well as females, that the dovecotes of the carrier pigeons are kept clean, olives packed properly, arrow shafts stored where they will not warp; they receive the minutest directions for the disposal of the harvest and what to buy in the open market, what to obtain in part exchange from other houses of the order. "Go circumspectly about the sale of your wine and oil, note the prices for good and inferior qualities; buy in oats as quickly as possible; take care that the wind does not uproot your new plantations and also see that they are not damaged by the cattle. . . . For our part we inform you that we are at present engaged in building a ship for 6,000 Solidi: In answer to your enquiry whether we would like you to send us a quantity of dates, we reply herewith that we should prefer cash. . . ."

Such attention to detail appears touching at a remove of eight centuries; but the indulgent smile fades as we pass from the particular to the general, from household management to wholesale trade, with all the sensuous associations of citrus fruits, figs, pomegranates, almonds; balsam from Engaddi, purple from Tyre; aniline, indigo, and ultramarine, i.e. the "pigment from Outremer"; saffron, gum, myrrh, mastic, terebinth oil; grapes from Gaza and Ascalon growing in such enormous clusters on vines trained horizontally along the ground that, as in the time of Moses, it needed two men to carry one bunch. Although the land once flowing with milk and honey, most fertile province of Byzantium, and brightest jewel of the early caliphs, now had only isolated productive areas, there were some cedars yet on Lebanon, and some manufacturing centers survived for cane sugar, silks, porcelain and glass, while the pearls and spices of India and the gold of the Sudan passed through Palestine to reach the West.

The imports of Outremer were large. Even without intermittent drought and earthquakes, the country was always on the brink of famine, and dependent on Europe, especially Italy, Sicily and Cyprus, for most of its grain — although some of this came from Moslem Syria. Horses and cattle also were in the main supplied from overseas.

The Temple had a finger in every pie. Display of wealth, from an incidental feature having its recondite metaphysical excuse, became more and more a business asset.

Many Moslems banked their money at the sign of the eight-pointed red cross, against the hazards of their own internal hostilities and, for that matter, of the luck of war. Although the sufferings of the helpless civilians in general outweighed those of the armed forces, war was yet far from total, and even when there was no truce, traffic between enemy provinces did not necessarily cease. The tolerance which this might seem to evidence did not mark the progress of humane enlightenment so much as it worked for cynicism. As principles relaxed, it began to be forgotten that wealth was supposed to be only a means to a fully circumscribed end: that the riches of the Templars, like the order itself, existed solely for the service of Christendom in Palestine.

The climax of moral confusion came when, in 1187, the Temple actually refused, and had to be compelled, to disburse its money for the cause which all along had been its justification.

After Sibylla and Guy had been crowned at Jerusalem, Guy's own brother Geoffrey remarked acidly, "If Guy has become King, for sure I shall end up as God." Count Raymond of Tripoli and the rest of the magnates took a similar view but expressed it in more practical fashion. If necessary, they would not stop at civil war to set aside the farcical coronation. Count Raymond and the High Court of Barons assembled at Nablus decided to put forward as rival Queen and King Sibylla's half-sister Isabella and her husband Humphrey — the youthful bride and groom of Kerak. But Humphrey was the stepson of Reynald de Châtillon and besides had no taste for war or kingship. He fled to Jerusalem and did homage to Guy. Without a legitimate pretender, the scheme fell to the ground. Raymond released the others from their oath, and one by one they went and made their peace with Guy — excepting Raymond himself and Baldwin of Ibelin who told the new King to his face that he, Baldwin, would forsake his lands sooner than pay homage. As good as his word, he left soon after for Antioch, where Prince Bohemond was happy to aid anyone of Raymond's party. Guy meanwhile had added insult to injury, deprived Raymond of his fief of Beirut, and ordered him to render an account of the public money spent during Raymond's regency. Raymond began seriously to consider saving the Crown by taking it for himself.

King Guy might count himself lucky in the truce with Saladin. But Reynald de Châtillon was still a law unto himself. The Moslem caravans were running again, and Reynald waited only for the biggest, to fall on it and fill Kerak with a haul of booty and prisoners to dwarf any of his previous takings. Guy must have been put in mind of his luckless predecessor, for when in answer to Saladin's protest he ordered Reynald to make reparation, his friend took no more notice than he had done in the previous reign.

Seeing that war was inevitable, Count Raymond entered into negotiations with Saladin, who promised to support his bid for the throne of Jerusalem. Had Raymond been impelled purely by selfish ambition, he had had years of better opportunities. Presumably he believed this to be the only way to save the country. It was treason all the same.

King Guy was not renowned for his martial spirit, but Gerard de Ridefort left him no peace and no excuse till he marched his army against Raymond, in the face of impending Saracen attack. But Guy was usually swayed by the last speaker, and so at the eleventh hour the head of the Ibelins succeeded in persuading him to offer acceptable peace terms to Count Raymond. The Lord of Ibelin undertook to deliver the offer himself, in company with the Archbishop of Tyre and the grand masters of the Hospital and the Temple — there was no hope of any lasting settlement with Raymond to which Gerard de Ridefort was not party.

They spent the night at Nablus, where the Ibelin lord was detained by business. He told the others to ride on ahead; he would catch them up next day.

At that same time Count Raymond at Tiberias received an envoy from the Moslems at Banyas, asking permission to pass through Galilee on reconnaissance into Palestine. Raymond had signed a separate truce with Saladin and could not well withhold permission. He sent out warning messages to all his people and to the approaching peace delegation of Jerusalem, and from his castle watched the ride past of seven thousand Mamelukes. A few hours later he watched them return — with a number of human heads, unmistakably those of bearded Templar Knights, stuck on the lances of the vanguard.

What had happened was that on receipt of Raymond's message to keep out of the way, Gerard de Ridefort against the protests of his companions had sent for the nearest Templar garrison, and coming upon the seven thousand Mamelukes watering their horses near Nazareth, recklessly charged them although even with the Templar reinforcements the Christian party was no more than one hundred and thirty strong. A few of the secular knights were taken alive, of the Templars all except Gerard and two others were slain.

In this somewhat backhanded manner Gerard acquired the merit of reuniting the Christians, for Count Raymond was conscience-stricken, annulled his pact with Saladin, and rode to do homage to King Guy. Pleading his wounds, Gerard for the moment kept his distance.

The cordial ardor of reconciliation was fanned by the herald breeze of storm. For years this storm had been forecast; its approach had been sighted for so long that men had accustomed themselves to it as one of the conditions of existence — like the end of the world, an article of faith, which never came. Suddenly it lowered close, threatening existence altogether — with the shock of the last trump sounding after all. The sinking of differences was genuine; and pride replaced the despondency of a nation that knew itself forsaken by the West.

The Patriarch Heraclius had his weaknesses, but cowardice was evidently not one of them. He had not minced his words in England, where King Henry II fobbed him off with a series of specious excuses for failing to carry out his promise to go on Crusade as part of his penance for the murder of Thomas Becket.* To maintain the fiction that an English Crusade was only deferred, Henry had, however, sent over a large sum of money to be held in trust by the military orders until the English host should appear. ("We seek a man, not money," the Patriarch had said.) The Grand Master of the Temple judged it right to use this money now, and transferred it to King Guy for equipping a brigade which in compliment to Henry was to march under the Plantagenet colors.

The spies reported tremendous Moslem forces from every quarter of Saladin's dominions massing in Egypt. From every part of Outremer the armed population flocked together to give battle; only the scantiest of token garrisons were left to guard cities and castles. Baldwin of Ibelin

---

* "Though all the men of my land were one body and spoke with one mouth, they durst not speak to me as you have done," King Henry told the Patriarch, who returned tactlessly: "Do by me just as you did by that blessed man Thomas of Canterbury, for I had liefer be slain by you than by the Saracens, for you are worse than any Saracen." "I may not leave my land," the King explained again with unusual self-control, "for my own sons will surely arise against me in my absence." To which conciliatory and prophetic words Heraclius made short answer, "No wonder, for of the devil they come and to the devil they shall go," and so re-embarked for Palestine.

prepared to come with troops from Antioch. Presently the army numbered twelve hundred knights in full armor, nearly two thousand light
cavalry, also Turcopoles and about ten thousand foot. The remainder of
the nation huddled defenseless, in many places without so much as a
town wall between them and the enemy, and strove for moral rearmament with prayer, vows, and a hysteria of public repentance. Here and
there a castellan's lady donned armor and took over the command of his
fief. These women were most resolute and steadfast in war, and, as if
conclusively to deny the reputed limitations of their sex, frequently of
astonishing cruelty.

On July 1, 1187, the Moslems crossed the Jordan, and on the 2nd took
the town of Tiberias after one hour's fighting. King Guy and his barons
held a council of war at Acre. Tiberias was Count Raymond's town, but
his advice took no account of that. The summer heat was at its height;
an attacking army, Raymond said, had the disadvantage. The Christian
forces should wait until the reinforcements from Antioch arrived and
the invaders had exhausted their provisions. To the majority of the council this sounded reasonable. Reynald de Châtillon and Gerard de Ridefort, however, accused Raymond of cowardice and treachery, and their
vehemence carried the King with them. He gave orders for the army to
move out towards Tiberias.

In the evening, as they lay encamped, with good water supply and
pasturing facilities, news came from Raymond's wife to say that though
the town had fallen, she was still holding the castle at Tiberias. The assembled barons rose as one man to rush to her succor. But Raymond,
with a desperation that convinced them all, repeated what he had already
said at Acre. Eloquently he pictured the folly of abandoning their present
strong position: should they be defeated, there were no other forces to
fall back on. In conclusion he cried that he would rather lose Tiberias
and his wife than see the whole kingdom thrown to perdition.

His conduct stood in crass contrast to that of the Patriarch Heraclius,
who had deputed the Bishop of Acre to carry the True Cross into battle,
on grounds of diplomatic illness thought to be connected with "Madame
la Patriarchesse," who was in childbed. One can sympathize with

both. Yet Raymond's austere heroism perhaps was rendered the more persuasive by the example of the Patriarch. Weeping, even the sons of the Lady of Tiberias bowed their heads in agreement. It was decided to stay and wait.

But in the middle of the night Gerard de Ridefort crept into the King's tent. "Sire, do you believe the advice of that traitor [Raymond]? He wishes to consign you to disgrace. You have but recently been made King, and no King of this country ever had so large an army, so soon after his accession. If you allow a city only six leagues distant to be lost, your shame will be everlasting. The Templars will throw off their white mantles and sell all they have, rather than not take their revenge on the Infidel. Sire! let the order be given for every man to take up his post, and with the Sacred Cross before us, let us advance!"

The army marched at dawn.

Count Raymond as lord of the fief commanded the van. The King and the True Cross were in the center, the Templars and Hospitalers and Reynald de Châtillon brought up the rear. There was no water and no shade on the parched hills. Soon men and horses, knights roasted within their armor, infantry fainting from thirst on torn and blistered feet, slowed down to a snail's pace.

I can do no better than quote extracts from two works whose summing-up cannot be improved upon.

The Franks had marched about nine or ten miles, when they began to be surrounded by swarms of [Saracen] skirmishers. Saladin did not display his main force, but enveloped their army with a cloud of horse-bowmen, pouring arrows into their midst and riding away before any counter attack could be made. . . . Only some six miles now separated [the army] from the town of Tiberias and the lake. . . . But between the weary Crusaders and their goal lay the hills of Tiberias, a range rising to about 1,000 feet above sea level: the northern point, Kuru-Hattin, is 1,191 feet high. Behind the crest of these hills (called the Horns of Hattin) the ground falls suddenly towards the deep-sunk hollow of the Sea of Galilee . . . 650 feet below sea level. All along the range the Saracens were arrayed. . . .

The Count [Raymond] sent back to King Guy, begging him to hasten the advance at all costs, as the day was drawing on, and the lake must be reached ere nightfall if the army was to be preserved. But the King and his counsellor were disheartened and no longer possessed the courage to order a final assault upon the heights where the enemy clustered so thick. Moreover, the Templars in the rear were sending messages to say that they were so hard-pressed that they had been forced to halt, and could not keep up with the advance of the column in front of them. . . . Fearing that the Templars would be cut off . . . Guy made the trumpets sound for [the whole army] to halt and encamp where it stood, on the hillside. Raymond rode back to join the main body, exclaiming, "Alas, alas, Lord God! The war is ended; we are all delivered over to death, and the realm is ruined."

That night the Franks camped, huddled together around the royal standard on the hillside. There was little food and hardly a drop of water. Even sleep was impossible, for the Saracens came close in under cover of darkness and kept up a constant shower of arrows into the camp. They also fired the dry grass to the windward of the Crusaders, so that stifling clouds of smoke were drifting over it all night. . . .*

At dawn on Saturday, July 4, the Franks were completely encircled.

The Moslem attack began soon after daybreak. The Christian infantry had only one thought, water. In a surging mass they tried to break through down the slope towards the lake gleaming far below. They were driven up a hillock, hemmed in by the flames and by the enemy. Many of them were slaughtered at once, many others were taken prisoner; and the sight of them as they lay wounded and swollen-mouthed was so painful that five of Raymond's knights went to the Moslem leaders to beg that they might be slain, to end their misery. The horsemen on the hills fought with superb courage. Charge after charge of the Moslem cavalry was driven back with losses, but their own numbers were dwindling. Enfeebled by thirst, their strength began to fail them. Before it was too late, at the King's request, Raymond led his knights . . . to burst through the Moslem lines [which] closed up again behind them. They could not make their way back again to their comrades, so miserably,

* Charles Oman, *A History of the Art of War in the Middle Ages.*

they rode . . . away to Tripoli. A little later Balian of Ibelin and [the lord] of Sidon broke their way out. They were the last to escape.

There was no hope left for the Christians; but they still fought on, retiring up the hill to the Horns. The King's red tent was moved to the summit, and his knights gathered round him. Saladin's young son al-Afdal was at his father's side witnessing his first battle. "When the Frankish King had withdrawn to the hilltop (he relates), his knights made a gallant charge and drove the Moslems back upon my father. I watched his dismay. He changed colour and pulled at his beard, then rushed forward crying: *Let us give the devil the lie!* When I saw the Franks flying I cried out with glee: *We have routed them!* But they charged again and drove our men back again to where my father stood. Again he urged our men forward and again they drove the enemy up the hill. Again I cried out: *We have routed them!* But my father turned to me and said: *Be quiet. We have not beaten them so long as that tent stands there.* At that moment the tent was overturned. Then my father dismounted and bowed to the ground, giving thanks to God, with tears of joy."

. . . The Holy Cross . . . was in the hands of the Infidel. Few of the horses had survived. When the victors reached the hilltop, the knights themselves, the King among them, were lying on the ground . . . with hardly the strength to hand their swords over and surrender. Their leaders were taken off to the tent that was erected on the battlefield for the Sultan.*

The only magnate to have been killed outright in the battle was the Bishop of Acre, who contrary to usage had concealed a mail shirt under his vestments. God had justly made an example of him for his lack of faith.

. . . Saladin received King Guy and his brother the Constable Amalric, Reynald de Châtillon and his stepson Humphrey of Toron, the Grand Master of the Temple Gerard de Ridefort, the aged Marquis of Montferrat, the lords of Jebail and Botrun, and many of the lesser barons of the realm. [Saladin] seated the King next to him and, seeing his thirst, handed him a goblet of rose water, iced with the snows of Hermon. Guy drank from it

* Steven Runciman, *A History of the Crusades,* Vol. II, also for the next two extracts.

and handed it on to Reynald who was at his side. By the laws of Arab hospitality to give food and drink to a captive meant that his life was safe; so Saladin said quickly to the interpreter, "Tell the King that he gave that man to drink, not I."

Saladin turned to Reynald and berated him for his crimes. Reynald answered back and Saladin there and then struck off his head; after which he gave orders that none of the other lay knights was to be harmed or offered any indignity. But with the exception of the Grand Master of the Temple, all captives belonging to the military orders were sent to execution. The gallant Countess of Tripoli was allowed to leave Tiberias with honor and to rejoin her husband.

The prisoners were sent to Damascus, where the barons were lodged in comfort and the poorer folk sold in the slave market. So many were there that the price of a single prisoner fell to three dinars, and you could buy a whole healthy family, a man, his wife, his three sons and two daughters, for eighty dinars the lot. One Moslem even thought it a good bargain to exchange a prisoner for a pair of sandals.

Before the end of August, Saladin had occupied the fortresses and towns of Acre, Jaffa, Aleppo, Sidon, Beirut, Jebail. In early September he appeared before Ascalon. With him were his two principal captives, the King of Jerusalem and the Grand Master of the Temple. Guy believed that he could purchase his liberty with the surrender of Ascalon, and harangued the citizens to induce them to give up. But the citizens upon the ramparts yelled their scorn at him and defended themselves with berserk fury. After a few days, however, they capitulated, and Saladin allowed every one to leave in safety. Under Templar discipline at Gaza, Gerard's call for surrender met with instant obedience, and Saladin released the grand master.

On September 20, Saladin began the attack on Jerusalem. There were only two knights in the whole thronged city. By chance and by extraordinary courtesy on Saladin's part Balian of Ibelin managed to get in and take command. He knighted every boy over sixteen of noble family and thirty men of the bourgeoisie. The silver was stripped from the roof of the Holy Sepulchre, and arms distributed to every man capable of wielding them. The defense fought fiercely in its hopeless cause, while a section of the native (Greek Orthodox) Christians entered into secret communication with Saladin, ready to open the gates.

But on October 2 what was left of the garrison laid down its battered arms in negotiated surrender.

Saladin had offered Balian that every Christian should be allowed to redeem himself at the rate of ten dinars a man, five a woman and one a child. But there were at least twenty thousand of the inhabitants too poor to pay these rates, and Balian asked Saladin to accept a lump sum for them all. Saladin agreed and suggested a hundred thousand dinars, but again Balian demurred, knowing that this figure was still too high. In the end a compromise was reached. For thirty thousand dinars seven thousand people should be freed.

The Moslems entered Jerusalem on the anniversary of their Prophet's ascension to Heaven. Not a building was looted, not one hair harmed on one Christian head. Among the Christians frantic activity began to raise their ransom money. Balian emptied the treasury, but what he found was still far short of thirty thousand dinars. He appealed to the Temple, the Hospital and the Patriarch; all were concerned only for themselves. Heraclius paid down his ten dinars and, groaning under sacks of gold strapped on his back, left the city, cartloads of his other movable possessions at his heels. After a great deal of argument the Hospitalers produced the remainder of King Henry II's conscience money, and the Templars with surly reluctance at last rounded off the sum. Many more thousands could have been freed, had the military orders cared to remember their stewardship.

The Infidel was more generous. The pitiful sight of the crowds who had been unable to ransom themselves, streaming into captivity, moved Saladin's brother to ask as a favor for his services in the siege that one further thousand of these poor wretches be liberated. The Patriarch Heraclius thereupon hastened to request that seven hundred more be freed in his honor, and this also was granted, as well as freedom for another five hundred for the sake of Balian, valiant defender. Then Saladin himself freed every aged person, and when Frankish ladies who had paid down their ransom but whose husbands and fathers were slain or captive came to him in tears, he released all heads of families, and sent widows and orphans on their way with gifts from his treasury.

At the sack of some of the other Frankish towns matters had been handled rather differently; and even at the Holy City many individual emirs and soldiers of Saladin ignored the humane lead and practiced wholesale blackmail and extortion. But at least they were not by fellowship and vow committed to protect and aid their victims. They had every reason to rejoice in their great victory. What reason can we accept as compulsive on the Emperor Isaac Angelus at Constantinople, to send an embassy of congratulation to Saladin? True, the Sultan repaid the courtesy by granting the reversion of the Christian Holy Places to the Greek Orthodox Church; and three days after the surrender Frankish pilgrims were again admitted to these places, for an entrance fee. Still this does not make such a degree of obsequiousness look any prettier.

The cross was the emblem of all Churches, of all Christian sects alike. The giant gold cross on the Dome of the Rock was torn out and cast down into the street and publicly desecrated. The building itself was washed with rose water inside and out, from top to bottom, and then reconsecrated to Islamic worship. The same was done at the Mosque of al-Aqsa, which had for so many years been in the hands of the Templars.

The Templars led the exodus of the homeless from Jerusalem. In three straggling columns, the Christian refugees moved to the coast, to seek the unwilling protection first of Tyre, then of Tripoli and Antioch. In many places the gates were shut against them, or they were robbed of the few possessions they had salvaged and of such gifts as Saladin had made them, by petty barons keeping alive the spirit of Reynald de Châtillon.

It may be argued that the military orders (and Saladin too, perhaps) were nothing worse (or better) than realists. As it was, with at most eight thousand five hundred displaced persons to provide for, a difficult problem had arisen, which in the majority of cases was never properly

SELJUKS

DANISHMENDS

ANTIOCH

EDESSA

LESSER
ARMENIA

• Tarsus

• Antioch

R. Euphrates

• Aleppo

Lattakiah •

Margat •
Marqab •

• Shaizar
• Hama

CYPRUS

Tortosa •

Krak des Chevaliers

• Homs

Tripoli •

Botrun •

Jebail •

Beirut •

Mediterranean
Sea

Sidon •

• Damascus

ATABEGS

OF

MOSUL

Tyre •

Banyas

Acre •
Haifa •

• Jacob's Ford
• Tiberias

Castle Pilgrim •

Nazareth •

Arsuf •

• Nablus

Jaffa •

Ibelin •

• Ramleh

• Jerusalem

Ascalon •

Bethlehem •

Gaza •

Dead Sea

Damietta •

Beersheba •

• Kerak

CALIPHATE OF CAIRO
(FATIMITES)

• Cairo

The
CRUSADER STATES
at the height of their power
in the 12th. century

R. Nile

E G Y P T

0   50   100   150

MILES

Constantinople

BYZANTINE
EMPIRE

SELJUKS

ARMENIA

LESSER ARMENIA

R.Tigris

Mosul

ABBASID
CALIPHATE
(SUNNITE)

Antioch

R. Euphrates

CYPRUS

Marqab
Tortosa
Tripoli

Krak des Chevaliers

Baghdad

Mediterranean
Sea

Sidon
Tyre
Acre

Damascus

Hattin

Jerusalem

Dead Sea

Damietta

Alexandria

Cairo

EGYPT

R.Nile

ARABIA

H E J A Z

Medina

Mecca

R e d   S e a

YEMEN

THE EMPIRE OF SALADIN

Saladin's Empire
in 1171

Conquests
in 1174

Conquests in
1187–1189

Territory under
Saladin's suzerainty

Conquests
in 1185

■ Principal remaining
Christian strongholds
in 1189

0   100   200   300   400   500   MILES

solved at all. What would have happened with more than double that number at a loose end makes disturbing surmise. By the same interpretation Saladin had shaken off the responsibility of an extra eight thousand five hundred-odd mouths to feed and depreciate his soldiers' plunder with another glut on the slave market. But there were other ways of disposing of such an embarrassment, as had been demonstrated at the Frankish conquest of Jerusalem eighty-eight years before, and as King Richard of England would demonstrate again in Saladin's lifetime. On the other hand if there were no other ways for the Templars to conserve lives — why, then, surely, it had been nobler for all to perish together, than to conserve wealth at the expense of the flesh and blood for whose service it had been subscribed. In fact, at the expense of its wealth, the Temple could have found the means of shipping every refugee to Europe, wind, weather and other accidents of travel permitting.

It does not do to be too "realistic" — a word, curiously enough, which is never used to describe a kindly action. For it is another curious thing that what is humane and just usually turns out to be materially advantageous in the end — though the end, indeed, may often be long deferred.

10 The Rot

THE ROT OF WHICH THE SPORES HAD LONG BEEN LIBERALLY SCATTERED, WAS setting in. Until the Holy City passed out of Christian hands, the New Jerusalem had retained an anchorage in actuality; until the Moslems won the citadel of Zion, Christian confidence in the Divine ally could maintain itself and the eleventh-century legend of Frankish invincibility survive growing contrary evidence; until calamity stripped the last veil from selfishness and a companion cowardice which had nothing to do with fighting gallantry, the last barrier of scruple and consequent inmost conviction of righteousness had not fallen. There is more to defeatism than military defeat, and more to disillusion than the effacement of a mirage.

The gateway was wide open, and the seven devils of corruption took full possession of the soul of Outremer.

In body, the kingdom hung on for another hundred years, "of Jerusalem" in name only save for a period of fifteen years between 1229 and 1244; after that it had more accurately been known as the Kingdom of Acre. For Acre was recovered from Saladin in the Third Crusade, after a two years' siege begun by King Guy and finished by Richard Coeur de Lion, and remained the center of government until it was razed literally to the ground in 1291. During the whole of that time the realm of Outremer never stretched beyond ninety miles of coastline, seldom more than ten miles wide and mostly less.

Raymond of Tripoli died in 1187, pleurisy the apparent physiological cause of a despondent end. The following summer Saladin released King Guy upon the latter's oath to leave Palestine and nevermore to bear arms against the Moslems. Guy immediately obtained the Patriarch's dispensation to break his oath sworn to the Infidel and proceeded to the siege of Acre. When Saladin afterwards reproached him, Guy virtuously pointed out that he was riding to battle with his sword *tied to his saddle,* so that his destrier, not he, was bearing arms. Gerard de Ridefort had been released on the same conditions and broke his oath without bothering about sophistical bows and ribbons to his sword; he fell in the first assault on Saladin's camp at Acre.

> *Fut occis le Maître du Temple ...*
> *Cil qui dit la bonne parole*
> *Qui lui vint de la preux ecole*
> *Quand les gens couards et hardis*
> *Lui dirent a cette envaie ...*
> *«Venez-vous-en, Sire, venez ...»*
>
> *«Ja à Dieu,» ce dit-il «ne plaise*
> *Que donc mès soit en autre place*
> *Ni qu'au Temple soit réprouvé*
> *Que l'on m'ait en fuyant trouvé.»*
> *Et ne le fit, ainsi mourut! ...**

* Then was killed the Master of the Temple,/He who spoke the noble rule/ That came to him from the knightly school,/When men that were strong enough and brave/Urged him again himself to save:/"Come away, my lord, come — "/he replied, "I go to God, whom it would not please/To see me wish for a safer place./Nor be it reproach to the Temple's might/That its master was discovered in flight."/And would not come, and therefore died.

Thus Ambrose, laureate of the Third Crusade. Moslem chroniclers relate that Gerard was taken alive and put to death by Saladin for his perjury. However, whether the trouvère be protesting too much or his Arabian colleagues indulging in wishful fantasy, all sources are united in honoring the Templars' contempt of death and their irreproachable discipline before Acre, as well as the order's amazing recuperative powers, when time and again it appeared on the point of extinction. At the time, there must have been some uncertainty as to Gerard's fate, for the office of grand master was vacant for a year and a half.

The West had for so long discounted the desperate appeals of Outremer, that the news of the fall of Jerusalem came as a potent jolt. The Pope imposed a special penance on all Christians and decreed special daily services in all churches. England and France patched up a truce and levied the "Saladin Tithe," a ten per cent tax on all goods except tools, jewels and knights' weapons, which was collected by groups composed each of one Templar, one Hospitaler, one royal official and one representative of the Church. All at once the potentates of Europe, hitherto unavoidably detained, found that they could get away. The Emperor Frederick Barbarossa made his peace with the Papacy and led the largest single army ever to have gone crusading by the land route across the Balkans. Henry II of England was dead; the new King Richard was as ardent for the rescue of the Holy Land as his father had been cool, and public opinion at home and abroad would not allow the King of France, Philip Augustus, to lag behind.

Even so it cannot be said that they hurried overmuch. The European preceptories of the military orders in Europe gave up waiting for them and despatched reinforcements right away, and many of the secular warriors whom the news had roused again went along with them. By summer, 1189, several thousand Western recruits had rallied around King Guy at Tyre, enabling him to march on Acre and almost take the city at the first assault. Foiled only by their lack of siege engines, the Franks settled down in a vast semicircle flung about the walls of Acre, themselves in turn beset by the crescent encampments of Saladin. Epidemics quickly sprang up, and long before the Third Crusade's arrival

Paul Popper, Ltd.

Aerial view of the Jordan Valley

Departure of Godfrey de Bouillon for the Holy Land

From Les Croniques de Jherusalem abregies, *Österreichische National-Bibliothek*

Conquest of Jerusalem

King Baldwin I of Jerusalem

From Les Croniques de Jherusalem abregies, *Österreichische National-Bibliothek*

Emperor Manuel Comnenus and
his wife, Maria of Antioch

Codex Vat. Graecus, *1176, Biblioteca Apostolica Vaticana*

British Museum

Seal of King Louis VII of France, obverse and reverse

Radio Times Hulton Picture Library

St. Bernard of Clairvaux

From Les Croniques de Jherusalem, *Österreichische National-Bibliothek*

Coronation of Guy de Lusignan *"à cause de sa femme"*

Cover of Queen Melisende's psalter, an example of
contemporary workmanship

Krak des Chevaliers

King Richard I of England;
the Great Seal

Public Record Office

British Museum

Templar seals

From Les Croniques de Jherusalem, *Österreichische National-Bibliothek*

The fortification of Jaffa

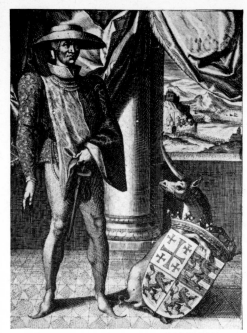

King John de Brienne (from a sixteenth-century print, Augsburg)

peror Frederick II, *"Stupor mundi"*

From his book, De arte venandi cum avibus, *c. 1260*

(*above*) St. Louis, King of France
(*right*) Pope Boniface VIII
(from the thirteenth-century stone
bust in the church of Menneval,
Eure)

A council of prelates and nobles at the Curia: Pope Boniface VIII receiving homage from St. Louis of Toulouse, son of King Charles II of Naples (from the fresco by Ambrogio Lorinzetti, San Francesco, Siena, c. 1330)

King Philip the Fair

From Cronica Breve de Re di Francia,
British Museum

Pope Clement V

British Museum

Ruins of Castle Pilgrim

Matson Photo Service, California

Paul Popper, Ltd.

Aerial view of Jerusalem, with the Temple terrace taking up
the foreground

Interior of the Temple Church, London, consecrated by the Patriarch Heraclius of Jerusalem in 1185 and burned out by German
incendiary bombs on the night of 10 May, 1941, restored and
rededicated 7 November, 1958. Some effigies of Templar Knights
are shown; only those with legs crossed have been to the Holy Land.

Guy de Lusignan had lost any title to the Crown, by the death of Queen Sibylla within a few days of their two daughters'.

Of the German host only a handful reached Acre; it had disintegrated upon the aged Emperor's accidental death in the river Calycadnus — even as his ill-embalmed corpse thereafter fell to pieces in transport. The English and French were delayed by a variety of wrangles and side-track campaigns; Richard did not appear at Acre until June, 1191 — that is four years after the battle of Hattin, nearly two years since the beginning of the siege, and one whole year since his army had left England. Philip Augustus had preceded him by only seven weeks. All their old contentions were resumed forthwith.

It was the thankless task of the new Grand Master of the Temple to preserve the appearances of harmony between the two allied Western monarchs, and at the same time preserve his order's good relations with both. He was Robert de Sablé, a friend of the English King, whose fleet he had commanded for a time in Sicilian waters, and like him something of a poet in the Provençal epic tradition. He is another eminent example of the Templar diplomat; and his abilities in this respect were heavily taxed.

Philip Augustus had done little since his arrival, and the coming of the English was greeted with frenetic expectancy. This did not serve to improve the friendship of the two contingents. Richard's first act on setting foot in Outremer was to offer four gold pieces to any soldier joining his army, in all too successful competition against Philip Augustus, who paid only three gold pieces. Next Richard fell ill. Everyone realized that only a concerted assault could succeed; Richard refused to allow his army to co-operate with the French until he was better; the French refused to wait. Their assault failed; each King and each army blamed the other. Then Philip Augustus fell ill, and nearly died — through Richard's fault, people said, for he had tried to hasten the French King's end as he lay prostrate of fever, with a false report that Philip's son Louis was dead — though others declared this to have been merely Richard's idea of a joke.

The two were at odds in all things; they had but transferred their neighborly struggles in Europe to an Eastern theater. The King of France sided with Conrad of Montferrat, who had saved Tyre from falling to Saladin after the loss of Jerusalem and who was the Frankish barons' choice for the vacant throne. The King of England gave his support to Guy de Lusignan who would not admit himself deposed. Personal animosity lent relish to their rivalry, and a pending match which should have made them brothers-in-law (Richard had ·been betrothed for years to the Princess Alice of France) embittered it. When a few weeks after the lone and unsuccessful French offensive the English attempted the same, Philip Augustus now withheld his help, and the Moslems rejoiced in another victory.

The Temple was placed awkwardly indeed between the upper and nether millstones.

As the Templars had become financial agents for the rulers of so many countries, their occasional diplomatic missions also had developed into an accepted function. Unlike the clerks who as the only professionally literate class acted as a kind of supra-national diplomatic pool (giving their name to generations of lay office workers), the Templars were not committed primarily to Church interests; and although they would never neglect the welfare of their order, this was conveniently bound up with the solvency of the sovereign to whom they had lent financial aid. The Temple could not wish to see Philip Augustus lose out, since it had sunk considerable capital in his venture, on which he could not possibly have embarked without Temple backing. Richard on his dilatory way East had taken the island of Cyprus and sold it to the Temple for 100,000 gold pieces; without the Temple's readiness to buy and put down nearly half that sum in cash, Richard would not have been able to offer that extra gold piece in army pay. Before Richard's time, Templars had played a prominent part in the difficult negotiations between Henry II and Pope Alexander, and between Henry II and Thomas of Canterbury. There were Templar Knights who spent their whole lives traveling back and forth from East to West on confidential embassies. Others were employed in leading household appointments to prelates and royalty; the papal chamberlain was nearly always a Templar, and Templars appear constantly as almoners to the various monarchs. Their great holdings, particularly in France and England, made the goodwill of the monarchs concerned an important consideration.

Quite apart from the mutual distrust of the Kings and the unceasing jealous tussles over precedence of banners and similar niceties within each faction, the camp before Acre was a hell on earth which well-nigh defeats the imagination.

The town was built on a peninsula protected to the landward by two great walls meeting at right angles. The Crusaders had sealed these off, but were in turn almost completely blockaded by Saladin and his navy out in the bay. The war had settled down. As always when enemy forces stay in fixed positions near each other for any length of time, they had begun to feel at home with one another. Christians and Moslems would at times invite each other to camp entertainments; their children met in mock battles, and duels between individual knights often took on a very friendly character, with intervals for conversation and exchange of presents. But shortage of food and water, accumulation of filth and wave upon wave of epidemic sickness spoilt the idyll.

Thirteen beans or one egg cost one silver penny, the price for a sack of grain was one hundred gold pieces; for ten pennies one might get some stew of horse entrails; the best horses were slaughtered, the worst died of starvation, and both were eaten, as was grass and bone meal; any available old leather was shredded and cooked for food. In the Christian camp there were from two to three hundred deaths a day. Besides Queen Sibylla and her daughters the Franks had lost the Patriarch Heraclius; Barbarossa's son, the Duke of Swabia (who had salvaged a few bones of his father's skeleton in the hope of giving them burial at the Holy Sepulchre); the Archbishop of Canterbury, four other archbishops, twelve bishops, forty counts and five hundred knights were listed, and uncounted numbers of dead among other ranks and camp followers. People died of famine, of scurvy, dysentery and typhoid, various fevers, of an infected scratch and a novel sickness called arnaldia in which the hair and fingernails fell out. Both the Kings of France and England were stricken with this; Saladin for a time was covered with boils from the waist down so that he got no rest day or night. Corpses were buried in the trenches and thrown into the sea; they floated in the harbor, lined the beaches, burst from their shallow graves. Flies, rats, vultures, scavenging dogs and vermin of all kinds helped spread disease; scorching heat or rain and mud maintained an even tenor of wretchedness. Primal instincts broke down: mothers ate their dead infants, or carried them about for days to prevent their being eaten. It makes all the difference to endurance whether such miseries are inflicted of deliberate human malice or embraced in a manner of speaking voluntarily. In a prison camp of such description surely no one would have survived, and, between life and death, all animation had been logged in lethargy.

Perhaps the spirit of rivalry kept the spark of truculence well alight, where even the uninterrupted action of siege engines, making no impression, could only quench it with fatal ennui. In the rivalry of Guy de Lusignan and Conrad of Montferrat the Crown of Jerusalem remained desirable. The rivalry of Richard and Philip Augustus eventually worked for single leadership. Not many months elapsed before the King of France took himself off and left the King of England to carry on in Palestine. Meanwhile, their rivalry had served to sharpen and complicate that of the military orders. Had the two Kings been in accord, they might have united Temple and Hospital against them both. As matters stood, whenever one order opposed one King, the other leaped to his support. Only in active combat did the orders treat each other as brethren: if a member of one became separated from his rightful banner, it was his duty to make for the standard of the competitor. Otherwise by mutual agreement any transfer was forbidden. During periods of peace or stalemate they kept their hands in and practiced on each other — the time was not far distant when they would fight pitched battles in daylight and cut each other's throats in dark alleyways at night.

The fact that all units participating in the siege had earmarked former property to be restored and booty to be won in the event of victory, did not help. The only point of unanimity was in a growing sense of hopelessness. Besiegers and besieged reached breaking point simultaneously. Both gathered themselves for a final effort, and both sent out peace feelers. Claustrophobically enclosed as the Franks were not, the Moslem garrison capitulated first. Saladin's intervention came too late. On July 12, 1191, the Crusaders re-entered Acre under honorable observance of the terms of surrender.

King Richard moved into the former royal palace and King Philip Augustus into the palace of the Templars; for the rest, the captured town was given over to the army at large. At once there was trouble. The Frankish battalions were full of people with prior claims, and the Templar Grand Master Robert de Sablé led their vociferous protests. The Kings had to yield and seek other quarters.

Three weeks later the King of France went home, though leaving behind him the greater part of his army and the solemn promise to respect Richard's French dominions. Less than three weeks after that, Richard, as a prelude to marching on Jerusalem, used a hitch in the payment of reparations to justify that black deed which accords so ill with his fame. He caused the twenty-seven hundred survivors of the Saracen garrison, with their wives and children, to be butchered by his soldiers, in full view of Saladin's outposts, who fought frenziedly but in vain to get near the victims; and the Frankish chroniclers praised God for it. According to a Moslem chronicler, Saladin had previously asked the Templars, "whose word he trusted though he hated them," to guarantee that Richard would keep his side of the bargain. Apparently the Templars had refused, because they already suspected that Richard would break his word.

Richard Coeur de Lion proceeded to the last great victories of Christian arms in Outremer, in a series of battles reflecting the greatest credit on both his generalship and personal bravery. He has been neatly docketed as a combination of Napoleonic genius and the oppressive moral earnestness of the Prince Consort Albert,* and while the comparison seems hardly fair to the latter, Richard's campaigns substantiate the former

* Alfred Duggan, *Devil's Brood*.

claim. He has been likened to an overgrown schoolboy, by others. Since our conception of a schoolboy was then unknown, this is meaningless — unless our faculties of projective comprehension are so poor that we can visualize all those who have lived by violence and had not much use for sensitive imagination, as monster caricatures of the football eleven.

Having spent less than three months in Palestine, Richard displayed a grasp of the particular strategic requirements, a degree of adaptability and organizing power, and a mastery over men such as no other crusading leader had ever possessed. With it all he was absolutely fearless, often fighting in the van, asking nothing of others that he would not himself overtop in performance. The battle of Arsuf, which opened the road to Jerusalem and showed that Saladin could be decisively beaten, was a triumph of military skill. The recapture of Jaffa, not quite twelve months later, was a triumph of improvisation and gallantry. Moreover, at Arsuf the Christian losses were under seven hundred; at Jaffa, incredibly, they totaled only two men dead, although many were wounded.

But Richard Coeur de Lion had pressing business in Europe and so had many of the host he had led to victory. Jerusalem was within their grasp, and Saladin was ill and old for his fifty-three years. But Jerusalem was some fifty miles from the coast, Richard could take the Holy City only at the cost of cutting himself off from the sea. A second Egyptian army stood guard over it, and, with Saladin in pursuit, the Christians would have been caught between the two. Also, as Templars, Hospitalers, and native-born barons combined to ask: supposing Jerusalem was recaptured, who would hold it thereafter, an isolated city deep in enemy territory? Richard might rest content that Saladin's conquest had been halted, and leave Outremer renascent.

Out riding one day and coming unexpectedly within sight of the Holy City, Richard veiled his face and would not look.

The army was bitterly disappointed, Western Christendom so uncomprehending that speculation as to his reasons was continued for centuries.

Sixteen months after his arrival King Richard departed from the Holy
Land. His luck changed. Shipwrecked off Byzantine territory where
he was in bad odor owing to the rape of Cyprus, he went on by land
disguised as a Templar to escape detection. He was making for Saxony,
dukedom of his brother-in-law Henry the Lion, but was recognized en
route at an inn near Vienna, betrayed and taken prisoner by the Duke of
Austria.

Richard now paid the price of the stimulating rivalries among the
Franks. The Duke of Austria had taken part in the recapture of Acre,
when, annoyed to find the Kings of France and England taking precedence, he had planted his banner beside Richard's on the town wall, and
Richard's soldiers had promptly hurled it down into the fosse. Duke
Leopold and his overlord the German emperor between them kept him
incarcerated for fifteen months; during which time Richard's brother
John and his late ally, King Philip Augustus, took every advantage of
their opportunities to stir up revolt against the captive King. After his
release, in the course of defending his inheritance, Richard Lionheart
was killed—the second English King to die by a stray arrow—five
years after these events. Saladin had preceded him in 1193, leaving
seventeen sons and one daughter—a profusion which augured well for
their enemies.

The pretext under which the touchy Duke of Austria had thrown
Richard into prison was the murder of Conrad of Montferrat, which
had taken place a few months before.

· This brings us to one of the most pathetic figures in the pageant of
Outremer: Queen Isabella, younger daughter of Amalric, the child-bride
of Kerak. At the time of that celebrated wedding feast Isabella had been
eleven years old. When on the death of her half-sister Sibylla she inherited the crown, she was yet only eighteen. She was happy with her
young husband, Humphrey, although he seems to have been a homosexual. This would in no way have disqualified him from sharing her
throne, but his undue comeliness was too feminine to command the
respect of the barons, whom he had in any case let down badly. Isabella

had no more desire for the throne than had Humphrey and she did not want to leave him, but in the end she was forced to consent to an annulment of their marriage. In the teeth of the violent protests of Guy's faction — stronger now by the support of England — Isabella was married to Conrad of Montferrat, the savior of Tyre. Conrad was said to have a wife living in Italy; otherwise he was eminently fitted to rule the Frankish kingdom in its protracted state of emergency. He immediately added to his qualifications by fathering a child on Isabella (again a daughter), but refrained from styling himself king until he and his young wife should be crowned. Guy meanwhile still refused to relinquish that title.

Richard had to see the dispute put by before he left. He called the knights and barons together and bade them choose between Guy and Conrad. Amazed that not one voice was raised for Guy, Richard bowed to the decision, and messengers were despatched post haste to acquaint Conrad with his good fortune.

Conrad received the news at Tyre. He fell on his knees and asked God that if he were unworthy of kingship, it should not be granted him. A few days later, having gone out to dine because his wife delayed in her bath, he was stabbed to death in the street. The murderers were Assassins; probably their motive was a recent act of piracy by Conrad against the sect. But many people preferred to lay the crime at Saladin's door, and many more to charge Richard with it. Neither was likely; but Duke Leopold of Austria took the latter view, as soon as he had Richard in his power, if not before.

The chief concern in Outremer was to replenish Isabella's bed. Count Henry of Champagne, nephew of both Richard and Philip Augustus, presented himself and was accepted by public approbation. One week after Conrad's assassination the widow married Henry, and they lived happily — alas, not for long.

Guy was at last disposed of. The Templars by unreasonable harshness had made themselves thoroughly unpopular in Cyprus and were not averse from getting rid of the island again. With Richard's permission

Guy bought it from them (the purchase price was never paid in full), and not long after closed any lingering rift by his death.

Henry was never crowned, possibly because there were some canonical doubts as to the legality of so hasty a marriage; in any event he made a conscientious King and was well liked. One day five years after his marriage he reviewed his troops from an upper window of his palace. A group of ambassadors was ushered into his presence. He turned to greet them, then, forgetting where he was, stepped backwards and right out of the open window. His dwarf, named Scarlet, made a grab for Henry's clothes; but Henry was heavy and took the little jester crashing down with him to the pavement of the courtyard.

This time Isabella was beside herself with grief; she had loved her third husband dearly. She had borne him two children — girls again. Her eldest, who was Conrad's daughter, was only five years old. As before, Isabella must remarry, the sooner the better. It took all of four months to bring about her next wedding. The new consort was Amalric de Lusignan, brother of the ex-King Guy and ex-lover of the ex-Queen Agnes, and Guy's heir to Cyprus. Thus the kingdoms of Cyprus and Jerusalem were united — until Amalric's death seven years after, on April 1, 1205, from a surfeit of fish. Queen Isabella bore this last bereavement more calmly, and took refuge in death from any further mating, before she reached her thirty-fifth year.

Her daughter by Conrad, Maria of Montferrat, succeeded to the throne aged thirteen. Isabella's elder half-brother, the Ibelin Lord of Beirut, was appointed Regent, and ruled quietly for three years. King Amalric de Lusignan and Saladin's successor had concluded a truce which lasted over a decade and which the Fourth Crusade, as will appear, did nothing to disturb. By 1208, it was high time for Queen Maria to marry and propagate her line. Few likely candidates came forward, although the King of France sponsored the search. At length he procured a bridegroom, John de Brienne.

Just as Isabella has the most woeful appeal, John de Brienne looms as the most staunchly practical, the most sober and industrious apprentice to the trade of royalty in the crusading era. Having neither fortune nor position, a younger son already past sixty, he had spent his life as a general in the French army and had so little to show for it that King Philip Augustus and Pope Innocent III had each to give him 400,000 silver pounds by way of nuptial equipment. He must have looked younger than his years (and must have borne himself more youthfully, too), for one of the rumors trying to account for his appointment to the throne of Jerusalem named him the lover of the Countess of Champagne — a scandalous liaison which Philip Augustus chose this step to sever.

However that might be, John proved himself capable and popular — what one may call a *steady* sort of king. He and the nineteen-year-old Queen were married and crowned together in the autumn of 1210. Before the end of 1212, Queen Maria died in childbirth. Once again the baby was a daughter, known as Yolanda, and King John was kept on as her regent until her turn came to marry.

One cannot escape from the terminology of a professional career in connection with John's occupation. He received an appointment, it was renewed under changed terms of reference, he did a job of work. When the job came to an end in 1225 upon the marriage of his daughter to the Hohenstaufen Emperor Frederick II, the professional king, undaunted by his seventy-five years, applied for the throne of England, narrowly missed the throne of Armenia, and finally took on the post of regent for an infant Emperor at Constantinople. Thus John de Brienne ended his life holding the highest diploma obtainable in his profession, the degree of Emperor, and died serenely in harness at the age of eighty-seven.

How there came to be a Frankish Emperor of Byzantium makes the sorriest tale in a sorry canon: the tale of the Fourth Crusade.

Innocent III, elected Pope at the early age of thirty-seven about the turn of the century, had conceived a burning desire to regain the Holy City, and succeeded to a large extent in communicating this to the secular lords and commoners of the West. No kings enrolled, but great names abounded, such as Tibald of Champagne, Louis of Blois, Simon de Montfort, Baldwin of Flanders, Boniface of Montferrat (Conrad's brother) and many more.

The merchant republic of Venice offered to transport them all, and there was a change of plans. Instead of sailing straight for the Holy Land, they would once more attempt to get at it through Egypt. So far, so good; only, as the expedition was about to embark, the Venetians disclosed that for their part they had other plans still. Venice had designs on the Dalmatian seaport of Zara, suddenly raised her transport charges, and held the Crusaders to ransom for their assistance. Afterwards they might proceed to Egypt.

Zara, once Venetian territory but in the hands of the King of Hungary at this time, was accordingly retaken, in a kind of digressional crusade. But that was not the end of the digression. The expedition which had taken three years to prepare never set sail for the East at all. Excepting only a few small disjointed units, the Fourth Crusade turned into a brutal and wholly mercenary assault on Constantinople — Constantinople, where the emblem of the cross was ubiquitous, but which was the greatest, the richest, the most magnificent and urbanized city in the world.

Irreplaceable treasures of antiquity and modern progress, learning and invention were destroyed, that Year of Grace 1204, in the sack of Christian Constantinople by the Christian Franks, and the sack of Rome by the Vandals pales beside what was done here. The atrocities, the vandalism as unjustly we still call it, perpetrated then are scarcely outshone by anything that has happened in the centuries since — one cannot say more. There was no excuse for it, not even in "political realism," for nothing but harm came of this outrage, either immediately or in the future. At the time excuses were not dispensed with altogether, but they were of the flimsiest.

A whole civilization was destroyed, a whole faith denied, a whole heritage had been perverted. The leaders of the Fourth Crusade claimed that they had done all this to ensure Byzantine collaboration for the re-conquest of Jerusalem, and incidentally to help a deposed Byzantine Emperor regain his rights. But when the smoke of burning and the effluvia of putrefaction cleared, not a Byzantine, but a Frankish Emperor was seen to be enthroned, and those of the Crusaders who had not gone home with their loot showed no intention of stirring from their new, fat fiefs.

What was more, henceforth the rich pickings of "Romania" continued to deflect the Western adventurers to whom overcrowded Outremer could offer little, and who styled themselves Crusaders still by grace of Romania's Turkish neighbors. Heiresses, too, were more plentiful and more rewarding this side of the Bosphorus, so much so that even the Queen of Jerusalem was no longer accounted a sufficient catch.

After 1204, the only remaining channel of recruitment for Holy War was through the military orders.

The trouble was that Holy War had ceased to know any bounds for the military orders as well. The Fourth Crusade had established the principle of religious warfare, not only against the Infidel, but also against deviationists of the same faith.

The Pope had thundered against the perfidy of the Fourth Crusade — but he had not scrupled to try and turn the conquest of Constantinople to advantage after the accomplished fact, which seemed to promise the complete Latinization of the Greek Church (the promise proved to be an illusory one). Thereafter, a crusade would be any war to which the Holy See saw fit to give that name and with it the same spiritual benefits as obtained for pilgrimage-at-arms to the Holy Land.

The Languedoc, bloc of the most southerly provinces of France,* was riddled with Christian heresy. In 1209 the first of a series of fully fledged Crusades was loosed on that country — the Albigensian Wars, which in

---

* This is an earlier instance of the extension of linguistic to ethnic terminology, like the German use of the denomination "Aryan." The "Langue d'oc" to start with was literally "the language of Oc," as opposed to the "Langue d'oeil," "the language of Oeil": two dialects respectively pronouncing the word for "yes" as "oc" and "oeil."

savagery and in the lasting damage they inflicted did not stand far behind the invasion of Constantinople, but to which one may cede the extenuating feature of misguided fanaticism.

The military orders distinguished themselves in these wars even as they did in Palestine. There were now three of them. The Teutonic Knights of St. Mary's Hospital of Jerusalem had first banded together in 1128 — without canonical status, however — to provide a hostelry for pilgrims of the German nation. Their hospital disappeared at the fall of Jerusalem and their activities lapsed. Then, during the siege of Acre, some German merchants had been moved by the sufferings in the Christian camp to revive the fellowship with generous endowments and active social service, and a few years later it became incorporated along the lines of the White Knights and the Black. Yes: the Templars had white mantles and red crosses, the Hospitalers black mantles with white crosses: what color was to be the uniform of the Teutonic Knights? It could not be a gay, worldly color, and the red of martyrdom, permitted in the Temple badge, when spread over an entire garment became a symbol of temporal glory. The Teutonic Knights obtained permission to settle on a white cloak with a black cross. The Templars protested in vain. So although the Hospitalers also viewed askance the rise of a third competitor, the Templars looked upon the white-cloaked Teutons as especially their rivals, black cross or no. Not that the third order waxed as influential as the other two. It fought as valiantly in the numerous sporadic campaigns and amassed property in much the same way as they, but its rebirth occurred at an economically unfavorable time, and it cherished no ambitions of political independence. The Teutonic order was not internationally minded; it bore out the implications of its name, geared to the interests of the German Emperors.

The Temple had for its next grand master a personal friend of Pope Innocent III, that Gilbert Erail who had been defeated in the election which brought Gerard de Ridefort to the top. As regard the Temple's policy, the pendulum of reaction was nearing the limit of its swing. About the turn of the twelfth century, the Temple tended to favor the prolongation of truces rather than the breach of them.

Friendship notwithstanding, the Pope found it necessary to remind Gilbert Erail that the Templars' first duty was to fight, not to nurse their revenues, and that they ought to fight the Moslems rather than the Hospitalers. He used strong language to rebuke them for their pride and threatened to withdraw their privileges if they persisted in abusing these. Next, however, we see *Omne datum optimum,* source and bulwark of the Templar pride, republished no fewer than eight times in the first decade of the new century.

The Fifth Crusade was taking shape, and the Papacy needed the loyalty of the Templars.

The Fifth Crusade began in earnest towards end of summer, 1217, after years of preaching and preparations — Pope Innocent III did not live to see it start. It went on intermittently during the pontificates of Honorius III (1216–1227) and Gregory IX (1227–1241) until 1229, and more than once came close to success. Time and again success was averted by the errors of the leaders — errors always typical, always imitating precedents of whose every classic form examples have been given in the foregoing chapters. An original sort of error sealed failure at the very end — when, indeed, an appearance of success was briefly created by the recovery of Jerusalem — original and interesting, in that it exemplifies the relativity of progress. What was modern, practicable and in fact desirable in Europe proved worse than unsuited to the nature and conditions of Outremer. The idea of the centralized state and autocratic government, the emergence of which determined survival and growth of the European nations, was inapplicable to the East. The crusading career of the Hohenstaufen Emperor Frederick II was directed by this idea and foundered on it.

Frederick II was the grandson of Barbarossa, by that Emperor's heir and the heiress of Sicily, and thus in upbringing a product of the fusion of Christian and Islamic cultures which prevailed in his mother's island realm. His was one of the most extraordinary personalities of the age of Crusaders — of any age. He was nicknamed *stupor mundi:* the wonder, the stupefaction of the world. For he was an intellectual — with every overtone of brilliance and opprobium that this designation carries. He was unique and he was solitary — a restless and vicious sociability notwithstanding — sensual and ratiocinative, tolerant and cruel; scholar, scientist, lover of the arts, politician, wit, despot, epicurean and a philosopher liberated from the belief in religious absolutes.

Frederick Stupor Mundi took the cross as early as 1215, but for over ten years contrived to avoid fulfilling his vow, while the Frankish Kingdom pinned all its hopes on him and the Moslems nervously absorbed reports of his greatness.

Much had happened in the years between his accession (1212) and his marriage to Queen Yolanda of Jerusalem — John de Brienne's young daughter — in 1225: troubles and upheavals and minor inter-Christian wars at Constantinople, at Tripoli, at Antioch, on Cyprus, and in Armenia.

Despite Saladin's seventeen sons, the leadership of Islam had gone to his brother Saif ad-Din al Adil, or Saphadin as the Franks called him. Saphadin had come and gone, his dominions divided between his sons and his nephews. The Assassins, still a party unto themselves, ever inscrutable and ever active, had passed from alliance with the Templars into alliance with the Hospitalers, for whom they had committed some sensational murders. Recurrent reports of a mysterious Far-Eastern Christian ruler known as Prester John had caused the Pope to write to this potential ally, whom the Pope fondly believed to have identified in the person of a Mongol chieftain by the name of Jenghiz Khan.

There had been the Children's Crusade, a fantastic phenomenon recalling the sway of Peter the Hermit and foreshadowing that of Joan of Arc. It was set off by a twelve-year-old called Stephen who presented himself to the King of France with a letter written by Jesus Christ. Though the King told him to go home, Stephen proceeded to preach all over France with marvelous eloquence, and in little over a month collected a following of several thousand children, none more than twelve years old, besides various kinds of hangers-on. He led them to Marseilles, where the sea was scheduled to divide for them, that they might march victorious all the way to Jerusalem. It was an unusually hot summer, and a great many of the young Crusaders perished long before the sea was reached. The waters failed to divide, but two merchants of Marseilles offered to transport the remnants of Stephen's force to Palestine, free of charge. Two vessels were wrecked and all the passengers drowned; the remaining five shiploads were handed over to a Saracen squadron by arrangement and taken to Algeria for sale.

Meanwhile the fame of Stephen had spread to Germany, rousing another boy-orator to action. His name was Nicholas, and unlike Stephen he did not intend to take Jerusalem by storm, but by converting the Moslems to Christianity. Within a few weeks he also had gathered an army of children, which he led to Italy. For them, too, the waters failed to divide. Numbers of those who had not fallen by the wayside accepted an offer by the city of Genoa to settle there. Nicholas himself and the scanty remainder went on to Rome, where the Pope received them in audience and told them, as King Philip had told Stephen, to go home. Only a few stragglers ever returned to their native land. Nicholas's father, who had encouraged him and whom his fellow-citizens held responsible for the loss of so many children, was apprehended and hanged. Yet to that boy goes the credit of having inspired the first missionary crusade, a concept which was to take root.

One greater than he adopted it in 1219, when the Fifth Crusade was fighting for Damietta in the Nile Delta. We salute him with the agreeable surprise of meeting a familiar face in incongruous surroundings. St. Francis of Assisi visited the Egyptian front on a private peace mission, it being his hope to persuade the Moslems of the error of their ways. He got permission to try his luck, made his way to the enemy camp under a flag of truce, and won a great personal victory. The Sultan could resist St. Francis's gentle charm of conversation no more than could the birds and beasts, but it was purely a succès d'estime.

After many battles, much contest, change and stiff-necked incompetence of leadership, the ravages of three years' siege warfare, floods, and diplomatic mistakes, and in spite of the Christian theologians' prediction by the Book of Revelation that the end of Islam was imminent, the Franks were finally repulsed from the gateway of Egypt.

The West could not understand it. The West had seen an uninterrupted procession of Crusaders going overseas for the best part of a hundred and fifty years and it had heard perennial tidings of Frankish victories. The West could not visualize the limitless manpower of the Moslems, which dwarfed that of the Christians even at the best of times, nor the insecure dispersion of the Latin commonwealth. The West was in no position to realize that over ten years of comparative peace had brought to Outremer a degree of prosperity hitherto unknown, and consequently lessened the native Franks' desire for war. The West knew only that God's special favor went with the Crusades, and that piece by piece the Holy Land was being lost all over again. Impossible, but it was happening.

There could be only one explanation: treason. The explanation preferred by the Church authorities, that God was visiting the notorious sins and vices of the Crusaders on their cause, need not be rejected — such treason would be sin enough to make God allow it to attain its object, by way of punishment.

The traitors were not far to seek. Everybody knew that Western arms were superior to the Saracenic, and that the military orders, notably the Templars, were invincible. On the Templars, therefore, fell the blame for everything that went awry, at this period, whether the pendulum of their policy swung towards intransigence — as under the Grand Masters Philip de Le Plaissiez, William of Chartres and Peter de Montaigu — or towards pacific conservation, as under Robert de Sablé and Gilbert Erail and again under Armand de Périgord later in the twenties. Ambivalence had frozen in one attitude, the adverse. When the Templars were responsible for the breakdown of negotiations, they were accused of sacrificing Jerusalem that they themselves might go on fighting and be covered with glory. When they counseled caution, it was pointed out that their bounden duty was to fight. In either case, they were selling the Holy Land.

It became necessary for the Holy See to issue instructions to the bishops and parish priests of all Europe, to preach the Templars' guiltlessness from every pulpit every Sunday. The Holy See could lay its hand on a much better sinner to fill the bill of responsibility for the failure of the Fifth Crusade.

He was the Emperor Frederick II, that sparkling cynosure of normality's distrust.

For ten years all exhortations had been vain, even Pope Honorius III, once Frederick's tutor, could not bring him up to scratch. It was left to Gregory IX, a pontiff of sterner stuff, at last to excommunicate the Emperor for what was considered his frivolous procrastination. At this Frederick did abruptly complete his now thirteen years of euphemistic preparations and took ship for the Holy Land.

A man under interdict was not allowed to participate in a Crusade, much less to lead one. The Holy See sought to restrain Frederick as fruitlessly as it had formerly urged him on. The pinnacle of irony was attained when the Holy See, which for a century and a half had done everything to impel Christians on Crusade, pronounced the ban on every Christian who had anything to do with the Crusade of the Emperor Frederick. As in the event Frederick succeeded where all others had failed and obtained the cession of Jerusalem — the Holy City, heart and soul of Christendom, was excommunicated lock, stock and barrel for permitting his entry. In the church of the Holy Sepulchre, without one single candle burning or one single priest to officiate, Frederick himself placed the crown of Jerusalem upon his head, with a shrug.

Characteristically this happened *after* he had lost his right to the throne by the death of his young wife Yolanda. There was a son, the infant-King Conrad, but the Frankish barons would have hesitated to entrust even the regency to one who was doubly excommunicate (excommunicated for having persevered with his Crusade though excommunicate). But then, to a man who could calmly disregard his exclusion from earthly and heavenly society, law and title were the least of worries.

The ban dissolved the oath of fealty; Frederick's army had shrunk to thirty thousand all told. The barons kept aloof. Of the military orders, the Teutonic Knights cleaved to him as a matter of course; the Templars and Hospitalers were faced with a dilemma. The fellow-soldiers of Christ could not go against the decree of Christ's Vicar; but neither was it wise to look on idly while the Imperial host stood to regain Jerusalem. So they did not march with Frederick's army when it set out from Acre, but parallel with it under their own officers — in this way they might disclaim any connection with the Emperor. Since, however, this ingenious arrangement enabled the Saracens to attack each army by turns, the two orders decided to join Frederick after all — so long as every command he issued was given, not in his own name, but explicitly in the name of God and Christendom! Thus did the army of the Pope take part in the Crusade the Pope had anathematized.

"See how God's blessing goeth with the Pope's curse!" the chronicler points out, with reason. By nothing more arduous than bluff and skillful bargaining with the Sultan, Frederick won Jerusalem and Bethlehem, with a corridor running to the sea at Jaffa, as well as Nazareth, western Galilee and the district around Sidon. Only the actual Temple area in Jerusalem, containing the sacred rock of Mohammed's Ascension, was excepted and remained in Moslem hands. A peace treaty was signed, for ten years, and both parties to it released their prisoners of war.

The Sultan's power had been seriously weakened by the family quarrels of Saladin's and Saphadin's descendants. The treaty, therefore, whilst not so advantageous for the Moslems as for the Christians, still had much to recommend it to Islam. It did not in fact recommend itself to anyone but the two signatories. Both Islam and Christendom were loud in execration.

The spiritual leaders of Islam contented themselves with abusing the Sultan, and ordered universal mourning. The Vicar of Christ, having already shot his bolt of excommunication several times over, went further. The Pope called out a Crusade against Frederick. John de Brienne, whom Frederick had gone out of his way to affront, with alacrity accepted command and began to ravage Frederick's Italian lands, with the diligent collaboration of the Italian branches of the Temple and the Hospital.

In Palestine, too, their tenuous alliance with the excommunicate Emperor was soon over. For many years no treaty had been ratified without the signatures of their grand masters; since their foundation, no King of Jerusalem had been crowned without the consent and participation of the military orders. Moreover, Frederick's achievement reflected discredit on them, the dedicated guardsmen of Jerusalem, who had not managed to get it back, by force of arms or otherwise.

The Templars even more than the Hospitalers were enraged. Without so much as asking their leave the Emperor had seen fit to throw away the Templars' Temple to the Moslems. He would advance the hated Teutonic Order at their expense. The grand master wrote to the Sultan, with a proposal to ambush and assassinate the Emperor; but the Sultan, true to his compact, merely forwarded the letter to the intended victim. Frederick's answer was to surround the Templars' headquarters and threaten to march on their Castle Pilgrim.

The threat was not executed. The Templar garrisons were too strong, and every hand in Syria was against Frederick. Without more troops than he had at his disposal, the best he could do was retreat in good order. There were anti-Imperial riots at Acre, and the papal invasion of his Italian territories was making headway. His presence there became imperative. Forced to compromise even in the matter of selecting the *baillis* he would leave behind, Frederick departed hurriedly six weeks after his coronation, amid the jeers of the populace and a shower of fish heads and offal. He had done little to enhance Christian reputation among the Saracens. They were repelled by his levity, which he had vented impartially in ostentatious tolerance towards Islam and in sophisticated deprecation of his own faith.

Immediately he landed in Italy, he seized all Templar property in Apulia. The Templars in Palestine avenged their brethren by chasing the Teutonic Knights out of Acre. At Jerusalem they set about rebuilding the dismantled fortifications of Mount Moriah — who were they to be bound by Frederick's pact, which he had signed over their heads? In fact refortifying Jerusalem was included in the peace terms, but Frederick now chose to interpret this as a personal concession to himself, to the letter of which he would adhere. The Sultan had made no move to have the work stopped; the Emperor forbade it on pain of confiscation of all Templar property in Germany and Sicily. Any attempt to renew the system of defense works for the Holy City in his absence would expose him to merited charges of perjury, he said, and he would not shrink from any means to guard his honor. Thus the walls,' the tower, ramparts and ditches of Jerusalem were never mended. Jerusalem remained an open city.

Jerusalem remained an open city until it was lost to the Franks for good in the year 1244.

The propelling force behind that final loss was Jenghiz Khan, once presumed Prester John. His stupendous sweep of conquest had displaced among others the Khwarismian Turks from their territory east of the Caspian Sea. These savage horsemen, who knew and cared nothing about either Christianity or Islam, had been wandering westward ever since, until their murderous search for land became concentrated on Syria. They had no other interest, and were perfectly willing to sell their services to the highest bidder.

Temporarily acting for the Sultan of Egypt, the Khwarismians in a whirlwind descent of terror swept the Christians from the open city of Jerusalem. (Like the Huns, whom they resembled in their way of life, this equestrian Turkish tribe was formidable in assault, but unskilled in siege warfare.) Only three hundred of the Frankish occupants got away; fire, slaughter, torture and pillage laid waste the citadel of two faiths. The remains of the Kings of Jerusalem, also of Godfrey de Bouillon, King in all but insignia, were torn from their tombs in the Church of the Holy Sepulchre and scattered like the myriad other bones already welded with the soil of Palestine.

The Christians vied in putting the blame on each other; and they were not far out, except in that each group accused only one specific entity, instead of all of them together. For the past decade rivalry had reigned supreme, and its realm was anarchy.

Though long since ousted from the internal affairs of Outremer, the Emperor Frederick, with a few years of life yet remaining to him, proclaimed the guilt of the Templars throughout the world. He accused them on the one hand of cultivating Moslem friendship and denying Christ by excessive religious tolerance — a very flagrant case of the pot denouncing the kettle's blackness. On the other hand, he said it was they who had driven the Sultan into the arms of the Khwarismians, by another breach of truce. Frederick did not mention, and perhaps he had forgotten, who was initially responsible for the want of fortifications that might have halted the unversed Khwarismians before Jerusalem.

The Templars were guilty on both counts, but the inference was false. The ultimate loss of Jerusalem was not due to their shortcomings, any more than to any one of the many other factors which in sum contributed to it.

Most devastating of all was the spreading paralysis of disillusion. In the East, belligerence and staying power were stifled in frustration and the sense of pointlessness. The Promised Land no longer promised either metaphysical or material rewards: the Divine ire which allowed Outremer to disintegrate had canceled both. In the West, recruiting preachers would find their audiences melting away, with bold asides to the effect that if a man wanted to commit suicide, he could find plentiful ways of doing so at home. The song-makers gave tongue to the pervasive pessimism, and so helped to spread it still.

The aggressive spirit which had deserted the Christians made its home among the Moslems, with a vengeance.

11 The Rearguard

RIGHTLY, IT HAS BEEN SAID THAT FROM THEIR FOUNDATION IN 1128 UNTIL the end of Outremer in 1291, the story of the Templars is that of the Crusades — one reason why it cannot be rendered down to the bare bones of a regimental biography. Also, in the Templar Order the nature of the parent-movement became demonstrable, as in a microcosm created on purpose to exhibit miniature models of a larger and more promiscuous whole.

The microcosm has now been explored, its salient features in the scheme of that whole have been covered. It remains to wind up this middle phase which, though steeply on the downgrade ever since the partnership of Guy de Lusignan and Gerard de Ridefort, was a long time dying.

The Mongols came to Syria.

Jenghiz Khan (1167-1227), paramount chief of the Mongol tribes, was the greatest conqueror the world has ever known and created the greatest empire the world has ever seen, stretching from Korea to Persia and beyond, and from the Indian Ocean to the Arctic Seas. The measurement of greatness here applies to dimension only. The Great Khan appropriated larger tracts of the globe and subdued larger numbers of people, than anyone before or since. But once he had this empire, he, in a manner of speaking, did nothing with it. Had he lived, he doubtless would have gone on conquering, as his successors did for some decades; had he been immortal, the Mongols would perhaps have overrun the earth, what was then known of it.* And then would his ferocious nomad horsemen have hung up their saddles and relinquished their tents, would they have used their hundreds of thousands of slaves on gigantic agricultural projects and evolved a new civilization in a synthesis of the various centers of culture on which they had remained content merely to levy tribute? In time, perhaps so. Yet the driving force behind their incredible dynamic has never been isolated with any certainty. If it was grazing lands they were after — there was more pasturage in the greater Mongol Empire than even their myriad hordes could consume; there was not enough of it in such places as Tibet, Afghanistan or the ice-bound coast of Siberia to have invited conquest. Their aggression served no religious proselytism, they being so far removed from bigotry that their creed has left no impression. Land-greed to us is no longer a respectable casus belli, forcible ideological conver-

---

* Personally and as a ruler, it appears, he was not without commendable qualities, and like Mussolini making the trains run on time, instituted (astonishingly) a good postal service.

sion is not now extolled, nor do we regard a higher standard of living as a satisfactory war aim; yet the empires founded on those have invariably produced some characteristic civilization. All left traces, monuments, artefacts, the memory of a cult — except the Mongols. The Mongols created nothing — save that featureless Empire itself. Their religious tolerance was the one positive expression of a surpassing indifference which applied particularly to human life. The blood they shed, the cities they incinerated, nowhere acted as fertilizer, but always as agents of decomposition.

It was so in Syria, too. The springflood of Mongol invasions, too transient to wreak complete destruction on Islam and its peoples, yet washed away the cultural cement of the old Moslem order. Islam arose resurgent, but, unlike the phoenix, in a bedraggled, changed, barbarized form. Almost its only emotive continuity rested in fanatical hatred of the Christians.

Scrambling over rubble, ashes and moldering bones, wading through blood and spurning the living alike with the dead, the Mameluke bodyguards of the Sultans of Islam fought and schemed, deceived and tortured their way to power; and the last vestiges of humanity and honor vanished from the Holy War.

Among the Christians, the wishful identification of Prester John died hard, even when Jenghiz Khan himself was no longer alive, and even after the Mongols had broken into Europe as far as Silesia and the Adriatic — showing that they waged war quite impartially and not only against Moslems and heathen. Because a number of the Khans had Nestorian-Christian wives* and had Nestorian clergy at their courts — together with the priests, shamans, witch doctors of other creeds — and because they too were ready to make opportunist alliances, the Franks clung to the belief that the Mongol scourge would act as a sort of weed-killer only, blighting the Moslems and leaving Christendom to flourish the better.

* Early in the eleventh century certain Turkish tribes of Outer Mongolia had been converted by Nestorian missionaries.

Indeed, when the Mongols entered Syria in 1259 and in a short space overran the country, when the Assassins were eradicated root and branch, when Baghdad was horribly sacked, Aleppo taken, and Damascus, when for the first time in six hundred years the Moslems were reduced into an oppressed minority, the Franks, although entirely surrounded by the Asiatic conquerors, were spared to look on, at the relatively inexpensive price of some humility. But already their own encounter in the forties with the Mongols' forerunners, the Khwarismians, had so exhausted the Franks that the piecemeal transfer of their kingdom into Moslem hands had been dizzily accelerated.

One small bright candle of integrity lightens the snarling chaos; one success story for a moment returns some glamour to the sordid Arabian Night; one enduring quality allows the episode of Outremer to close, as it had begun, with a degree of epic grandeur. The first was Saint Louis, the second appertains to the Mameluke Sultan Baibars, the third is the heroism of the Templars.

In an era of enthusiasm, the whole Christian world bowed down before Bernard of Clairvaux. In an era of despondency, the whole world that knew of him, Moslem as well as Christian, reverenced King Louis IX of France. We may take him as representing the ideal man of his time, his character compounded of all the virtues which society recognized but usually honored in absentia. First and last, he was sincere. In our day, too, sincerity is prized, to the extent of rendering all sins pardonable — which suggests that it may be as rare now as it had become in the thirteenth century, at least among those who were in the public eye.

Louis was a highly conscious person; his piety, his justice, his asceticism were not spontaneous, easily come by, but wrought of hard work upon the material that was himself, products of unrelieved whittling, polishing, improvement, to the end of his days. We too attach great value to conscious awareness, and we respect the soul-scourer (as surely one should), although humorlessness today is suspect, even slightly in-

PORTUGAL
LEON-CASTILE
ARAGON
MOORS
MOORS
BRITAIN
FRANCE
HOLY ROMAN
(GERMAN)
EMPIRE
E   U   R   O   P
BYZANTINE
EMPIRE
A   R   A   B   I   A
A F R I C A

THE WORLD OF THE MIDDLE AGES

Showing the Western States about 1200 and the extent
of the Mongol Invasions in the 13th. century
Palestine is shown in black

MILES   0   500   1000   2000   3000

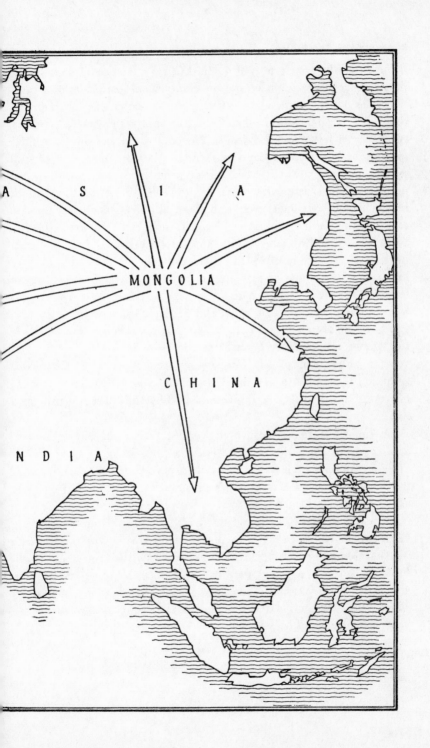

decent, slightly grotesque. But Louis IX was canonized for it. Jesting implies a lack of seriousness, and the ability to see both sides of a question rules out the passionate obtuseness of the genuine zealot. Louis IX could be charged with neither failing, even by the devil's advocate, twenty-seven years after his demise. Nor was the devil's advocate likely to bring up sins which today Louis's unimaginative sincerity might still excuse, but which would nevertheless obviate perfect goodness in our judgment. The cruelty with which he proceeded against civil miscreants, rebels, heretics and unbelievers — in short, all offenders against the two causes with which he identified himself: state and religion — the tyranny he exercised over his family, and the breathtaking egotism which interpreted his defeat in Palestine (to the tune of thousands of lives lost and a nauseating sum of human suffering) as a divine stratagem to teach him, King Louis, humility — none of these presented itself so to his coevals. He knew his duty, and he never swerved from the pursuit of it. He always kept his word. His gentle, uncomplaining fortitude throughout two months of harsh imprisonment in a Moslem dungeon was an inspiration to his companions who could never afterwards speak of it without tears; the very jailers, when they saw him off, affectionately joked that such a man should by rights become their next ruler.

Yet this good, honest man and deeply conscientious King, this sincere Crusader, dealt the coup de grâce to the Christian cause. For if a living saint like Louis was suffered to be defeated by the Moslems, the theory of defeat as the wages of sin fell to the ground once for all.

Faith was shaken in its foundations. Either there was no God, or else Christendom had been mistaken for close on two centuries as to His will, and He had never desired them to win back the Holy Land at all. For close on two centuries they had spilt their blood for a delusion, and so far from pleasing God, had angered Him beyond patience. In either case, whether Heaven be empty or incomprehensibly perverse — hope was truly dead.

The Sixth Crusade again attempted to free the Holy Land by subjugating Egypt, and again it opened with some success. Louis IX took Damietta and transformed it into a Frankish city with a cathedral and a bishop and sectors allotted to the military orders and the consulates of the Italian cities. For one summer Damietta was the capital of Outremer. But inaction in the humid Delta did its inevitable work. When the arm of occupation eventually pressed on towards Cairo — against the advice of the military orders — it was in a low state of organization and morale, and steadily dwindling. It was then decimated at Mansourah, partly owing to the indiscipline of the Count of Artois, Louis's brother,* and partly by the talents of the enemy commander, a former Mameluke slave named Rukd ad-Din Baibars, "Bundukdari," the Arbalestier. Out of two hundred and ninety Templar Knights five survived the first battle of Mansourah; and it can have been small comfort to them that they had tried to restrain the Count of Artois — particularly as the count was himself among the fallen. In a second battle King Louis was technically victorious, but his losses almost equaled those of his brother in defeat. The Grand Master of the Temple, William de Sonnac, who had lost one eye in the first charge, lost the other and died of his wounds.

As best they could, the remnants of the Christian army fortified their camp, and all the horrors of the siege of Acre repeated themselves in more concentrated form. When finally the King could no longer postpone retreat, his engineers forgot to destroy their pontoon bridges behind them. Incredulous of their good fortune, the Moslems followed, and with ease rounded up the entire army, sick and weary as it was. The King himself, having fought with great gallantry, was seriously ill, and they dragged him from his bed and in chains led him to prison. In spite of the heavy Frankish losses, the prisoners still were so many as to threaten their captors with famine. Everyone too enfeebled to walk was executed on the spot, and for a week three hundred soldiers were decapitated at the end of each day's march.

* Louis's biographer, Joinville, blames, not the Count of Artois, but the defective eardrums of a deaf knight whose job it was to hold the count's warhorse.

The ransom for King Louis and the remaining prisoners was fixed at five hundred thousand livres Tournois, or one million besants, over and above the surrender of Damietta. When the city had been handed over, Louis was released to collect the money. He found only a hundred and seventy thousand livres in his coffers. Until a first installment of two hundred and fifty thousand was paid, Baibars would not release Louis's brother Alphonse of Poitou.

The Templars were known to have a large store of money on board their flagship in the bay; and the King's friend, counselor and biographer, Joinville, approached them for a loan. The Templars refused: the money was not theirs, they but held it in trust for the Pope and could do nothing without Papal authorization. Joinville wasted no further words. He hastened out to the Templar galley with an axe and threatened to break open the treasure chests. The gold was disbursed. Some say this was only a gesture, hatched between Joinville and the Marshal of the Temple, to get around the letter of a principle. Seeing that the ransoming of pilgrims had been one of the Templars' earliest charges, and that previously they had not hesitated to hand out King Henry II's money at their own discretion, it is at best an embarrassing story.

The Count of Poitou and other noble prisoners were released and sailed with the King to Acre. The wounded soldiers left in captivity were one and all put to death.

In spite of urgent despatches incessantly requesting his return, Louis selflessly remained in Palestine for another four years.

His nature had not changed, his tenets were not modified; but the situation was not what it had been when he first arrived. Then he had absolutely declined, even to his cost, to negotiate with the Infidel. He had consented to approach the Mongols — the heathens were a different proposition from the Infidel. He had sent them an embassy, bearing what he considered the most suitable present, namely a traveling altar shrine, which for the moment elicited nothing more useful than a demand that he acknowledge himself a vassal to the Khan.

King Louis was hard up for allies. The Pope (Innocent IV) was supporting, not Louis, but another "Crusade" to help the Frankish Emperor of Constantinople against the insurgent Byzantines; Louis's brothers had their hands full at home and sent him no reinforcements; and Henry III of England, who had taken the cross in 1250, obtained indulgence to postpone his expedition. A popular mass movement in France to go to the rescue of the saintly King petered out in a medley of civil disorders. The saintly King went to the only source of armed assistance against Egypt left for him to tap: the Ideal Christian joined forces with the Assassins, professional murderers. Doubtless he was able to persuade himself that, as the heretic opponent of the ruling Moslem sect, in negation of a negation, so to speak, the Assassins did not rank as Infidels either. At the very end he was forced after all to conclude a pact with Egypt, with Islam, but it was too late to undo the damage which his whole ill-starred enterprise had brought upon the land of Outremer.

It remained on his mind for the sixteen years that followed, a time during which the internal affairs of France again and again prevented King Louis from attempting to make good that tragic failure. Then at last Louis, worn out and old before his time, led another Crusade, the Seventh and last ever to set out under royal command from the motherland, the most confused of plan and the most fruitless of all. Almost upon arrival in North Africa, he died of another camp epidemic, on August 25, 1270. But his last words were "Jerusalem! Jerusalem!"

The Mongols in Syria eventually encountered an unyielding obstacle: the Mameluke Baïbars "Arbalestier," the victor of Mansourah.

He was then fifty years old, a Kipchak-Turkish tribesman from the Russian plain between Volga and Don, who, when first put up for sale in Syria as a youth, had been rejected by several prospective buyers. Knocked down cheap to a more perspicacious Mameluke emir, Baïbars proved himself no inconsiderable bargain, and rose rapidly in the Sultan's bodyguard. After the Mongols had been halted and driven back, in the early sixties, he gave his attention to home affairs, stabbed the Sultan in the back on a hunting party, and sat himself on the throne.

In time he became the mightiest Moslem ruler since Saladin, universally respected like St. Louis, to whom he was counterpoised as the pattern of evil, unloved even by his subjects, but held in awe by them as by the enemy.

Like St. Louis, Baibars may serve not only as an allegorical figure, but also as an instance of a social-political principle. Outside his crusading enterprises, Louis is the epitome of modern monarchy struggling out of feudal toils; Baibars exemplifies the essential egalitarianism of Islam. In origin he could not have been more base. It is impossible to visualize his European counterpart, let us say a Christian serf of foreign race, taking power in any of the countries of the West. Though such a Christian serf might conceivably have murdered the sovereign of the land, that would have been as far as he got; whereas in the case of Baibars the entire general staff of the Egyptian army did homage to him immediately the deed was done. His suzerainty was never contested on grounds of his birth, and two of his sons occupied the throne after him.

His relentless prosecution of the war against the Christians left Outremer the merest rudimentary collection of coastal cities at the time of his death in 1277. Antioch had been crushed and depopulated nearly ten years before; Acre, Tyre, Sidon, Tripoli, Jebail and Tortosa were all that remained, with Lattakieh and the two impregnable castles of the Temple and the Hospital, Athlit (Castle Pilgrim) and Marqab, clinging on in complete isolation, cut off from the rest except by sea.

The Franks of Palestine were no longer colonists so much as birds of passage. Few of the older great families survived; temporal wealth was mainly concentrated in the grasp of the Italian city consulates, temporal power an adjunct of Western princes whose chief interests lay elsewhere. The Palestinian Church was a feature rather than a force. The barons were storm-tossed and rudderless on the breakers of policy; the humble cowered, in resignation or despair, and without that sense of solidarity and pride which a common danger will sometimes engender. Colonial and native elements had never been more sharply divided in recriminations and self-seeking. English, Spanish, German, Greek, Italian expeditions came and went; the Crown and its heiresses passed from hand to hand. The military orders still had permanence, in essence the military orders were the nation — though by the same token evincing not a few of the above national weaknesses.

What with the absolute secrecy of the senior Order of the Temple and the massive front it presented to the outside world, the material for individual portraits is scanty. Just as that country is happy which has no history, so the faces of the "good" grand masters remain dim. An Odo de Saint-Amand, a Gerard de Ridefort stand out clearly enough. On the other hand, the last span of the order's existence became subject to exhaustive judicial investigation, so that a good deal is known about the last grand masters, without necessarily impugning their characters.

Philip de Le Plaissiez, grand master between 1201 and 1208, initiated the constructive-defensive period foreshadowed by Gilbert Erail and continued by William of Chartres who died in the pestilential camp before Damietta, and by Peter de Montaigu, under whom Castle Pilgrim had formed the climax of an extensive building program. On Peter de Montaigu also fell the mantle of Cassandra, and the unenviable task of holding the balance between the rival leaders of the Fifth Crusade, again at Damietta. The date of his death is uncertain, save that it occurred in the uneasy period of the Emperor Frederick's peace. His successor, Armand de Périgord, must have been elected around 1230. Under him Templar diplomacy won some of its greatest triumphs. By skillfully playing off the various Moslem princes against each other Armand managed to have the whole Temple area at Jerusalem restored to his order. At this same time the predominance of Temple over Hospital became final, since the foreign policy it advocated in opposition to the Hospital was adopted. That is to say, the barons renounced the remote-control of the Emperor Frederick and broke the pact with Cairo, in favor of a new agreement with Damascus. When thereupon the Egyptian Sultan invited the Khwarismians to do their worst, Temple and Hospital abruptly buried their differences and their recent pacific ten-

dencies. Armand de Périgord perished at the hands of the Khwarismians in the catastrophic Frankish defeat at Gaza in November, 1239,
along with three hundred knights of his order and two hundred of
the Hospital. Although thirty-six Templars survived the battle, none
knew what had become of their grand master. Failing definite information to the contrary, there was a possibility that, like the Grand Master
of the Hospital, he had been taken alive. For an unknown period, therefore, the next election was deferred.

The first document showing the name of William de Sonnac over
the grand master's seal is dated 1247. He it was who bore the brunt of
St. Louis's virtue, in the early days of the Sixth Crusade, when the
French King reproached the Templars for favoring negotiations with the
enemy. However, William died unexceptionably at Mansourah, and the
clash of policy did not come to a head until the next term of office,
when the grand master was Reynald de Vichiers and the King had to
swallow his resolve not to treat with the Infidel. Then Louis's compact
with the Sultan was nearly wrecked by the Templars' refusal to break
off relations with Damascus. So by one of the ironies of history which
can be so amusing at a distance, the positions were reversed, and Louis
administered a stern public reprimand to Reynald de Vichiers. The
resulting procedures of the grand chapter are shrouded in mystery as
ever, but Reynald either resigned or was deposed, since he did not die
until 1256, and the signature of his successor is first recorded under an
earlier date.

The English Templar Knight Thomas Bérard, then, became grand
master in the fifties and stayed in office until his death in 1272. His
connection with England was preserved in copious correspondence —
Cassandra-style — with King Henry III. But so far from being able to
lend the required assistance, the English King's financial embarrassment
at the time was such that he had to pawn the crown jewels to the Temple
at Paris, ". . . golden wands, golden combs, diamond buckles, chaplets
and circlets, golden crowns, imperial beavers, rich girdles, golden pea-
cocks, and rings innumerable, adorned with sapphires, rubies, emeralds,
topazes and carbuncles. . . ." against an immediate loan.

When at last old age saved King Henry from redeeming his ancient crusading vow, his son and heir, the Prince Edward, went in his stead. To Thomas Bérard belongs the honor of having provided the saving antidote when Prince Edward was wounded by a poisoned Assassin dagger.

However, none of this gives any very positive indication of Bérard's character, which is of importance because many years later he was charged with having set the Temple's downhill course. He may have been thus accused merely because he was safely dead while still alive in memory. Yet it may be to the point to remark that in Thomas Bérard's day fell the cataclysmic onslaught of the Mongols, overrunning Syria with the horrifying density of a carnivorous insect plague or a Martian invasion, enough to upset the equilibrium of many a European mind. Coming on top of the pall of Godforsaken pessimism which hung over Outremer, the terrible phenomenon might well have appeared as an announcement of apocalyptic changes in the very nature of the universe; and if there was any truth in the subsequent allegations of a sinister cult practiced in the secret places of the Temple, certainly this would have been a fertile season for its inception.

Less than two months after Bérard's death in 1272, William de Beaujeu was elected, the last grand master to be invested in the Holy Land. We have a deceptive impression of more intimate acquaintance with him, because the chronicler of the last decade of Outremer, the "Templar of Tyre," was this grand master's secretary and naturally allotted a fair amount of space to his employer's role. But this could scarcely have been glossed over by any contemporary reporter, and when we come to scrutinize the secretary's description of the man, we find it does not tell us much more than a tombstone would. "He was a great gentleman, related to the King of France, and also very generous and great in almsgiving, for which he was much renowned, and in his time caused the Temple to be greatly honored and respected." While it does deviously transpire that William de Beaujeu was proud, self-willed, ambitious, an intrepid warrior and acute politician — these qualities were typical of almost any Grand Master of the Temple.

The first historic appearance in public of William de Beaujeu is at the Council of Lyons of 1274, four years after the death of St. Louis. The council was summoned by Pope Gregory X with the object of making the next Crusade the greatest and final one. His concern for the Holy Land was the more lively as he had been the first Pontiff to visit it, when yet only Archbishop of Liége, in the entourage of Prince Edward of England — an experience he never forgot. But his trump card, that same Prince, now reigning as King Edward I, did not turn up at the conference, nor did any of the invited galaxy of potentates with the exception of King James I of Aragon. King James, who was no youngster, enjoyed himself as the sole crowned head in the assembly of prelates and fighting monks, and talked big. He was willing, he said, to provide a thousand knights on the spot and lead them to the Holy Land himself, and would likewise undertake to furnish and fit out no fewer than ten ships — just to spur on the sluggards a bit, he added pointedly, for William de Beaujeu's soothing attempts to reduce the royal offer and thus bring it down to earth into the realm of possibility had made the old King very angry. This minor fracas, which greatly entertained the Pope and his cardinals, was later to be used in evidence against the Temple.

Otherwise the Council of Lyons produced small results. The Franciscan and Dominican Friars received official recognition, and representatives of the Emperor of Constantinople promised the reunion of their Church with the Church of Rome — for the Pope in return promised them to check the imperialistic ambitions of Charles of Anjou, a surviving brother of St. Louis, who was the specter then particularly haunting Europe. But the union of the two Churches was a fiction, since neither the clergy nor the people of Byzantium would have any part of it; and as for the Crusade to end all Crusades, it never went beyond the talking stage.

Charles of Anjou had made himself King of Naples and Sicily by right of conquest and by right of purchase had acquired a claim to the throne of Outremer. William de Beaujeu was a kinsman of his, and so the Temple supported Charles against Hugh III of Cyprus, another sprig of the Lusignan stock and lately become King of Jerusalem, by right of heritance. Having the Templars behind him helped further to embolden Charles's arrogance and brutality, so that the Templars may be said indirectly to have had their share in the bloody expulsion of the French from Sicily. The Sicilian Vespers, which disrupted the whole balance of power in Europe and marked the beginning of the end of papal world suzerainty (therein exercising a most portentous influence on the destiny of the Temple) — that crucial rebellion was only seven years off.

In Syria a succession of Moslem civil wars had given Outremer another respite. The Franks used this to repair their fortifications and to break them down again in civil wars of their own.

For instance, in an operation resulting from yet another breach-of-promise feud, the Prince of Tripoli, Bohemond VII, destroyed the Temple preceptory where his antagonist, Guy of Jebail, had taken refuge, and for good measure cut down a nearby forest also belonging to the order. William de Beaujeu led his knights against Tripoli to stage a demonstration outside the walls; on the way back they set fire to the castle of Botrun in conclusion of its fateful if humdrum history. The Prince of Tripoli came out in pursuit and they joined battle, with fearful losses on both sides, which deterred neither from continuing their war at sea, in a series of full-scale naval engagements, suicidal in their effect. The end of that incident was no prettier than the rest, and no less wasteful in the upshot. The Hospitalers tried their hand at mediating between Bohemond and Guy, and the latter surrendered on receiving Bohemond's promise to spare his life. As soon as he had them in his power, Bohemond put out the eyes of Guy's companions; Guy himself with two brothers and one cousin were buried up to their necks in a ditch and left to starve to death.

Presently war broke out, and like an ignited powder train seared the Palestinian coast from end to end, between the Pisan colonists and the Genoese. It burned itself out at last; but only the energetic intervention of the grand masters of Temple and Hospital prevented the Genoese from sending their fellow-Christian prisoners of war to the slave markets of Egypt.

The Moslems were the first to pull themselves together. Marqab fell to them. Lattakieh fell.

Tripoli fell, and need not have been lost. One of the Sultan's emirs was in the pay of the Templars and gave them warning. William de Beaujeu hurried to Tripoli with the news, but not òne of the factions then struggling for supremacy within the city would believe him. It was thought that he had invented the story in the hope of fishing in artificially troubled waters; and nothing was done to strengthen the defenses of Tripoli until the army of Egypt was actually at the gates. The garrison fought gallantly, the Templar posse died to a man; only the Genoese and the Venetians defected and sailed away. Of the inhabitants all grown men were butchered, the women and children taken into slavery. The carrion stench drove off a Moslem historian coming to inspect the scene, a few days after. Then Tripoli, the three-cities'-town of Hellenic times, was systematically demolished, never to rise again on its ancient foundations.

This happened in late April 1289. The tragedy was repeated the following year at Acre.

It was the end of summer, and with a new truce in force prosperity had returned. The harvest had been good, and trade was flourishing. The markets of Acre were thronged with Moslem merchants and farmers, and enlivened by the arrival of a ragged expedition from North Italy. The soldiers of this Crusade, composed of peasants and unemployed, were wholly devoid of discipline, and their pay, moreover, was in arrears. They had come over to fight the Infidel and fill their wallets, and fight the Infidel they would, truce or no truce. A drunken riot started, and ended in the massacre of every civilian wearing a beard, in spite of the efforts of the military orders, who succeeded only in saving a handful of the Moslems and making a very few arrests.

The Mameluke Sultan Qalawun swore that for this he would root out every Christian from the Holy Land. William de Beaujeu advised the commune of Acre to beg the Sultan's pardon and deliver up to him all the Christian criminals currently in the city jails, under pretense that these were the culprits, whose extradition was the only earnest of good-will Egypt would recognize. But the city council refused to go beyond expressing their regrets and trying somewhat feebly to make out that the riot had been started by the Moslems.

The Sultan mobilized his army, but gave out that its destination was Africa. Again William de Beaujeu's emir agent betrayed the Sultan's real plan which was, as might have been guessed, to march on Acre. Again William passed on the warning, and again he met only with disbelief. The inference suggests itself that the grand master had in the past cried wolf for his order's own ends, too often.

But he was not so easily discouraged. On his own authority William sent an envoy to Qalawun. The Sultan offered to spare Acre for as many Venetian gold pieces as there were inhabitants. When the grand master apprised the city council of this, he was howled down, jeered out of the High Court, and insulted by the public waiting outside for news. The sanguine temper of the city was intensified when shortly afterwards Qalawun died.

Unfortunately this Sultan's successor — named al-Ashraf Khalil — measured fully up to his father's stature. He regarded his father's vow not to leave a single Christian alive in Acre as part of his inheritance, and was determined to carry it out. After the customary palace revolt had been quelled and the winter rains subsided, he brought into Palestine an army said to number sixty thousand horsemen and a hundred and sixty thousand infantry, not counting engineers and miners, with several hundred siege engines of all kinds collected from all over al-Ashraf's dominions. There could now be no further doubt, no further willful blindness, as to his intentions.

The population of Acre was between thirty and forty thousand strong. At most two thousand were fighting regulars, six or seven hundred of them knights and mounted serjeants. Arms were distributed to all able-bodied citizens. The military orders rushed in all their available troops, a party of English, Swiss and others came over in the nick of time, and

Henry of Cyprus, King of Jerusalem, sent an expeditionary force under the command of his brother to take charge of the defense.

Upon the whole, Western response to the belated cries for help of the threatened city was exiguous and unofficial. Those who rose to the call did so from motives of piety and compassion, without the least confidence that the tide could now be turned. The best they could offer was their willingness to die and sell their lives dear — a policy individuals might indulge in, but not expedient from the point of view of governments.

The same expectation of doom suffused the embattled city; it might be the militant defeatism of martyrs, but ruled out the contingency of victory.

The walls were manned in four divisions, respectively under the Cypriot Prince Amalric, the English knight John de Grailly and the Swiss Otto de Grandson, the Venetian and Pisan garrisons, and the military orders. Shiploads of women, old men and children were despatched to Cyprus. (The third of the Italian outposts in Palestine, the merchants of Genoa, had been squeezed out of Acre by the other two, and they made a separate peace with the Sultan.)

The last siege of Acre went on for forty-three days. The Moslem armies sealed off the land front and bombarded the great double walls, night and day. They had two enormous catapults, named Ghadban, the Furious, and al Mansour, the Victorious, which had required two hundred wagons to transport their timbers prior to assembly. These, and quantities of lighter mangonels, without pause hurled their ammunition against the city — huge bolts of timber, rocks, and pottery containers filled with burning tar or Greek fire, which upon impact burst and scattered their incendiary contents far and wide. Continuous showers of arrows sprayed the walls and the platforms of the eleven outer towers, each of which was assailed simultaneously by an estimated one thousand engineers burrowing to undermine them. The Christians yet had command of the sea, and one of their ships was fitted with a catapult which inflicted creditable damage on the Egyptian camp by the Bay of Acre. Food still reached the town, from Cyprus, but the shortage both of armaments and men was felt more and more. Many sorties had been made to destroy enemy siege towers, mangonels, and miners, but such success as had attended these sallies was offset by the expenditure in irreplaceable men. The Templars, assisted by Otto de Grandson and the soldiers under him, staged a moonlight raid on the Northern Moslem sector and took the enemy by surprise, but most of them tripped over tent cords and were captured or killed. The Hospitalers made a similar attempt in total darkness and were driven off before ever they reached the camp. Thereafter sorties were abandoned. The defense could not afford them, even though the King of Cyprus and Jerusalem had arrived with reinforcements of a hundred horsemen and two thousand foot.

During the week of May 8 to 15, the fifth since the beginning of the siege, the outer defenses ceased to hold. Some collapsed, others were set on fire by the garrison retreating to the secondary defense zones. Al-Ashraf now gave orders to accompany the attack with incessant, organized tumult and the appalling din of three hundred drummers mounted on camels and leading an all-out cacophony of war cries, trumpets and cymbals, made up for the absence, in those days, of shell-shock.

On May 16 the Mamelukes forced their way through the ruins of the central gate, having filled up the ditch with carcases of men and horses and piles of wood, stones and earth. Mounted Templars and Hospitalers charged down upon them and with great carnage forced them backwards through the narrow streets until those who survived so long could be hurled off the walls. However, from the next day's fighting the Moslems emerged in possession of the outer enceinte, and on the morning of Friday, May 18, they attacked along the whole eight-hundred-yard stretch of the inner wall from St. Anthony's Gate to the Patriarch's Tower at the most southerly point by the sea. Moslem suicide squads sacrificed themselves, like ants aiding the progress of their comrades over their dead bodies, endlessly, without any visible reduction

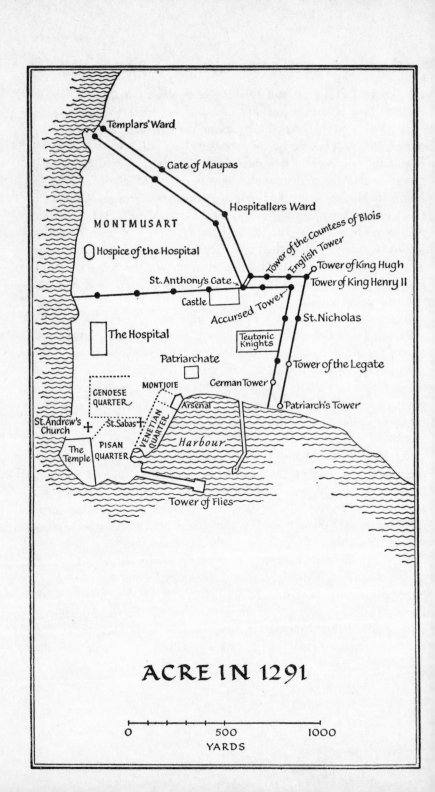

Templars' Ward

Gate of Maupas

Hospitallers Ward

MONTMUSART

Hospice of the Hospital

Tower of the Countess of Blois

English Tower

Tower of King Hugh

Tower of King Henry II

St. Anthony's Gate

Castle

Accursed Tower

St. Nicholas

The Hospital

Teutonic Knights

Patriarchate

Tower of the Legate

German Tower

Patriarch's Tower

MONTJOIE

GENOESE QUARTER

Arsenal

St. Andrew's Church

St. Sabas

VENETIAN QUARTER

Harbour

The Temple

PISAN QUARTER

Tower of Flies

ACRE IN 1291

0   500   1000

YARDS

in the oncoming masses; whereas every single Christian slain opened wider the gaps in the defenses. Before long the Moslems occupied the key tower, called the Accursed, of the eastern salient; Templars and Hospitalers, united, threw themselves at it in rapidly falling strength, again and again without avail. On the eastern wall John de Grailly and Otto de Grandson held out for some hours, but the Moslems pinned them there, cordoned them off, and suddenly appeared behind them in the city.

Every street, every house, every corner was contested inch by inch, while the evacuation of civilians commenced. William de Beaujeu fell, and even as he got his death wound, he was accused of cowardice. An arrow had penetrated to a hand's depth into his armpit, unnoticed by those around him. He rode on as best he could in the press of battle, erratically as his powers failed. This was at last remarked, and a troup of Crusaders intercepted him, exhorting him not to flee and leave them. He replied, *"Seigneurs, je ne peu plus, car je suys mort: vées le coup,"* and sank into the arms of his attendants, dead.

By contrast, the Grand Master of the Hospital, also seriously wounded, weeping and protesting, was forcibly carried down to the harbor and on board a ship. Henry and Amalric of Cyprus with their remaining soldiers had already weighed anchor. The only commander still on his feet was the Swiss Otto de Grandson. To the best of his ability, he directed the rescue operations from the Venetian quarter of the harbor.

A panic-stricken multitude struggled to get on to the quays and fought for the rowing boats, pitifully few and incapacious, to take them out to the galleys anchored off shore. The elements turned against them too; a heavy storm broke over Acre. The aged Patriarch, himself wounded, had been placed in a small skiff, but allowed so many other fugitives to climb in that the craft sank and they were all drowned. There were men who laid hold of boats and auctioned off the berths. But the total number of craft was inadequate to cope with more than a small percentage of the frantic population.

Within a short time the Moslems had established themselves in the city and spread right through it, slaughtering everyone, regardless of age and sex. The yellow flag of Islam flew from the barbican; the crescent had supplanted the cross.

One group of fleeing Christians, including women and children, had been rescued by some Templar survivors who hacked a way to the palace enclosure of their order, which formed the extreme northwesterly tip of the promontory.

By nightfall this compound was the only spot not in Moslem hands and it continued to hold out for days. The Templars repulsed every attack, until the Sultan offered to spare the lives of everyone inside if they would surrender. The marshal of the order, Peter de Sevrey, accepted, and in token of good faith admitted a hundred Mamelukes, commanded by an Emir, to hoist the crescent flag while the Christians made ready to embark on the waiting galleys that had returned from Cyprus for them. But the Moslem soldiers, drunken with victory, began to molest the women and younger boys, at which the Templars set upon them and killed them all. They pulled down the Moslem flag and barricaded the gates again.

At the approach of darkness the marshal sent off the Temple treasure with the commander of the order and as many noncombatants as could be packed on board. Next day the Sultan offered the same honorable terms as before. The marshal and a few other knights ventured out under safe conduct to discuss the surrender. No sooner had they been escorted to the Moslem camp than they were seized and beheaded on the spot.

The rest, who had been impotently watching, fought on. As before, they repelled assault after assault, but they had no means of stopping the enemy's mining operations. Ten days after the sack of the city itself, the landward walls of the Temple began to weaken under the constant bombardment, reinforced by the fires burning in the tunnels under the foundations. A breach appeared, and the Sultan threw two thousand Mamelukes into it. As the Moslems battered their way in, the whole building came crashing down, and the Templars, like Samson, were buried with their enemies in the flaming ruins. Al-Ashraf had accomplished his father's vow.

Nothing remained but to level the ruins of Acre to the ground, and sow the earth with salt.

Nothing remained of Outremer but Tyre, Sidon, Beirut, Haifa, and Tortosa and Athlit. Within another two months they were one by one eliminated. Tyre gave up without a struggle. So did Beirut and Haifa. Sidon resisted for a spell: the commander of the Temple with the treasure and a few knights had landed there, and braved a Mameluke army of vast numerical superiority, until first the town and then the castle became untenable. Only then did they take ship for Tortosa. The commander, Tibald Gaudin, whom they had elected grand master, was already gone on an errand of raising troops and ships for them at Cyprus.

No troops, no ships ever sailed from Cyprus — whatever the unknown reason. Sidon was razed on July 14. On July 30 Haifa was taken, and on the thirty-first, Beirut. Tortosa and Athlit, both of them impregnable, but manned only by the merest fraction of their proper complements, were evacuated respectively on August 3 and 14.

The Sultan laid waste the coastal lands of Palestine at his leisure, and at this task his armies worked for the next few months, leaving no tree unfelled, no irrigation system whole, not a farm or castle standing within reach from the sea. They had not only made an end of Outremer, a political entity; they immolated an entire countryside.

The Templars were the last to quit Palestine. Castle Pilgrim at Athlit had been the last Christian stronghold to be abandoned on the mainland; but two miles off Tortosa they had still a small island, Ruad. Though Ruad had no fresh water, a Templar garrison stayed here for another twelve years.

What was left of Outremer congregated on the isle of Cyprus, where the Temple also made its new headquarters, and where the human debris of the Frankish kingdom outstayed its welcome, as a perennial reminder of a lost cause.

But the Temple did not give up its own cause for lost. The Temple had no need to do so. The Temple still had the greater part of its possessions and its power, intact, all over Europe.

Part Three

The Destroyers

12 The Next Crusade

THE PRECEDING CHAPTER THREW A BRIDGE ACROSS THE TURMOIL OF DIS-
solution which fills the last decades of Outremer; the present one is
the companion arch, over which the story of the Templars and
the Crusades as a whole passes from the East into the West. Cyprus
formed only an exalted transit camp of displaced personages and ideas,
an interlude which, though protracted, could not last, and nobody believed it to be more than that.

The belief in a Christian future for the Holy Land had almost wholly
faded. Palestine now was more inaccessible than it had been at the
time of the First Crusade. Then Islam had been divided; it was united
now. True, then as now all the landing places had been in Moslem
hands — but not barren graveyards in a desert of scorched earth.
Then the land route had been protected, however passively, by the
East Roman Empire, rearing a solid cliff against which Christian aggression might brace its back; now Byzantium was only one state
among many engrossed in a foredoomed struggle to hold its own.
Then unguessed sources of fervor had spurted forth at the tapping of
the Pastoral staff, like the water that gushed from the rock for Moses.
Now, exploited intensively over two centuries, these fountains had
run dry.

"To win a foreign country, none of which will come to *me*, should
I desert wife and child, fief and heritage? Cannot I worship God as
well in Paris as in Jerusalem?" demands a spokesman of secular knighthood. "The way to Paradise does not necessarily lie across the sea. The
great lords and prelates that share out the riches of the world — well
may they take an interest in crusading! For my part, I live at peace
with my neighbors and have no complaints against the quiet life — why
would I go in search of war to the ends of the earth? If you be thirsting
for fame and adventure, do you go and cover yourself with glory, by
all means. You may then tell the Sultan from me that if he wants to
attack me, I shall know how to defend myself. But so long as he

leaves me in peace, I shall do the same by him. High and low have made the Pilgrimage — presumably to become saints. Strange that only brigands have returned. . . ."

"Cross and Creed are of no account," sings the Templar trouvère, "since neither is any protection from the fell Turks — may God confound them! But then, it seems that God wishes, rather, to preserve them, for our undoing. . . ."

As for the common people, we hear that when the friars came round with their alms sack to collect for the succor of the Holy Land "in the name of Christ," the man in the street would brusquely refuse, call some beggar and throw him a coin, with the words, "In the name of Mahomet, who is mightier than Christ!"

Even if this happened only once, even if poet and satirist expressed a common attitude with uncommon acerbity — still it is clear enough which way the wind was blowing: not to the East, not any more. Only the papal vane stood set to the Orient, unwavering banner, signpost, rallying signal to the next Crusade.

To be sure, the Holy Places must be rescued: overtly the secular rulers of the West would not allow that there could be two opinions about this, let alone confess that they considered it impracticable, nor that they were fully occupied with other business. No monarch, however great, arrogant or impious had ever dared decline a direct invitation to take the cross, not even the Emperor Frederick II, not even Henry II of England, both of whom had merely postponed carrying out their vow year after year, in their time. Now as ever, ostensibly, plans for a new Crusade were under constant consideration by the Western monarchs, who perhaps evinced their theoretical willingness the more glibly as the loss of Outremer must delay execution of a project which now needed to be entirely revised.

The next Crusade (which, we may as well say here, never took place*) became a catchphrase of European diplomacy. With it on their

---

* Though eventually various sporadic attempts were made from one quarter and another until the middle of the fifteenth century, no other "General Passage" was ever launched.

lips secular rulers were able to protest their amenableness to the Pope even when in other matters defying his dictates; it could be used for bargaining, for deflecting attention from any less patently righteous activities and for raising money.

Just as no king had the face to set himself against the sacred cause, so the murmuring of his people tended to be muted, against taxation in the same behalf. Such levies had not always found their way into the prescribed channels, even when Outremer was still in existence. Funds which are not immediately employed for their destined purpose have a way of evaporating — hardly into thin air, however. So the next Crusade was a useful administrative device to keep on hand. While it is well to be careful with imputations of calculating hypocrisy, the Crusades of the past had in truth served to introduce universal taxation as an instrument of state economy, and the ephemeral Grand Pilgrimage of the future was soon to serve as a perennial pretext for fresh levies.

The Papacy, however, was sincerely anxious for the Holy Land — so sincere in its anxiety, of late, as to acknowledge the part played by the Church herself in discrediting the great movement. After the fall of Jerusalem in 1187 Gregory VIII sounded the first note of implied Church self-criticism, with an announcement that his cardinals had all sworn to become poor itinerant preachers and in this capacity would go with the Christian armies to Palestine. Self-criticism became more and more explicit in the course of the next hundred years.

From the last quarter of the thirteenth century onwards, until the whole matter subsided during the Renaissance, the Holy See commissioned numbers of reports on the subject of spiritual as well as material rearmament, in all of which a significant amount of space was allotted to the clergy's failure of example. One of the earliest, written by a Franciscan, was candidly entitled *Collectio de Scandalis Ecclesiae*. Another, by a leading Dominican, pointed out that, while large sections of the laity held aloof from the holy work and even cursed an enterprise which had already caused so much bereavement in Christendom, their pastors encouraged the indifference of the flock from sheer avarice.

"The same clerics who cheerfully rake in their tithe of the peasant's hard-won harvest rebel against the inconsiderable contribution for which they themselves have been assessed and refuse to give up the smallest of their luxuries in aid of the Holy Land. . . ." No wonder, the writer goes on to say, that "along with their faith in Christianity Triumphant, men are losing Faith itself. . . ."

Both authors belonged to the great missionary orders, whose growing influence is apparent in these and other treatises, all arguing that God Himself had evidently countermanded conquest by bloodshed, and that conversion rather than extermination of the Infidel should henceforth be the Christian objective. But the main concern of every report was how to rekindle enthusiasm and how best to finance future expeditions, of whatever kind. And almost invariably their suggestions fell under three main heads: Christian unity, Church reform — and reorganization of the military orders. Schismatics and heretics must be brought into conformity with the true Church and wars must end between the Christian nations before they could properly launch the final offensive against the common enemy; the clergy must be purged of wealth and sloth if it were to regain the confidence of laity and Deity; and none of these conditions would be met so long as any ambiguity was permitted concerning the role of the military orders. So long as they, who were by name and statute exclusively wedded to the Holy Land, blithely pursued their interests in the West — so long would European peace be in doubt, so long could religious bodies be charged with worldly preoccupations, and so long would the layman see no reason why *he* should sacrifice himself.

About the turn of the century the Spanish preacher Raymond Lull, although most famous as a mystic, submitted the most concrete conspectus yet. While he agreed with the missionary view (and in fact founded schools of Oriental languages, without which any missionary projects would have remained in the realm of pure fantasy), he acknowledged the necessity of parallel military action. He went into the history and geographical conditions of the Holy Land, discussed strategy, routes and the matter of supplies, and proposed that a particular

King, entitled "Rex Bellator," should be appointed leader of the new pilgrimage. The military orders, to form the backbone of this King's army, should be amalgamated under his command, with the style of "The Knights of Jerusalem" (leaving no room for quibbling as to where they belonged and what was their sole function).

All these writers were themselves in holy orders. Presently their lay colleagues ventured into the field with similar publications designed primarily for lay consumption. A new professional class had appeared in the West, that of the lawyer as distinct from the cleric, working for the interests of the temporal power rather than in overriding attachment to the Church. It was the job of the legist, the man versed in law as of set occupation, not fortuitously as a sideline, to substantiate (or contest) accomplished fact with legal theory and make this binding as a basis for future act and argument. Inevitably this led him to anticipate potential fact, ramified for every contingency, and so an inch gained under law was an ell in embryonic guise. Thus in perfect mundane logic the legist Peter Dubois, who produced the weightiest memoir, *De recuperatione Terrae Sanctae,* of the early thirteen hundreds, amplified the previous conclusions. Concerning the military orders, he proposed that upon amalgamation their common funds should be administered no longer by the knights themselves, but by the Pope; that the residence of the synthesized order should be confined to the East, and all its holdings in the West be converted into schools of Oriental studies and Crusader training camps. In other words, it was to be expropriated and banished — always on that pretext, Heaven-sent and papally sanctioned, of the next Crusade.

For the secular ruler had espoused that three-point program of Christian unity, Church reform and delimiting the status of the military orders, with a will. If practical theology had entered a new, rational phase, so had practical politics. The secular ruler would gladly assist at putting down schism and heresy — to his territorial gain; the head of the state applauded the head of the Church in an austerity campaign which would help to curtail ecclesiastic influence in temporal affairs; and he did not need to be told to keep a wary lookout for the fighting monks who, technically homeless, in fact owned large chunks of his dominions: homes from home, and potential military bases.

This was especially the case in France.

The bridge spanning the maelstrom of historical development, our short cut from East to West, debouches straight into France; in France the story of the Templars and of the abortive next Crusade took its final course.

France had played a dominant part in the whole crusading movement, with a special responsibility towards it. France had furnished the ruling class of Outremer and the great majority of the continuous reinforcements; France had remained the motherland, however disengagedly. France also owed a special debt to the Crusades, which had depleted the nobility and enabled the monarchy to expand, and through which the *langue d'oeil* had graduated as the standard speech of French and the standard secular language of war, diplomacy and political intercourse, just as Latin was the language of learning and sacerdocy. Any major Crusade was unthinkable without special reference to France.

France had always been the Western headquarters of the military order. There were rumors that the Templars contemplated transferring their permanent chief residence to France, though only the Hospitalers had actually put out feelers in that direction. Since then, however, the Hospitalers had started transforming themselves into a maritime police force to combat Moslem piracy in the Mediterranean; if Cyprus was too cramped for them, they would be looking for another island home. The Teutonic Knights had retired to the Baltic provinces of the Empire to give their full attention to the heathen Slavs. Whether the Templars would adjust themselves to a similarly useful and circumscribed function remained to be seen. They protested in heart-felt tones against any suggestion of amalgamation, they held up their sacrifices and their fidelity to the Holy Land; but they had not volunteered any proposals of their own. Their written responses might be dulcet, even lugubrious; their physical stance was unmoving. Another suggestion that had been made was that the whole order might throw itself into the unremitting struggle of Spain against the Moors. But as far as anyone could see, the Templars in Spain went on fighting the Moors, the Templars of other countries likewise stayed where they were apart from traveling on business. Men did indeed remember the heroic merits of the Temple; the Temple's claim on the gratitude of Christendom was not the least of its assets, and not the least likely to become an embarrassment to other people.

Imperialist ambitions, thwarted and aspiring, were in the air; the German Emperors still strove to regain the supremacy that had been Charlemagne's; the Plantagenet Kings of England, the Capetian Kings of France, the Italian city states, the Norman dynasty of Cyprus, the Angevins in Naples, the Holy See, all dreamt of empire, and any who could not in reason aim so high dreamt of independence. Whatever the intentions of the Temple, to which no outsider would be made party — their independence had long been beyond question. They were as they had always been, self-contained and self-centered, for good or for ill a social and political anachronism.

France in the last hundred years had grown into the most powerful and most coherent realm of the West. In France the modern, national state was well on in gestation, with absolute monarchy already well implanted, patriotism already changing from a peasant reflex answering invasion into a mainspring of centralized government, and chivalry becoming a code of manners rather than a separatist force. Gone were the days when "France" was merely the compact little dominion of the Counts of Paris who were the Kings of the French; when every vassal could strike his own coinage, when every castellan was his own hanging judge and tried every civil case out of hand, on its own merits, and according to his temper. Though the realm was still a patchwork of duchies and counties in the hands of provincial dynasties, the authority and significance of the King of France now extended everywhere French was spoken. The royal succession had become independent of election, the symbol of fealty a Capetian family heirloom, and leadership the prerogative of legitimacy, not simply a prize that went to the strongest.

However, gone, too, were the days when the King had not to defray the costs of justice and administration and the upkeep of his household on circuit, nor to hire soldiers, all of which it had been the object of the old order to supply. Along with the régime of feudalism the feudal economy had been broken down, and the Crown was hard put to it to find new means of support. Almost invariably taxes imposed for one specific purpose passed into permanence, and still fiscal organization failed to keep pace with social progress. It was a case of interminable leapfrog: for the Crown would raise money by the sale of civil liberties, which freed increasing sections of the population from economic bondage also and thus indirectly perpetuated the deficit. In ever-widening circles, contracted service was replacing unlimited servitude; with the growth of communities answerable to none but the central government, agriculture improved, learning flourished and spread, and commoners grew rich and proud, so that Jeanne of Navarre, Queen of France, holding court in a provincial merchant city, was moved to observe, "I thought I was the only Queen here, but I see more than six hundred." *

But there was another side to this, not so galling. The suzerainty of the vassal fiefs was further disrupted by areas over which the lord had no authority and persons on whom he had no call. A novel relationship between King and subject was evolving, direct, without intermediaries, regardless of station. The clear-cut class structure of the old system, the simple feudal pyramid, disintegrated at the entry of the *bourgeoisie du roi,* commoners released from any obligations other than allegiance to the King, to be poised against the remnants of seignorial opposition.

Seignorial territories could pass into outright possession of the Crown by sale, escheat and marriage, and even thus the Crown demesne had been steadily enlarged. These processes did not apply in the case of the military orders, of which the Temple was the one that counted for most.

---

* It is related that about 1300, a merchant of Valenciennes came to the court of the King of France, wearing a cloak of furs covered with gold and pearls. As no one offered him a cushion to sit on, he spread his cloak on the ground and sat there. On leaving, he did not attempt to take up the cloak. A servant called his attention to it, and the merchant answered disdainfully: "Where I come from it is not customary for visitors to carry their cushions away with them."

The Temple was "always buying, never selling" and like the Church, it was immortal and celibate. The Church and the Temple did unto the Crown as the Crown through the agency of the rising popular forces was doing by the aristocracy. They interposed a cystlike autonomy against absorption by the state, whose organic growth they thus obstructed; at the same time, in exactly the same way, they encroached on the freedoms and the prosperity of those rising popular forces. Just as the royal jurisdiction and revenues were impaired, civil complaints and lawsuits multiplied against the tenacious incubi. This at once strengthened and, in a manner, forced the King's hand.

Purchase being unlikely, acquisition by escheat and marriage impossible, the only remaining means of reducing the possessions of such bodies were conquest or confiscation. Barter, negotiation, persuasion, as it were, would be scarcely worth the attempt.

The sacred body of the Church was hard to touch, the more as in France it, too, had played a special part in fortifying the ascendant monarchy. The first Capetian Kings had had only the support of the Gallican bishops to pit against the nobility who did homage to the Crown but from whom the Crown was as yet unable to exact obedience; and the Gallican Church, therefore, had a certain national standing. More recently, the co-operation of Church and Crown had given rise to particular anomalies in Toulouse, the most southerly province of the realm and not long united with it, which exemplified the dangers of a policy of accommodation.

During and after the Albigensian Crusades (1209–1229, off and on), centering on Toulouse, the temporal officials of that country had been made subordinate to the bishops for the better prosecution of the campaign to stamp out southern heresy (a campaign which had stamped out an entire, advanced culture). The bishops in their turn had been superseded by the Inquisition, an institution hitherto an engine of ecclesiastical justice and now for the first time endowed with authority in its own right. The carnage over and the ruined country pacified, reconstruction was an uphill task that called for extraordinary measures. The Inquisition accordingly offered its protection to all who wished to be attested as true children of the true Church, and the laity flocked to seek bodily security and economic rehabilitation in holy orders. Before the end of the thirteenth century, Toulouse was swarming with shopkeepers, butchers, bakers, artisans and smallholders who could claim semiclerical status — and who were thus outside royal control and taxation. To attain this status one had to do little more than sport tonsure and cassock; there was no question of celibacy, on the contrary, a man's wife and children came with him into the privileged category. How long before there would be no laymen left save outlaws and vagabonds? The Church authorities themselves were forced to take repressive steps — without, however, relaxing their consistent attempts to prevent the temporal power from coming into its own in the new province.

Nothing of quite this order had happened in any of the areas under Temple rule, but it was a matter merely of degree and, possibly, of time. The Church, for all its puissance, was not itself composed of trained warriors; for all its wealth, the Church was not in business on such a scale as was the Temple. The Templars might be the "fellow-soldiers of Christ," but the Pope was His anointed deputy. The Pope's meddling in the wars of the nations was for peace (towards the next Crusade); the Templars on occasion were not averse from lending a hand — as they had against the Scots (1296) in alliance with the King of England (who was also the traditional enemy of the King of France). They were quite liable to become a standing international mercenary force at the disposal of whomsoever had most to offer them — which would be unfortunate for that combatant who had failed to secure their services, since they had their garrisons in his dominions too.

Hence the recurrent endeavors to draw the teeth of the Templars and remove them from all danger zones — especially in France.

This, roughly, was the relevant position when Philip IV had become King of France and was considering the part of Rex Bellator.

13 The King

PHILIP IV OF FRANCE WAS BORN IN 1268, YEAR OF THE FALL OF ANTIOCH, betrothed to the child-heiress of Navarre and Champagne in 1276, two years after the Council of Lyons, their marriage solemnized in 1284 which was two years after the Sicilian Vespers, and he succeeded to the throne in 1285, when Outremer had only another six years to run. He was distinguished from his predecessors of the same name by the epithet of "the Fair" — meaning beautiful, not equitable.

Philip IV (the Fair) was the son of Philip III (the Bold, or Rash), grandson of Louis IX (Saint Louis), and great-great-grandson to Philip II (Augustus — a compliment bestowed under the misapprehension that this title of the Caesars stemmed from the verb *augere,* to increase, for Philip Augustus had mightily increased his kingdom). The fourth Philip came into a far larger realm than had belonged to any of his forebears, with the monopoly of the royal mint restored, a codified system of uniform justice in force, and the beginnings of a new type of civil service to draw and improve upon. Standard currency and law code owned their existence to St. Louis, who yet did not become known as "the Coiner" or "the Law-giver" — any more than his grandson was dubbed "Hammer of the Church," "Coin-clipper," "Father of Parliament," "Architect of Absolutism," nor yet "the Fortunate," "the Rapacious" or "the Cruel." One was *Saint* and the other was *le Bel.*

Beauty, it is said, lies in the eye of the beholder. The annals from which this story is culled abound with men and women famous for their beauty; it seems that plain or downright ill-favored folk were exceptional among persons of rank and renown.

Among such persons, King Fulk of Jerusalem, also his grandson Henry II of England, the stupefying Emperor Frederick, St. Louis himself, and Saladin's precursor, his uncle Shirkuh, are especially mentioned for their undistinguished appearance. In the same breath as the chronicler castigates the moral decay of the Franks in Outremer, he will emphasize their general physical excellence. There is no end of the tall, magnificent men and luscious women — who yet followed one another in a bewilderingly rapid turnover of the generations, such as we would associate, rather, with debility.

For Philip IV of France to have been surnamed the Fair, he must have been handsome indeed — for it was not as if he had lacked other outstanding characteristics, or as though his reign had been without moment.

The eye of the beholder is conditioned by race, place and time. There appear to be no naturalistic contemporary portraits of Philip, so that we cannot apply the standards of our present taste, nor even deduce the ideal of his day — though surely nowadays his label would not have weathered the first reports of his growing obesity, as early as 1290, when he was only twenty-three.

He was putting on fat, they said, the fat of indolence — indolence, forsooth! The indolence of the spider in its web, perhaps, or of some mythological fowl hatching the egg of destiny. Lack of exercise, maybe: playful games are not for the mystery man; tennis, dancing, jousting will not serve an enigma. Elusive, reticent even when he allowed himself to be seen and interviewed, King Philip left only his beauty in men's grasp for them to know him by.

His beauty, his reserve and his piety the chroniclers agree on. They are divided as to whether he was a great man or merely the mouthpiece of his advisers.

Leaving aside the concept of greatness, as variable as that of beauty, the intelligence, determination, and, yes, the sincerity of Philip the Fair can hardly be in doubt. If from the start he surrounded himself with very able men — what does that argue, especially in a King aged seventeen at his accession, but shrewdness and sagacity? Rare and gifted the ruler who knows where to go for advice and who, moreover, heeds it, who knows exceptional ability when he sees it and places it where it will have the maximum effect. In general drift his policy was a logical continuation of his whole dynasty's, of which he was so far the most autocratic monarch. His ministers might be the authors of all manner of daring schemes, but they were schemes devised to further his ambitions and submitted for him to authorize. A monarch of a different stamp would stifle daring rather than give it scope, and a certain grandiose naïveté in forming the more startling of Philip's notions would seem to attest that they were his own. Megalomania is never vicarious. However bold of intellect, his ministers were men of affairs with their feet on the ground; whereas Philip's visions could occasionally soar clean into the clouds and well beyond the bounds of commendable confidence.

There is evidence that at one stage of his career he conceived of himself in the role of a universal monarch along Caesaro-Papal lines: a priest-king, a royal pontiff in dual control over Christendom. While one can see in this the logical conclusion of a sequence of ideas beginning with the need to eliminate Church interference in temporal government and leading naturally to the realization that without spiritual authority temporal power would never be entire — this would hardly be the sort of blueprint devised by eminently practical underlings, and that for a master who was a nonentity. When — a step in the same direction — Philip contemplated acting Rex Bellator to the next Crusade, he calmly proposed that:

1. The Kings of France (beginning with himself) should be hereditary grand masters of the combined military orders;

2. The incomes of all prelates, including archbishops, should be limited to a fixed minimum, the surplus to go to Rex Bellator for the conquest of the Holy Land;

3. Propertied monks should be sent out into the world only for preaching and hearing confession, mendicant friars live immured, and their revenues beyond the same fixed annual rent likewise accrete to Rex Bellator's coffers;

4. The hereditary royal grand master should command four cardinal-votes at papal elections.

And these, we are told, formed only a small part of Philip's demands.

Philip never employed bluff. Even when he employed blackmail, he would carry out his threat in the end. In his time he made a genuine effort towards winning the grand mastership of the Temple; so those preposterous conditions are unlikely to have been a mere feint. His able servants served him well and loyally at all times; they would have shown themselves neither able nor loyal had they foisted on him such extravagance, though to aid and abet him in it might be compatible with both qualities.

It is a strange fact that we are inclined to prefer the avowed cynic to the honest bigot, even when the consequences of their actions come to the same thing. Perhaps that is the reason for the aura of coldness and antipathy surrounding Philip the Fair. Impossible that cynicism could have upheld him in a lifetime of relentless consistency, full of actions which only the serenest conscience could endure to carry through. It is true that on his deathbed he took full responsibility for the *evil* advice of which he had all along availed himself (*Malo consilio ductus et quod ipsement erat causa mali consilii sui* — he had spent his life among lawyers); but in face of death and imminent Divine Judgment, even the most sincere obtuseness has a way of crumbling.

King Philip was very devout. There was no need for him to pretend piety — not an indispensable virtue in a king, as shown only too often; also, during the greater part of his reign he was at odds with the Holy See. No, King Philip loved God with the complete devotion of the man who knows God in his own image. He knew best what was in the mind of God, and therefore had no qualm in interpreting God's wishes by the actions of the King of France. Just as he was at one with the Deity, himself and the weal of the realm were one; expediency squared with good works, and power with rectitude. Power was holy, God-bestowed, the talent it behoved a king to increase, so that in Philip the craving for it would not spring from that beast of all burdens, the inferiority complex. He did not worship power, he was of it and lived for it, on it, by it; all of a piece in himself, too, wholly the political man, devoid of other passions. This would explain his preference for remaining behind the scenes, to act through the agency of others, act, even, under simulated pressure. Power is at its most potent and at its least sensual when it directs, unseen, in apparent denial of personal gratification. The royal ascetic hugged the brooding shadows and shunned the limelight of fruition as far as possible; he played Grey Eminence to his own throne and left the part of figurehead to a wraith masked in beauty.

Philip IV has been accused of perfidy, greed, injustice, and nothing can acquit him of these charges, nothing stand him in ethical excuse. He has been hailed as the liberator of his people and the father of parliamentary legislation, and nothing can disguise the purely adventitious nature of these genuine achievements. Nevertheless, and granted that a man of different character in the same position at the same juncture doubtless would have resolved his problems differently, he makes his entrance upon a stage fraught with an air of terrible inevitability.

He stepped straight into an imbroglio of financial difficulties and inherited wars, which were not unconnected. From some of them he could not, from others would not altogether extricate himself, so that their fusion immediately determined his actions. Throughout his reign, it can be safely said, economic compulsion sped political conflict and political conflict showed a tendency towards taking an economic turn. That was his especial burden and his peril, and therein his especial strength came to be manifested.

One of Philip's first acts as King was directed against the Templars in France. He passed legislation putting a stop to any further territorial aggrandizement of the Temple, and moreover revoked benefits that had accrued to the order inasmuch as similar edicts under certain of his predecessors had been left in abeyance. This was again primarily an economic maneuver, not necessarily of any wider significance. He was only following in the footsteps of his ancestors, from Louis VII onwards, who had nevertheless maintained the friendliest relations with the Temple. For the most part, periodical conflict of interests had been settled by compromise and later smoothed over by renewed grants and presents to the order. As for the Crown's repeated efforts to abolish Temple ownership in mortmain, on the whole it had been a routine of one step forward followed by two steps back. Philip was going to block that backward slide and start again where his ancestors, or more precisely St. Louis, had left off.

To be sure, the restrictive ordinances of St. Louis, and now of his grandson, applied to the military orders as a whole, but by the nature of the orders' respective positions they were in practice aimed particularly against the Temple. As usual, the Temple provided the first test case, and showed that it had no intention of complying with the "new" law, thus giving Philip the opportunity he needed. He confiscated all landed property which the order had acquired in the past thirty years — that is, since the date of the last serious attempt to limit Temple holdings to their then extent — a proceeding which former Kings had on occasion threatened, but never executed.

Philip IV executed the threat. The new broom swept clean — not only in the first flush of its untried vigor, not only because it had an Augean mess to cope with. There could be no better proof that the next Crusade was hanging fire. The leniency of former Kings was not merely an index of Templar resistance — rather, such resistance had been stiffened by the Crown's recurrent need, *in times of Crusade,* to fall back on the Temple. Without the assistance, financial and military, of the Temple, no Crusade after the First had ever gone ahead; the Kings of France had admitted as much.

Philip evidently did not think he was going to need the Templars — no hard feelings, for in other ways he continued to avail himself of their usefulness. In spite of the growth of the royal civil service, individual Templar Knights, widely traveled, experienced, and fast-moving, still made the best confidential envoys, and in Paris itself the Temple treasury served the Crown as an unofficial ministry of finance.

Philip had gone one better than his fathers. One year after his accession, royal officials were actually in charge of the sequestered Temple estates. But in the early spring of 1287 he ordered provisional restitution to the Temple of the usufruct of those possessions while the principle of ownership remained pending. Was he going the same conciliatory way as his fathers after all? He was, and again he went further than they. First he desisted. Then, reserving the right to put the matter before a grand assembly of his vassals, he granted restitution of all the order's confiscated lands and suspended rights. And then he dropped even the

reservation. In 1292 he confirmed all restitutions as absolute and unconditional, and over the following decade issued a spate of letters patent
confirming the confirmations in unassailable detail. As late as 1304, on
the eve of the next royal volte-face, yet another confirmatory proclamation
was couched in the most explicit and flattering terms of all, lauding the
Templars' piety, their charity, liberality and valor to the skies and making even privileges hitherto holding only in exceptional cases, valid for
the whole of France.

What had happened?

For one thing, Philip had let it be known that he would be willing to
lead the next Crusade. But this in itself was only a symptom.

During the first few years of Philip's reign, the uncompromising tenor
of the royal decrees shows that the money was coming in. He had succeeded in financing his wars with England and Flanders by a series
of hitherto unheard-of taxes on persons, property and business, which
caused great hardship among the poorer classes and which did not
respect the immunity of the Church. By 1292, the growing opposition to
these methods could no longer be ignored. Philip did ignore it and imposed the last straw: *Maltôte,* the Ill-levied, as it came to be called, which
was a purchase tax on all commodities, affecting the whole population
regardless of income. Riots broke out in the capital and nation-wide
rebellion threatened. For the Church, too, it now was no longer a matter
of intermittent extortions, the rights and wrongs of which were individually arguable; a fundamental principle was at stake. The three Estates
which the Crown had so long played off against one another, clergy,
nobility and commons were united in resistance. The Crown must find
support where it could, or give way.

The import of the royal decrees against the Temple was abruptly
altered. What had been a genuine plan of action became a bargaining
factor. Another such was, of course, the next Crusade, more versatile in
that it could be brought to bear on the Holy See as well as on the Templars, for thus the scheme of amalgamation came once again under re-
view. As the Pope had the next Crusade deeply at heart, and as the King
of France was a thorn in the side of the Church, a coalition with Philip

equipped the Templars in their turn with a lever, which effectively shelved the amalgamation proposals.

A beautiful friendship flowered in Paris. The King appointed his good friend the Treasurer of the Temple Hugh de Peraud, receiver and warden of the royal revenues. When the King betrothed his daughter to the heir of England, the Temple advanced her dowry in full. Although the original rule of Hugh de Payens and St. Bernard had forbidden knights of the order to accept baptismal sponsorship, the Grand Master William de Sonnac had stood godfather to St. Louis's daughter born in Palestine; now Philip the Fair requested and obtained like honor for one of his sons.

(King Philip did nothing without reason, and his every reason was multifaceted. His little son's godfather was the Grand Master Jacques de Molay — who had been elected, it was said, in successful rivalry against Hugh de Peraud, the two candidates representing two different factions within the order. Whether the King had a mind to make use of an internal split in the Temple, or whether he merely wished to preserve his good friend and *homme de confiance,* Hugh de Peraud, from undue complacency, we shall never know; but it is worth a side glance.)

The year 1292, then, was the year of the first *Maltôte* riots and of the first formal restitutions rendered by the Crown to the Temple. In 1294 the holy cipher Celestine V was induced to abdicate after a pontificate of a few months, and the most forceful of his cardinals supplanted him. The struggle for supremacy between the temporal and the spiritual powers crystallized in two well-matched protagonists: Philip the Fair and Boniface VIII; the pace quickened, and the buttons came off the foils.

In 1296, deaf to increasingly energetic Church representations, Philip exacted another forcible subvention from the Gallican clergy. Pope Boniface replied with the bull *Clericis laicos,* which laid down that no levies could be imposed by Kings or paid by clergy without the previous consent of the Holy See, on pain of excommunication. Philip by return prohibited all exports of bullion from France — thus freezing the Gallican tithe and creating havoc among the Italian bankers entrusted with the conveyance of the papal moneys.

The Pope yielded. In summer 1297 he conceded the King's right to levy taxes designed for the protection of France on the clergy within the orbit of protection. As every tax King Philip imposed was initially a war measure, that settled the matter. But Philip pursued his advantage; various concessions followed; within a month the Pope let go a bargaining factor which he for his part had kept in reserve as long as he was able, namely, the canonization of Louis IX. As from St. Bartholomew's Day, 1297, the King of France had a saint and powerful intercessor in the family.

Ever since St. Louis's death twenty-seven years before, miraculous visions and occurrences had testified to his rightful place on high — which in all likelihood he would never have attained but for the sublime fortitude he had displayed as a Crusader, seeing that he was the first monarch of his line to curb the powers of the Church in his dominions, unwilling, for all his piety, to leave the Church in full possession of feudal rights which he was taking away from the nobility. St. Louis also had once and for all established the revival of Roman civil law, with a secular bureaucracy to serve it: in other words, he it was who nurtured the most inimical agency the Church had yet encountered within its sphere of influence. While the canonization of his grandfather must gratify King Philip, this particular saint was hardly likely to sponsor lasting peace between Church and state.

The pivotal point of conflict between Church and state, everywhere — in England and the Empire as in France — was the immunity of clergy from secular jurisdiction. So long as transgressions against the law of the land where he resided were not punishable under that law, in any affiliate of the priesthood, so long would the Pope wield unbriefed temporal authority. In France there was an additional twist to this. The civil law, administered by the new class of lawyers, was based on the code of ancient Rome; literacy and latinity were dispensed by the clergy; it followed that clerical training was an indispensable qualification for the civil service. Although the civil servants held no ecclesiastical offices, most of them had taken minor orders at some time in their lives. For the Church to claim authority over the acting executive of temporal government was a contradiction in terms and of function.

The concessions to King Philip regarding emergency taxation of the clergy had left the foundations of ecclesiastical power yet untouched.

The Templars were the army of the Church; at the same time they had for decades past drawn upon themselves the fierce resentment of many churchmen. By flaunting his preferential treatment of the Temple in the faces of the regular clergy, Philip might do two very useful things. Simultaneously he might cause infinite irritation to the Church and seduce away its sworn champions. In addition he might blandly claim that in his dealings with the Temple he was only upholding clerical independence; and he made certain that the French prelates would not raise one finger to help the order in the event of any future attack by him.

For the present the honeymoon was yet in full swing.

Pope Boniface VIII had ambitions as large and compelling as were those of Philip the Fair — in fact, their ambitions were each other's mirror image, eternally irreconcilable. Both men were equally ruthless dynasts, both equally contemptuous of the herd — but Boniface despised all who were not of his own blood where Philip believed in the God-given superiority of kings. Boniface was the prey of passions, where Philip if anything suffered from the lack of them. Boniface's breast hid a volcano, Philip's a glacier: two opposites, each of them inexorably active.

Jubilee year, A.D. 1300, was approaching: the turn of the century which was always celebrated with great sacerdotal pomp. It was long since a Pope of Boniface's caliber had held sway; in six years he had built up St. Peter's throne to an eminence where it seemed in truth to tower high above those of the Kings and Emperors. He had brought about the seemingly impossible: cessation of hostilities between France and England; he had defeated the antipapal forces, thought to be irrepressible, in Italy; he had avenged himself on those cardinals who had opposed his election, with a "Crusade" which devastated their possessions and sent them fleeing for their bare lives (and whither did they flee, where else were they granted asylum, with a pension to boot, but under the protection of the King of France?). Now he would embark on world conquest. Pilgrims in their hundreds of thousands, from every corner of Christendom, flocked to Rome to pay homage and make offering, and to obtain plenary indulgence in return for a stay of fifteen days. The gifts far surpassed the most sanguine expectations of the Holy See; all Italy profited; and the Pope paraded before the enormous throng of the faithful with the insignia of empire, calling himself Caesar, and having two swords borne before him in token of temporal and spiritual dominion.

His triumph was real; but in the experience Boniface forgot, perhaps, that he had organized it. He fell victim to a common phenomenon, the spell of his own publicity, and proceeded to overreach himself.

He returned his attention to the King of France and demanded nothing less than Philip's unconditional acknowledgement that he held his realm by the grace of the Pope. A declared antagonist of Philip was appointed Bishop of Pamiers and Legate to France. This bishop-legate was a close friend of the Pope's and a man of similar fiber; he lost no time in making himself extremely troublesome to the Crown, nor did he care on how many other toes he trod while he was about it. Thus assured of the widest sympathy, Philip had the Bishop of Pamiers placed under arrest and arraigned on a wonderfully comprehensive set of charges. Treason, blasphemy, simony, fornication made up only a portion of the list, which for good measure included the most heinous crime of having "called our holy father Boniface a devil incarnate." The Pope showed himself unappreciative of Philip's solicitude. He issued a bull, *Salvator mundi,* which revoked all privileges and concessions granted to Philip since the publication of *Clericis laicos* and, hard on its heels, another *Ausculta, fili,* which explicitly condemned the French King and summoned the Gallican clergy to a General Council to be held at Rome in November, 1302.

The next move was up to Philip.

The ministers of the French Crown had blazed a trail in political polemics by means of the multiple trumped-up charges against the Bishop of Pamiers, and had done so with impunity. They would forge out along another new if parallel path. For a start they circulated a forged abstract of the papal bull, which was even more violent and abusive than the original and carefully omitted all points based irrefutably on doctrine. Still no thunderbolt fell; the nation's response was everything the Crown could wish; it remained to utilize it. A third precedent was set, of the utmost consequence. The King called on the three Estates of clergy, nobles and commons to appear before him at Notre Dame in April, 1302, and listen to a full recital of the facts.

It was the first time such an assembly was called in the reign of Philip IV; it was the first time the Third Estate was called at all. The model had been furnished by Philip Augustus, who convoked an assembly of clergy and nobility to express their formal condemnation of King John of England, in a fine display of fair dealing and serried unity and with the ultimate result of knocking out the bulky Plantagenet wedge from French territory. Now the same propulsion was applied against the wedge of papal encroachment, with the added strength of a commonalty which was by nature anticlerical. The institution of the *Estates General* was born and immediately proved itself a lusty child.

The voice, the vote of the nation as yet was required only for purposes of demonstration; it was invited to express approval, not to offer advice or make demands. But this was quite sufficient innovation to be epochmaking. The range of the nation's voice as yet could be only a matter of volume, it might be loud, it might be faint; however, at this its fullstrength debut it fairly resounded through the world.

The papal bull was publicly burnt. The King pronounced a curse on his descendants should any of them ever admit that he held France from anyone but God. Nobles and commons sent manifestoes to Rome absolutely rejecting the Pope's pretensions and calling in question his legitimate tenure of the Holy See. The clergy did not commit themselves to quite that extent. However, they assured the King of their loyalty — they who had only one loyalty, to the Church — whilst begging his leave to attend the council at Rome in the autumn. This the King refused. The prelates hesitated, between the two fires of expropriation by the King, if they went, and excommunication by the Pope, if they stayed. In the end half of them made their escape across the frontier, half stayed behind and forced the Pope to drive them irretrievably into Philip's camp.

Yet the position of King Philip had been appreciably weakened in the meantime — or so it appeared on the surface. A month after the assembly of the Estates General, the people of Flanders rebelled against French oppression and staged a bloody uprising, called the Matins of Bruges to point the resemblance to the Sicilian Vespers. French knighthood in its magnificent entirety rushed to arms and rode to Flanders, and was routed utterly by the Flemish pikemen in the battle of Courtrai, "the Day of Spurs": four thousand gilded spurs were hung up in Courtrai Cathedral by the victors, a popular army of commoners on foot. The old French nobility was all but wiped out, at this one blow. As yet no one could see beyond so devastating a defeat; however, the Flemings had unwittingly done the French monarchy a service. Feudalism was dead, killed at Courtrai.

We must repeat, this was far from evident at the time. Yet Philip's supporters stuck by him. The fact wants to be emphasized, for all his life he inspired complete loyalty in those that served him, which points to one human aspect of his personality that is anything but negative.

Pope Boniface, however, was not within reach of that personality and only took account of the apparent situation. In the most peremptory and comprehensive bull of his pontificate, *Unam sanctam,* he proclaimed the inferiority of all kings to the Pope, in all things and for all time, as kings like all other men were sinners, and all sinful mankind subordinate to Christ's Vicar. This theory was of ancient standing, but reproduced at the wrong time — a time of nascent liberation of the peoples. Like the Flemings, Pope Boniface unintentionally officiated at the birth of a nation. His assertion of complete ultimate supremacy, jumping all temporal ties of authority, as it were, struck at everybody, against privilege and against freedom; the lords cried, "Anarchy!" The people seconded it with "Tyranny!" The difference was lost in the unanimous roar of protest, to which the previous declarations of the Three Estates had been the merest prelude. All internal dissension was obliterated.

With such concert behind it, the French Crown retaliated unabashed. The indictment of the Bishop of Pamiers was as nothing to the indictment of Boniface which Philip's ministers drew up now. The twenty-nine charges comprised every crime the heart could desire: adultery, for one thing, the Church having been lawfully wedded to the deposed Celestine V — so that Boniface's election was no more valid than a bigamous marriage; sorcery, sodomy, heresy, blasphemy; intercourse with demons; murder; misappropriation of funds for the next Crusade; denial of the immortality of the soul and denial of the very existence of the soul in human beings of French nationality, and more besides.

This document, which one might think would have invited ridicule, was, rather, admirably calculated to suit the contemporary fashion in credulity — but have the Gothic style and the Gothic receptiveness to propaganda ever wholly gone out of vogue? A campaign was launched to acquaint every district of the country with these accusations, which created the expected furore in all quarters. Over twenty bishops, hundreds of lesser clergy and the local leaders of the military orders joined in the nation-wide demand that the Pope be removed from office and brought to trial.

These events took up the spring and early summer of 1303. Before the end of summer came the Holy See's announcement that on September 8 the entire Kingdom of France would be laid under ban and all men sundered from allegiance to King Philip.

This was a serious matter. For all that kings had been excommunicated before now, had braved the ban or succumbed to it and, sometimes, recovered afterwards — still excommunication was no joke. King Philip could not afford to snap his fingers at a threat which endangered his security in the very public opinion he had marshaled and which would delight his enemies as an incentive to invasion. Yet to retreat at this point would be a humiliation of no smaller consequence.

On August 10 a strange document was signed by the King, the Queen, two of their sons and a distinguished witness, the Count of St. Paul — a secret document which, though later retrieved into Crown possession, by some oversight equally strange was never destroyed. It was a private undertaking given to Hugh de Peraud, treasurer of the Temple and receiver of the royal revenues, by which King Philip pledged his unqualified and undying support, also on behalf of his heirs and successors, to the Templar Order in general and Hugh de Peraud in particular, in a pact of mutual defense under all and any circumstances but especially against the present head of the Church (never once referred to as the Pope, but by name only) — the head of the Church, sole overlord of the Knights Templars.

It is uncertain whether the Grand Master of the Temple, Jacques de Molay, had any knowledge of this strange agreement. But it is a fact that about the same time Pope Boniface sent Hugh de Peraud a personal invitation to a colloquy at Rome, which Hugh de Peraud never attended.

14 The Propagandist

AN UNINVITED VISITOR, HOWEVER, CROSSED THE ALPS AT THE END OF THAT summer, 1303, in secret. He was William Nogaret, King Philip's minister and chief diplomatic adviser since the death at Courtrai of the Chancellor Peter Flote. Speed was essential, and he traveled light, with only two attendants and little ready cash, but carrying drafts on some Italian banking houses and, most valuable of all, a warrant of full authority by his sovereign. As far as remuneration went, he had been paid in advance, with the Godspeed of an annual 300 livres payable to himself, his heirs and descendants in perpetuity, on account of "faithful service, meriting gratitude in the highest degree, rendered Us for some time past and *such as shall be rendered in the future.*" * His instructions were imprecise; he had carte blanche.

As Nogaret's German biographer Holtzmann points out (writing in the heyday of the Hohenzollern Empire), this, too, was a novel manner of approach. "The gallant German Emperors had pursued the same end (i.e. undermining the power of the Holy See) sword in hand, at the

* My italics.

head of their armies. The minions of Philip IV came sneaking in, armed only with blank checks and license to conduct negotiations with any sort of elements" — no, it was not at all chivalrous behavior.

Indeed Nogaret was no true knight and no aristocrat. He had been raised but recently to a very recent order of nobility, modeled on the old chivalry, but recruited from that new professional class, the legists. For our purposes he shall represent that class, more particularly in its intimate service to Philip the Fair, although more properly he was one of a team, if a leading member and for much of the time acting captain. In spite of this prominence, and although his actions emerge clearly where Philip operates in a distorting mist, the person of Nogaret remains as indefinite as that of his master. Quick, unobtrusive, Jack-of-all-trades and master of the lot, he merges with his changing backgrounds as by consummate functional mimicry.

His entry into Italy went unremarked, more especially by the power' most concerned, the Papacy, which continued in ignorance throughout the quiet enemy's advance. He advanced implacably. Whether propelled by loyalty, or by his own brilliance, by love of his work or the innate impulses of his rising class — behind it all there was a driving force still more explosive. His father (and probably his mother also) had been burnt as a heretic in the mopping-up operations after the Albigensian Wars. That fire burned on in the son.

The family were of Toulouse and had belonged to the Manichaean sect of Catharans. They had some house property in the town, where they must have followed a trade, and their surname was taken from a small fief they held nearby. William, who like many upstarts became a stickler for any title to which he had a right, yet adopted a nut tree (*noyer* — *noyeret*) for his crest when elevated to the new chivalry, punning on the humble name rather than disowning it. He describes himself as small in stature; that is all we know of his appearance.

Little more is known about his early life. It is probable that as an orphan of the religious persecutions in Languedoc he was brought up under the tutelage of the Inquisition and received clerical training as an antidote to the heretic taint. Evidently he took minor orders. Although he married and had children, he liked to style himself *savio clerico* besides knight, counselor, also doctor of law and professor of philosophy, long after he had ceased teaching at the university of Montpellier — which is where his name is first recorded, in a document dated 1291 and concerned with the purchase of a house.

Like his namesake Shakespeare, William Nogaret left few personal documents apart from records of business transactions and his will. His writings were almost as prolific, and almost as prodigious in their particular field, although the internal evidence they give of his character and experiences is at once more exact and less substantial. As one of the originators of pamphleteering warfare and one of its most outstanding exponents, his pen proved worth a battery of swords.

Publicist, administrator, lawyer, politician, Nogaret was the perfect factotum to a ruler of Philip's cast. Yet he had already reached the middle years of life and career before he came to the King's notice. Though the civilization peculiar to the southern provinces had been trampled down, the humanistic studies there initiated had survived, and the universities of Montpellier, Toulouse and Avignon were especially centers of Roman jurisprudence; Peter Flote and many other colleagues of Nogaret had graduated there. King Philip in the nineties acquired part of the rights of the town of Montpellier, hitherto an episcopal enclave in his Provençal territories, and it was in the delicate groundwork towards eventual possession of the whole that a competent jurist could make himself very useful to the Crown.

Directly the two of them had come together, Nogaret's rise was swift and sure. Within a few years his name heads the list of royal counselors on sundry commissions; and on all occasions of important business he accompanied the King. In 1229 he was ennobled, in 1300 he paid his first visit to Italy as the King's ambassador to the Holy See — on which he drew for some of his most effective propaganda writings later on.

The Pope — so Nogaret would relate — was entirely preoccupied with his own selfish ambitions; when various weighty matters were to be settled he "stopped up his ears after the manner of otters" (pleasing item of nature lore!); he showed that he did not care a jot for the fate of

the Holy Land, and every time he opened his mouth emitted nothing
but vituperation, slander, oaths, and curses against the rulers of France
and Germany and their peoples. "Knowing his [Boniface's] abject de-
pravity," says the son of condemned heretics, mournfully, "and fully
cognizant of his religious and sexual aberrations, his habitual simony,
depredations, murders and other crimes galore . . . my heart bled for
Christ on Whom he had brought such shame, and for the Church whom
he imperilled . . . I wept for the Roman Church, held captive by that
adulterer; I wept for the Gallican Church, whose destruction is his
avowed mission in life . . ." At the time Nogaret must have kept his
bleeding heart well under control, for there was then no breach in
diplomatic relations.

The Pope, too, must have made his notes and held them in reserve
until a more appropriate time, when, in the bull *Ausculta, fili* a special
passage was devoted to the evil influence of King Philip's counselors.
"There are some, endeavouring to excuse you, who say that it is not
you but your advisers who are guilty. But in fact responsibility does rest
with you alone, for employing men known to all the world as false and
godless . . . men that fatten themselves on the tears of the poor, the
widow, and the orphan, even as they batten on the rich . . . who will
fan the flames of war at any price, who find no means too foul if thereby
peace may perish from the earth. . . ."

As regards invective, it seems the Pope could hold his own with the
professional publicist. But as propaganda instruments his bulls did not
compare with the work of the French pamphleteers. For one thing, his
strictures were not in themselves so unusual. Violent they were, but kept
to the facts — even if these facts could be variously interpreted. The
papal bulls were statements of infallible opinion, they did not stoop to
persuade. The publications of the French Crown were carefully designed to just that end. To extend a metaphor, the voice of the nation
had been trained by the most skillful choir masters, who as skillfully
continued to conduct its performance in denunciation of the Pope before
the world.

Nor did they neglect to lay down a sound foundation of theory. They buttressed their case with legal arguments, and did not neglect to find scriptural chapter and verse. The Pope, it was expounded, might be the temporal lord of the Emperor, since the latter had to be confirmed and crowned by the former; but no such authorization had ever been needed in France or could be recognized in the future, therefore. It would indeed by the best thing for society if the whole world were subject to French rule, for "it is a peculiar merit of the French that they have a surer judgment than other nations. . . ."

On the eve of his departure for Italy, Nogaret still took a leading part in council sessions to justify the Crown's stand. In his last great speech he passed on a personal message of support imparted to him by St. Peter, and modestly likened his own forensic eloquence to the voice of Balaam's ass. The meetings continued after he had gone on his way — much as if policy were still under discussion. At the same time the King somewhat softened his official tune. He no longer demanded immediate deposition and imprisonment of the Pope, but merely recommended that the Pope himself convene a General Council of the Church which should investigate the twenty-nine charges laid against Boniface by the French Crown. The Pope went on composing his bull for the 8 September.

It is hard to credit that he got no information of Nogaret's arrival in Italy; but since right up to the last he remained inactive, no other conclusion seems possible. Perhaps he was too rigid in his assurance of supremacy and his contempt for others to spend money on intelligence. Yet one would have thought that anyone stumbling on evidence of Nogaret's mission would volunteer to bring it before the Pope, sure of reward.

Nogaret's travels must have left some evidence at every step. Though he halted only to take up moneys here, and there judiciously distribute them — hiring messengers, winning allies, enrolling mercenary troops and purchasing silence — he could scarcely do so much and attract no notice whatever.

His personal courage was on a par with his efficiency. The highways and townships of Italy were notoriously unsafe, teeming with predators of all kinds upon the unprotected wayfarer. But Italy was teeming also with enemies of Boniface. Philip's kinsman, the Neapolitan King Charles of Anjou, was one, while the traditional conflict of Guelphs and Ghibellines, the pro- and antipapal parties, maintained a constant, vested opposition to any Pope. In the equally traditional feud between the noble families of Orsini and Colonna, Boniface and his kindred belonged to the Orsini bloc, which automatically made every adherent of the Colonna his natural foe — even had he not exacerbated enmity by his "Crusade" against the two Colonna cardinals, which had involved the whole clan in ruin. Not content with that, Boniface had meanwhile alienated the Orsini faction as well, by his incontinent nepotism, arousing against him everybody whom he did not count a blood relation.

Even so, it needed finesse to integrate all these proud, self-centered elements into one working conspiracy, and that under the aegis of a foreigner who was not even a soldier, nor yet of distinguished birth.

Pope Boniface VIII was staying at the small town of Agnani, his family stronghold near Rome, deep in putting the final touches to the interdict on all France, and unaware of the infiltration of French bribes, up to his doorstep by and by, and under his own roof. Everywhere in the surrounding countryside, in the town and in the papal palace, French subsidies caused latent discontent, greed, pique and ambitions to mature. The leading citizens, the rabble, gate watch and chamberlains, none had been forgotten, and none was moved to warn the old man, the Vicar of Christ in their midst.

Outside in the Roman Campagna an army of three hundred knights and two or three times as many infantry stood ready under a Colonna commander. The attack was scheduled for Saturday, September 7. At the last moment the Italian allies bethought themselves of a stratagem to evade responsibility for their actions and came to Nogaret demanding to march under the French colors. Nogaret ingeniously countered this by pairing the banner of France with the standard of the Papacy, in token that the enemies of Boniface came not as enemies of the Church, but on the contrary as her defenders. At last the signal was given, and under cover of darkness the march began.

The gates of Agnani were reached before dawn and opened instantly by order of the commandant of the papal guard. With the names of the King of France and the House of Colonna for their war cry, troops poured into the sleeping town. The inhabitants sprang from their beds and rushed into the town square, where all men fit to bear arms were sworn in and forthwith joined in the assault on the loyalist centers which were few enough — the palaces of three cardinals and that of the lord of the district, Boniface's nephew, besides the Pope's own residence.

In little more than an hour the three cardinals' palaces were in allied hands and the owners fleeing for their lives. The papal residence and the stronghold of his nephew still withstood the siege, although increasing numbers of courtiers and servants deserted as it went on.

At six in the morning the Pope asked for a truce until three o'clock in the afternoon. This was granted. Too late, he tried to get the populace on his side with pleading and promises. All else having failed, he entered into negotiation with Nogaret and the Colonna leader.

It is at this point that the would-be Caesar confronts us as an old man pure and simple, a pitiable old man pitilessly oppressed. The conditions which the confederacy offered him were purposely framed so that he must reject them.

There were four:

1. The two deposed Colonna cardinals to be restored;
2. Restitution to be made of *all* Colonna property, whether war-damaged, sequestered or otherwise alienated;
3. The Pope to abdicate;
4. The Pope to surrender his person into the custody of the confederates.

On these conditions would his life be spared.

The Pope refused, and on the stroke of three the attack was resumed with unconcealed glee and redoubled violence. The church abutting on the palace was set on fire, and with it perished the strongest point of defense. The last of the old man's retinue forsook him to save themselves. The assailants were intoxicated even to frenzy by having nothing left to lose if indeed setting fire to St. Mary's Church and hunting down St. Peter's successor ended their hopes of salvation, as might well be the case.

The aged Pope was found lying on his bed, with a crucifix carved from a fragment of the True Cross clasped to his breast, and in a loud voice offering himself up for martyrdom. The soldiers made to take him at his word — affording Nogaret an ultimate refinement of satisfaction, in that ever after he could claim only his personal intervention had saved the Pope's life. A murdered Pope would be a greater nuisance than any live one; a captive Pope was the object desired.

Thwarted savagery had to be vented. There was much to loot, to desecrate and smash and burn; the palace contained Church treasure as well as private property. The soldiers tore down costly hangings and trampled underfoot any works of art that were not made of gold and silver and precious stones. Sacred relics that were encased in such materials they broke to pieces for fair distribution, and in a fury of disappointment dismembered the remains of various martyrs that had been preserved unadorned. A bowl of the Holy Virgin's milk was emptied out, and according to subsequent inventories, innumerable charters granted to the Holy See by generations of emperors and kings were lost forever. The orgy of destruction found its climax in the wine cellars, where eventually it was spent.

"The Lord hath given, the Lord hath taken away, praised be the name of the Lord," the Pope quoted Job in sole comment. He was then in his eighty-seventh year.

Throughout his ordeal Boniface behaved with a touching dignity which adds to our difficulties in allocating sympathy. For the whole outlook of our civilization, which here met a decisive turning point, must be hostile to Boniface VIII, whose aim was universal totalitarian theocracy. Yet we melt to the old man's tears, to his steadfast refusal to abdicate, and to his ingenuous statement, later, that he had had nothing to eat but one egg during his captivity.

As to that, reports conflict. Some say Boniface was deliberately kept without food, some that he went on hunger strike, and some that he declined what was offered him for fear of poison. He may have had small desire to eat, as grief and despair commonly kill appetite. Doubtless each account is colored by the wish to strengthen the case for or against him; and no one knows whether Boniface was in truth subjected to physical ill-treatment — pulled by the beard, buffeted about the face with a mailed glove — as alleged. His face, presumably, would have shown traces of this on his release, when hundreds of eyewitnesses saw him — when, also, an old woman gave him "four eggs and a little bread to save him from starvation." No bruises or lacerations are mentioned, and starvation was not really imminent, as his release took place twenty-four hours after his capture. The woman with her four eggs was only one of many: all the women of Agnani flocked to comfort the old man with food and drink in such quantities that the floor of the palace "ran with wine, there being too few vessels to contain it." The repentant compassion of country women would be apt to take such a practical, maternal form, whether or not the Pope was in actual need of sustenance; and whether or not he was actually beaten and insulted, the blow and the insult of his kidnapping could hardly have been more crushing.

In the night from Sunday to Monday, the people of Agnani had sat back and taken stock. Bribes had been earned, a high riotous time had by all; now, while the confederates chaffered about what to do with their prisoner and the soldiery disported itself brawling and carousing in the town — now came the first pause for reflection. Darkness awakened foreboding, remorse, all sorts of holy terrors centering round the Lord's anointed Vicar who had been so shamefully abused. They had to bolt and barricade their doors against the soldiers they had themselves let in and who were in no mood to differentiate between friend and foe. What was going to happen to the Pope? If he were murdered in their town, the consequences both here and hereafter were likely to be terrible. The women, the mothers, wives and sweethearts of yesterday's citizen-warriors beset them with wailing and scolding, imprecations and dire prophecies; from curtain lectures to impromptu gatherings it was but a step; behind all the closed shutters the deliberations went on until dawn.

By Monday morning the swing was accomplished. The civic militia reassembled and fell upon its erstwhile allies, with cries, this time, of "Long live the Pope! Death to the foreigners!" Soon there was fighting in every street, the whole town turned into a battlefield before midday; the soldiers, taken by surprise after well-nigh twenty-four hours' dissipation, never recouped themselves and were slaughtered by the handful. At three in the afternoon a deputation of citizens was able to wait on the Pope and announce his liberation.

The last, terrified stragglers of the allied army had been hunted down; Nogaret and the Colonna commander escaped in disguise; behind them in Agnani the French banner was torn to pieces and dragged in procession through dust and filth.

The old man who had dreamed of ruling the world now bore himself with heart-rending democratic simplicity. He emerged from his battle-scarred portals and sat himself down on the top step of the entrance, to address his friends and deliverers, the people of Agnani, who thronged around. He forgave them, he pronounced absolution upon them all. He said that any who had looted his personal property were welcome to it. Church property was a different matter. All the Church property hoarded here, said the Pope, had been collected for the next crusade, and it was not for him to acquiesce in its dispersal. However, everyone who restored such plunder within three days was assured of absolution.

Pope and people wept together in one of the most moving scenes of public reconciliation ever to be described. But the gentle old man who sat on the bare stone in communion with his humble friends, was proof of his own downfall. Simplicity, pliancy, forbearance were not in his nature; his demeanor did not betoken change of heart but exhaustion, dissolution. The terrible impotence into which he had been cast, even for a bare twenty-four hours, could not be cured by unlocking his prison. He was weak and he was ill, he was destroyed in body as in spirit.

A painful kidney disease, from which he had suffered of old,* flared up afresh; his attempts at political recovery were muddled, fitful and short-lived. The prestige of the Papacy, which in the person of Boniface VIII had attained such overwhelming proportions, collapsed under the same blow that felled the man himself. He had himself taken to Rome, where a solemn ceremonial reception was staged for him — only to find that he was now the prisoner of his Orsini escort.

The *official* ambassador of the King of France called, to strike the iron so well heated by two fires, but the Pope was too ill to see him. Four weeks after the coup of Agnani, Boniface was dead.

The unofficial envoy, the unbidden visitor who had engineered the attempt remained close by, hiding out in the town of Ferentino under the protection of the mayor, who gambled on the favor of the King of France against the uncertainties of the future. Whatever the future might hold, to whatever extent the attempt had failed, the strength of the anti-papal forces — once they banded together — and the long arm of the King of France had been amply proven. Also, Nogaret had succeeded in his chief task; the wholesale excommunication of France, announced to Christendom long in advance, had been prevented. God could not have desired it, in fact.

15 Popes and Heretics

THE OLD POPE WAS BURIED IN ST. PETER'S WITH VERY LITTLE OF THE POMP that was his due, owing to exceptionally bad weather — wherein many saw a sign. Not only that; it was reported from various parts of the country that at the hour of Boniface's death subterranean voices had been heard to rumble in awful exultancy, "Boniface is coming! Hurry up and let him in for his share of eternal torment!" Everywhere men repeated a quip to the effect that Boniface had snatched the tiara like a

* And which adds physiological motivation to his irascibility.

fox, ruled like a lion and died like a dog. They had it on the best authority that in the rage of frustration he had gnawed the flesh off every part of his body which his teeth could reach; that he had taken his own life by dashing his head against the wall of his chamber; that his familiar demon had carried him off in clouds of sulphur. Nogaret, most gifted propagandist of his day, was still in Italy, and the brief access of compassion for Boniface the old man had not restored the shaken reputation of the Papacy.

Boniface had won sympathy such as he had never commanded in the time of his greatness, mainly by his rocklike resistance to pressure for his abdication. He had stuck staunchly to the contention that for the true pontiff there was no such thing as abdication. The rightful Pope was Pope, by God's ordainment, and that was that; he could not throw off his condition. Admirable; but that being so, then what had happened to his predecessor, Celestine V, and where did that leave Boniface? None, not even Boniface, had ever questioned that Celestine had been rightfully Pope. Therefore, Celestine's resignation from office was void and with it Boniface's election — precisely as his Colonna opponents had posited from the start, and the King of France after them.

We have to deal with *two* poor old men, competing for our sympathy. The victim of 1303 in 1294 had victimized the other.

In those days Boniface, then Benedetto Cardinal Gaetani, had been the moving spirit in a campaign of persecution which drove the unworldly Celestine to lay down St. Peter's keys. The story went that Benedetto-Boniface had drilled a hole into the wall by the Pope's bedside, to which he would repair each night and, representing himself as God's messenger, in an eerie whisper command Celestine to retire on account of his age, infirmity and unfitness to rule. Such stories are the all-purpose loopholes of historiography, to be accepted, rejected, used in evidence of calumny or *ben trovato* confirmation, according as they fit into the framework of one's thesis. Nothing is too extravagant to find belief — but then, nothing is so extravagant that it cannot possibly be true, especially in the sphere of intrigue.

At all events, no sooner was Benedetto Gaetani ensconced as Boniface VIII than he seized the ex-Pope and committed him to solitary confinement. Even that was not enough; though politically ineffectual, Celestine had won great love among the people, who worshiped him as a living saint. Saint he might be (and he was subsequently canonized), but within a few months he was living no longer. There is no proof either way of the strong suspicion that the fierce old man Boniface murdered the meek old man Celestine; but the dimensions of Celestine's prison, a cell so small and narrow that he could scarcely stretch out to sleep, in themselves were not designed to prolong his fragile life.

Alas, Celestine is no more blameless a victim than his persecutor. Weakness and unworldliness cannot acquit him of responsibility in having helped to create the situation of which Boniface took advantage. Celestine owed his election to the King of Naples (kinsman-satellite of the King of France). In gratitude he had at once appointed ten new cardinals, seven of whom were French and three Neapolitan — thus building up the very, united front that in due course rallied to Benedetto Gaetani.

That transaction — which, in all innocence and mannerly kindness, smacked of the market place rather than the temple — with its wide-branching ill effects, is only one example among an embarrassment of riches signifying the decline of the Papacy from the august position it had occupied. Through the agency alike of strong pontiffs and feeble, biddable saints and unscrupulous power-mongers, by indiscriminate "Crusades" and by blunting that most potent weapon of the Church, the ban, with overuse; by a thousand compromises, ambiguities, acts of expediency — the Papacy had met the efforts of its enemies halfway.

The next Pope, Benedict XI, was elected with despatch, again under the influence of the King of Naples who appeared in Rome with an army during the deliberations of the cardinalate. The new Pope was accordingly prepared to take a conciliatory line with France. Only a few obstacles needed to be cleared out of the way — such as the excommunication of King Philip and the interdict on his kingdom which, though formal proclamation had been averted, yet had not been rescinded in intention.

Pope Boniface in his last days had been unable to see the accredited ambassador of France. Pope Benedict declined to see him on the grounds that the ambassador's credentials were addressed only to Boniface. Sending for new credentials or appointing a new ambassador took time. Nogaret hurried to Rome under armed protection and sought audience with the new Pope. He was refused on the grounds that Boniface had absolved only the Italians who had taken part in the outrage of Agnani, and that the Pontiff could not consort with an excommunicated person. A definite ruling having been obtained on his own case, Nogaret abstained from further efforts for the present and returned at last to France.

King Philip received him graciously — even ostentatiously so, under the circumstances. Nogaret had made a point of publicly assuming full responsibility for his actions in Italy, thus exculpating the master in whose service he had committed them. It would have saved the King of France a deal of trouble to disown him now. He could probably have relied on Nogaret's continued services in an unofficial capacity, and by ostensibly throwing him overboard would have facilitated his own absolution. But he returned loyalty for loyalty, and while it would be churlish not to give him the credit in so many words, it was another instance of the waning papal power that Philip could so defy it.

A new embassy was despatched to Rome with a congratulatory address of which Nogaret was the author, felicitating Benedict XI on his accession and lauding him at the expense of the deceased Boniface. The ambassador was empowered to *receive* absolution for King Philip "in case for any sort of reason the King might have happened to fall under the ban" (delightful inconsequential picture). He also rammed home, over again, a point Nogaret had already made and which was to become of increasing importance. All communications by the King of France were based on the assumption that the ecumenical council to follow up the French Crown's charges against Boniface had been definitely de-

cided on, and that Boniface himself alone had criminally delayed it. On
this assumption the King of France pressed for an immediate posthumous
trial of Boniface. No such thing had ever happened. The very demand
for it was a hair-raising precedent. The more often it was publicly renewed, the more threatening became its implications — unless the Papacy
had been strong enough to punish the King of France for his temerity,
which it most certainly was not. A new blackmailing lever had come into
operation.

After devious maneuvering Pope Benedict granted absolution to his
"dearest son in Christ, the illustrious King of the French," and moreover
nullified the most damaging passages in the bulls his predecessor had
directed against Philip. By doing this the Pope went as close as
he could to condemning Boniface and ranging himself with Philip;
further than that he dared not, would not go. He refused to yield an inch
in the issue of Nogaret, the man who had actually laid hands on a Pope.
Even *Absolutio ad cautelam,* a form of provisional remission bestowable
on persons engaged in contesting the validity of their excommunication,
was denied.

Philip might have reasoned — and Nogaret the trained logician could
not have blamed him, Nogaret the lawyer could not have complained —
that as an excommunicate Nogaret was of no further use to a master who
had become reconciled with the Church. However, Philip chose that
moment to show Nogaret still greater favor, and did his utmost to drive
the Pope into a corner. He left the Pope no option but to declare himself
unequivocally and either explicitly sanction the attack on his predecessor
or explicitly denounce it. Benedict XI chose the latter course, proclaimed
that the perpetrators of the coup were to be brought to trial, and prepared
to excommunicate Nogaret in style. He died before he could carry out his
purpose.

The symptoms of Pope Benedict's sudden illness were those of severe
dysentery, which contemporary medicine had learned to associate with
various forms of poisoning. While in the Middle Ages any unexplained
indisposition was readily attributed to poison, it is not impossible that
agents of Philip's were responsible. The subject lent itself to exhaustive

literary treatment by both sides. The clerical chroniclers asserted that the Pope had been foully murdered, and Nogaret's busy quill penned numerous variations on the theme of divine intervention against unworthy Popes.

This pontificate had lasted eight and a half months. For nearly a year the Holy See remained vacant. Benedict's chief aim had been to make peace between the nations and end factional strife in Italy; his efforts had all come to nothing and left peace-making itself discredited. The cardinalate split into two parties, whose one point of tacit agreement — that there could be no middle way for the Papacy — made their division irremediable. One party wished to revive the aggressive policy of Boniface, the other desired alignment with France. The successive candidates were surrounded with intrigues and discussions so turgid and so cynical, there was so much dirty work all around, that popular wit inserted an r into *Consilia lat(r)inorum*. At length it was decided to seek a candidate outside the ranks of the cardinals themselves. Still no progress was made. One member of the conclave in exasperation proposed his cook.

Miraculous indeed that deadlock was not perpetuated longer, that a candidate emerged at all, capable of being made acceptable to both the Bonifacians and the French and French-controlled Neapolitan cardinals. He was the Archbishop of Bordeaux, Bertrand de Got. He had sided against Philip in the dispute with Boniface; on the other hand, he was a Frenchman, of Gascony, whose every tie of interest bound him to France. The Bonifacians initially proposed him, and by degrees it was found possible to work out a balance of promises to both sides. The King of France was sounded and to everyone's astonishment showed himself agreeable.

A story went the rounds that a secret meeting had taken place, with the suitably dramatic venue of a ruined abbey, where the King offered Bertrand de Got the tiara on six conditions and the archbishop, intolerably tempted, swore on the Host to comply. He was told five of the conditions, as to the sixth, it was not to be revealed until after his coronation. The sixth condition was the abolition of the Temple.

In point of fact — unless this conference was so secret that none but the King and the archbishop ever knew of it at all — the two did not meet until after the election. Of course the King's ambassadors were present immediately before and during the election and closely in touch with the candidate, so that such a midnight bargain was hardly needed. And while in the realm of human ambition nothing can be dismissed out of hand — while Philip would be unlikely to trust to luck and hope for the best of an old antagonist raised to the highest eminence on earth — we know that he was a shrewd judge of men. He was acquainted with Bertrand de Got of old. If Philip exercised his judgment here, certainly Bertrand de Got, as Clement V, bore it out. "All the world knows by now," a competent observer was to write before long, "that the Pope is a nought and the King of France can accomplish anything he wishes by getting the Holy See to do it for him."

Clement V was no villain, nor lacking in will and views of his own. His trouble was a particular type of imagination, the kind that often afflicts the ultra-thin-skinned. He was an affectionate creature, easily hurt and shrinking from giving pain to others which would cause them to think ill of him. He liked to be loved, to see fond and smiling faces about him; he liked to make presents, accede to requests and receive thanks, to praise and to gratify men by bursts of stressed, informal affability. This made him equally susceptible to blandishments and to threats, for threats implied dislike and shattered the sunny feeling that he was making everybody happy. Boniface had been acrimonious and sarcastic, Benedict virtuous and remote, Clement was charming and polite. He hated to utter rebuke. He avoided working with the Inquisition. Once, when in consistory session a certain prelate delivered himself of heretical opinions, Clement on being tackled afterwards said serenely that he had not happened to be listening just then. It was different when he felt himself personally slighted, when his warmth and kindliness met with cold rebuff, when people would not let themselves be made happy by his mode of dispensing happiness — or when he was forced to reverse a previous friendly attitude against his inmost conviction, which he must drown with strident harshness.

Withal he, too, was a sick man. He suffered, at times excruciatingly, from what were probably stomach ulcers — which completes the picture.

Throughout his pontificate this excessively vulnerable man was haunted by the difficulties of doing justice to all the different interests which had combined to make him Pope yet remained at variance, and by chronic money troubles. If it be true that he had bought the tiara, he paid for it, exorbitantly.

No need to kidnap Clement; he remained right where the French King wanted him: in France. Rome was closed to him by civic unrest — the papal election had taken place at Perugia — and he was crowned at Lyons. He created ten new cardinals, nine of them fellow-Frenchmen. The tenth was English. The Italians were outnumbered. Bull followed bull, conferring benefits on the French King. First of all Philip received absolution for the manifold forced money contributions he had extorted from the Church, and that without any suggestion of restitution. Next came an invaluable patent. Under Boniface, under Benedict, and now under Clement, Philip had periodically talked of leading the next Crusade. Now he obtained the papal dispensation that neither he nor his successors were to be held to any crusading vow they might have taken, should the security of the realm demand the monarch's presence at home. Furthermore, the monarch himself should be sole assessor of the situation. After that came the so-called "Flemish Peace Bull." Philip had retrieved the defeat of Courtrai in 1304, but had had his hands too full meanwhile to ensure that his hard peace terms were observed. The Pope at his instigation threatened Flanders with the ban in the event of any future rebellion against France, absolution to be granted only at the request of the French King! This Philip had not obtained without a struggle. It was a fundamental principle that any excommunicate must be absolved once he had made atonement, whether his enemies liked it or not. But in the end the Pope gave in; that he had put up a struggle made Philip's victory the more complete. In future Clement not infrequently would submit the first draft of a bull for Philip's approval and dutifully adopt Philip's suggestions.

On one point only the Pope would not yield. In the matter of Nogaret's excommunication Philip made no progress. Clement had finally vindicated the Colonna cardinals whom Boniface had expelled and despoiled, in terms such as no Pope before him had ever used in reference to a predecessor. But that was as far as even he would go. He would not condemn Boniface outright, he would not sweepingly extend pardon to everybody implicated in the outrage of Agnani. He would have no hand in setting a precedent for bringing a Pope to trial — any Pope, alive or dead; even if it meant refusing a dear friend, even if it meant antagonizing the ruler of the land where he was staying.

Philip was in no hurry. He had Clement's measure. In future, whenever there was anything he wanted, Philip brought the matter up again; whenever he had got what he wanted, he would temporarily drop it. But Clement for his part made the discovery that the question of Nogaret's excommunication could serve him as a counter lever.

All this goes to suggest that the story of the sinister bargain at the ruined abbey was indeed a fiction. The five conditions Philip was supposed to have specified were: absolution for the conspirators of Agnani; erasure of the bulls of Boniface from the records of the Holy See; indictment, exhumation and burning of the bones of Boniface; reinstatement of the Colonna; and conceding the French Crown's right to tax the Gallican clergy one-tenth of their revenues for five years. In spite of all his subservience to Philip, Clement made no move to fulfill more than the fourth and fifth — and the latter with considerable reservations.

Moreover, there was a matter which Philip had so much at heart that it is impossible to believe he would not have included it in such a set of conditions. For some years now Philip's brother, Charles of Valois, had been seeking to make good a claim to the Holy Roman Imperial crown, in right of his second wife, and Philip spared no pains to secure it for him, always unsuccessfully. The chance of adding the Empire to the heritable estate of the Capetian dynasty was too momentous to be at any time neglected, and Philip importuned the Pope for his support. So far from having made sure of Clement beforehand, he in fact yielded some advantage by acknowledging his need of papal support.

One means of evasion which Clement had was his state of health. It will not do to be over-ready with facile charges of psychosomatic illness, nor to be too dogmatic as to the correspondence of nervous strain and peptic indisposition; also, during one very harassing year (1307–1308) the Pope was, quite unusually, free of saving ailments.

However, that was almost the only crisis which did not coincide with his recurrent bouts of illness. He had scarcely been crowned (1305), scarcely begun to decide the priority of the many pre-election promises he had now to honor, when he was incapacitated by rheumatic troubles, and soon after retired from affairs for many months in the grip of a series of gastric attacks which were so severe that convalescence was long-drawn-out. Not until the beginning of 1307 did he reappear from his seclusion, in which only four close relatives were suffered near him while the Curia sank into unmitigated disorder. Then came that spell without relapse, but from 1309 onwards not a year passed when he was not prostrate and inaccessible for long stretches, continually postponing, yet never finally escaping, the unpleasant decisions he had to make.

The regularity with which this happened inspired the inevitable ribald rumors that the Pope absented himself to wallow in clandestine amours, and it was no better when he reappeared too weak to hold a pen, too apathetic to return a smile of greeting. Would-be petitioners roamed the fields and byways in the hope of seeing him, as he avoided the public roads, but he would jog past torporously, without the energy so much as to raise his hand in benediction.

Corruption multiplied all around him. Prices soared where the papal court sojourned. The incomes of the curial functionaries were to a large extent dependent on their residing in Rome. As they were not residing in Rome, they made up for what they lost in any way they could, and took heavy bribes even to admit foreign ambassadors in audience. The Pope himself, when he was well enough, could never refuse a needy kinsman, never resist a sufficiently adroit appeal; in any case, his own coffers were always empty. Purchase of preferment had become the rule; worse, prelates-elect must pay for the privilege of taking office. One, informed that he had been made a bishop and that the charge was twenty thousand gold pieces, declined the honor, since to accept, he said, would evidently ruin both the health of his soul and the economy of his designated diocese. Others were not so scrupulous. The state of the Holy See as it lay open to the gaze of France was not designed to recover the esteem which Boniface had squandered.

There was one way of mending reputations, replenishing coffers, side-tracking creditors, all with a good conscience, too. The next Crusade was still in the offing.

Even without that compact of five conditions parceled up with a mysterious sixth, King Philip and Pope Clement very probably had discussed the Templar problem at their first meeting after the papal election, inseparable as that problem was from the whole crusading issue.

Philip had made his bid for direct control of the Temple, and had failed. He had done no less than seek admission to the order, with a view to becoming grand master in due time: he had more than toyed with the idea of abdicating in favor of his eldest son. Admittedly this was soon after the death of his Queen, so that one may assume an abnormal state of mind over and above his sudden eligibility as a widower. That derangement would pass once he grew used to his loss; nevertheless he was unlikely to be pleased at having been headed off with polite excuses by the Temple. He would now try other means.

Though by all accounts the faculty of humor was not highly developed in Philip, he surely must have seen the sardonic joke of going straight to the top, as it were, and, in order to denude the Pope of military power, getting at the military orders through their one and only lord, the Pope.

The fact was that the Papacy, too, had reason to distrust them. They had always made great play with acknowledging the authority of the Supreme Pontiff, but in practice ignored it as often as this suited them. Any Pope would recollect that they had been forbidden to march with the excommunicate Emperor Frederick and had nonetheless marched with him (while any secular ruler would keep well in mind that they had afterwards ravaged the Emperor's lands at the Pope's behest). The French Templars had endorsed Philip's attack on Boniface; the Aragonese Templars had backed the Count of Toulouse against the Inquisition in the Albigensian Wars. A former Pope Clement (IV — 1265-1268) had threatened to disband them for certain obstinate transgressions "best left unnamed"; when Boniface VIII had given Temple property (Church property, theoretically) in pledge to the King of Aragon, over their heads, their clamor had been shrill.*

Philip reopened talks about the next Crusade. Court and Curia got very busy. Reports and memoranda, old and new, shuttled back and forth. Plans were drawn up. It looked as if the new Crusade were really about to start. Oddly in transference of their respective spheres, the Pope concerned himself more with the military considerations, the King with the economic planning. The Pope canvassed all expert sources for advice and urged a definite date; the King's ministers produced infinite plausible arguments why the Church ought to defray the total costs. Helpfully, they showed how Church assets might be liquidated without hurt to the Holy See. For example, by suppressing the Templars and annexing their enormous wealth. What, out of the blue, for no reason at all? Out of the blue, yes, like a thunderbolt, the more sudden the better; but by no means without reason. Certain horrendous information had reached King Philip concerning the Templars, which he would be glad to communicate to the Pope. King and Pope once again went into private conference.

At the end of these discussions, in which King Philip put his terrible discoveries before the Pope, Clement is said to have told him, *"Fils, tu enquerras diligemment de leurs fais et ce que tu feras, tu me rescripas."* True? False? Absurd? *Ben trovato?* After these discussions, at

---

* This happened just about the time of the secret agreement between Hugh de Peraud, treasurer of the Temple, and Philip the Fair: the two events would not be unconnected.

all events, which were to have been followed up by another meeting not long hence, the Pope fell ill. This was the illness which tided him over the best part of a year, from the turn of 1305 until towards the end of 1306, during which time he would see no one save the four kinsmen who tended him, and transacted no business whatsoever.

The next Crusade had been postponed again.

But there were other forms of Crusade, and Moslems were not the only infidels. One did not have to go far afield to find heretics and Jews. Making war on these enemies of the faith involved no expense, little risk and sure profit. King Philip had said he would go on Crusade, and he showed willing. Open heresy in France had been destroyed, he had a campaign up his sleeve against a more insidious movement, for which, however, he must wait the Pope's recovery. Meanwhile he launched a systematic persecution of the Jews — a recurrent event in each reign of his dynasty. Nogaret was entrusted with the task.

In this way a whole flock of birds might be killed with one stone. As too often, King Philip was in grave straits, the fiscal shading over into civic. For some time past he had been adulterating the currency of the realm, and had clipped it so often that by 1306 it had fallen to half its fixed value. Rioting broke out again all over the country; in Paris the master of the royal mint was lynched, and the King himself had to take refuge from a bloodthirsty mob in the tower of the Temple (no doubt this did not ameliorate his feelings towards the Templars, as witnesses of his humiliation). He could now create a diversion, replenish his purse somewhat, and at the same time show his mettle as a militant Christian ruler. Nogaret would acquire merit and progress a step towards absolution, this being more urgently desirable than ever, since only Nogaret could be considered equal to organizing proceedings against the Temple, which were only hanging fire while the Pope was ill. The proceeding against the Jews, moreover, might serve as a dress rehearsal for the suppression of the Temple — which could only be encompassed in collaboration with the Papacy, which would not admit an excommunicate as a collaborator, and so on.

The plans for the suppression of the Temple were, in fact, already well advanced. Philip's brother, the professional pretender Charles of Valois, could not refrain from bragging of his privileged knowledge, to the effect that there were matters brewing, connected with the Templars and weightier than any the kingdom had known for sixty years. There was no other leakage. Relations between Crown and Temple seemed never to have been better.

The operation against the Jews went through without a hitch. Without breach of secrecy of any kind, on one and the same day, July 22, 1306, everywhere in France, the Jews were imprisoned and their property "taken into custody." A few days later, the surviving Jews were exiled. Their money had already disappeared into the royal exchequer, the rest of their goods were auctioned under Nogaret's supervision, and Philip issued a decree commanding immediate repayment of all debts owing to Jews — repayments to be made to the King. The Crown announced another victory for Christ.

To win like victory over the Templars, they too must be shown up as detractors of Christ. The prospective money-yielder, the potential danger to the state, had to be enemies of God.

In a sense it was true that the enemies of the state were the enemies of God, and vice versa. Christianity, originally an evangel of the lower classes, had spread so prodigiously, had so recommended itself to the rulers of heathen peoples that they had not only embraced but forcibly propagated an intrinsically humane and leveling religion, largely because this religion was a powerful unifying factor politically. The moment any branch of the faith began to act as a disruptive factor, therefore, deviation from established religious dogma became a political crime. It followed that political crime was religious heresy.

Again, the false syllogism had some justification. In many countries of the West conversion of the heathen had been accomplished by terrorism. Thus driven underground, the various pagan creeds by a natural process became cadres of lingering political resistance movements, and political discontents would generally assume a religious coloration. And even such heretical teachings as derived, not from some ancient pagan canon, but from Christian mysticism itself, constituted attacks on vested authority — in particular on that of the ruling clergy. (When such a movement was successful — to vary an old dictum — men called it Reformation.)

For although every heresy had a basic doctrine of its own, they one and all aimed at the purification of faith and priesthood. Their name was legion. In the East, home of introspective monotheism, you had Maronites, Monotheletes, Monophysites or Jacobites, Paulicians, Nestorians, Manichaeans, to list only the principal divisions, besides the Armenian and Greek Orthodox Church. In Europe there were the Patarines and Humiliati of Lombardy, the Waldensians of Lyons, the Bulgar Bogomils, and the Albigensian Catharans — the latter "puritans" by literal translation, with headquarters at the town of Albi. The Paulicians denounced St. Peter as an impostor, the Luciferians worshiped Satan as the *elder* son of God, the Waldensians advocated the classless society and asserted the competence of every individual to commune with God directly; the Jacobites held that Christ had one nature only, the divine, the Nestorians that He had two natures, the divine and the human, but one single will. The Bogomils and Catharans, who were the most influential offshoots of the Manichaean sect with its concept of godhead compounded of the Spirit of Good and the Spirit of Evil — these "Puritans" pursued to the ultimate logical extreme the postulate that all things material pertain to the Spirit of Evil, and denied the dogma of Redemption in the belief that only by total, personal Renunciation of the physical world might salvation be attained. They were, one might say, the nihilists of their day, and as such had been put down with particular rigor. But antisacerdotalism was the common feature of them all.

However, the Church oligarchy could not well declare war on heresy expressly in self-defense, and error as such was no sufficient indictment for popular consumption. The mass of the people were themselves inclined against the priesthood; heresy must be made thoroughly unattractive to them, by means of concrete delicts which the common man and woman could understand and wholeheartedly execrate.

Two types of delinquency had become synonymous with heresy: witch-craft and sexual perversion. Under a religion built up on miracles, any unauthorized manipulation of the supernatural was of course cosmic high treason. And to go against the God-ordained form of copulation — ordained solely for the purpose of procreation — was blasphemy, robbery, murder, rolled into one.

Sodomy was not rare in the Middle Ages, and no stigma of effeminacy attached to practices which numbered many adherents among doughty Crusaders and distinguished princes such as (probably) Coeur de Lion and Edward II. Nevertheless, popular revulsion from unnatural sexual intercourse went deep. To this day many regard such revulsion as instinctive, whereas its origin surely lies in the need of the early conquering Israelites to increase their population — a need which banned also the time-honored usage of infanticide and earned the death penalty for venial offenders like Onan, son of Judah, who merely let his seed spill on the ground. In this as in so many other matters the spirit of the Old Testament informed the New, which had shaped the morality of Western culture. A curious circumstance, in this context, is that the Jews were never charged with sexual aberration by their medieval persecutors — even the charge of ritual murder lacked any sexual tinge. The Moslems, too, were merely accused of superlative incontinence. But homosexuality was so thoroughly identified with religious dissent that Bulgar (Bogomil), or *bougre,* has come down to us in the form of "bugger."

No doubt a vicious circle ensued again, in that defiance of established tenets of belief led to deliberate breach of the eugenic rules associated with those tenets, while natural inverts would be driven to seek a spiritual justification in heresy. The same applies to sorcery. The point is that any departure from established ritual was in itself classed as magic, to which were attributed natural catastrophes like plague, drought and flood: what we call acts of God were works of the devil then, performed by the devil's minions on earth, the witches and warlocks. Being credited with such powers, naturally the underground opposition would begin to experiment along those lines and purposely call down plague, drought and flood, warts, boils and abortion on their enemies. Whether or not the magic worked, witchcraft was practiced, in all the secret covens of disaffection. With religion in the place of political ideology today, this was the form the higher treason took, genuinely or as a pretext for persecution.

Like the sexual urge, whether normal or perverted, like superstition which after all is dabbling in magic, heresy defied lasting suppression. This is why, at first reluctantly, successive Popes had endowed the Inquisition with increasing powers. Heresy was the specific province of the Inquisition; the secular arm had no authority in this field. But the Inquisition could call on the temporal power for assistance, even as the temporal power could call the attention of the Inquisition to suspected heretics. The Inquisition then paid the temporal power for its trouble: the property of the convicted heretic was automatically forfeit to the state, and he was handed over to the secular arm for execution.

On these facts pivoted the plans of Philip the Fair against the Templars.

The Pope's illness showed no signs of lifting, time was passing. Philip decided to go ahead, confident that he could get Clement's approval at his leisure, afterwards. In the latter half of 1306, Nogaret detailed twelve agents to apply for membership at various preceptories of the Temple, with instructions to fulfill all the order's customs, to penetrate as far as they could into its secrets, and to find the required evidence.

16 *The Templar*

Before Pope Clement V went into his painful retirement of 1306, when he was yet trying to hasten on the next Crusade, letters had gone out to the grand masters of the two military orders on Cyprus, summoning them to a consultation with their holy liege at Poitiers, for the autumn of that year. They were asked to travel as secretly as possible and with the smallest possible retinue — after all, they would find plenty of their knights to attend them in France, and it was important that the Moslems should not learn of their departure.

The Grand Master of the Hospital, Fulk de Villaret, immediately excused himself. The Hospitalers were in process of transferring to Rhodes, and he could not desert his brethren at a critical point in the reduction of that island. The Grand Master of the Temple, Jacques de Molay, accepted, though not so promptly, and he took his time to obey.

News traveled slowly, and in any case nobody was to know, from week to week, how much longer the Pope would continue sick. But Jacques de Molay made no attempt to reach France before the year 1307 had got well into its stride. And then he came accompanied by sixty knights with their full complement of followers conveying a vast train of sumptuous equipment and apparel, which included twelve horseloads of gold and silver. Their progress was leisurely and attracted the widest publicity. It was, in modern terms, as though a reigning prince had traveled incognito from Marseilles to Paris (one of the most frequented routes in the world), with the noise and show of a circus procession headed by sixty tanks. All the way the heroes of a thousand battles, haloed in effulgent wealth, were greeted with homage and acclamation.

Paris, not Poitiers, was their first destination. Jacques de Molay entered the capital like a king and like a king was received by Philip the Fair, amid the usual public festivities and the most amicable private conversations. Both must have been masters of dissimulation — one hesitates to rank them equals in that art only because for the grand master the strain of keeping up the diplomatic bonhomie must have been greater. Philip knew what he was about; Jacques de Molay as yet had only vague intimations. It takes strong nerves to await a blow in the dark, knowing neither when nor in what manner it will fall, with patience, let alone while bandying pleasantries — be a man's conviction never so strong, that he is invincible.

That Jacques de Molay had had warning is beyond doubt. The case of Boniface who had no inkling of the plot of Agnani is not comparable. Boniface had not been invited to France for discussions which, had the dissolution of the Papacy (in this case, amalgamation of the military orders) plainly on the agenda. In the case of Boniface only the person of one individual was to be seized, that of a man of peace whose guards were venal. The simultaneous seizure of five thousand trained warriors all over France required infinitely more organization with proportionately greater opportunities of leakage. Seeing that the King's own brother could not keep his mouth shut, other indiscretions are indicated — enough for adepts at intelligence, who had a finger in every worldly pie, to put two and two together, even had they no more definite information.

During the grand master's stay in Paris, the Temple Treasurer Hugh de Peraud (closer to court circles than anyone) told a knight who requested dismissal from the order that he was wise and should not lose a moment to get out, for a catastrophe was at hand. The Master of the Temple in France, who in the presence of the grand master would not have acted on his own authority, circulated an ordinance to all preceptories that no brother under any circumstances was to give information concerning customs and ritual of the order, no matter who asked for it. A number of former Templars, who had been dismissed the order or left it of their own desire, had been rounded up by Nogaret's agents and placed under protective arrest — impossible that this should not have come to the ears of the Temple leadership, however carefully it had been done.

The long delay between the grand master's acceptance of the papal invitation and his landing in France suggests reflection and had furnished ample time for any preparations Jacques de Molay might wish to make. His ostentatious progress through France, in contravention of the papal orders, showed what decision he had come to. He felt secure in his order's military strength and material power, and would take this opportunity to remind others thereof; he felt secure in the goodwill of the Pope — so secure that he would wait on the King of France first of all — and in the influence of the Pope's Templar chamberlains at the Curia. Perhaps he wished to estimate how much popular support the Temple could command in France and what were the chances for stirring up civil war. Jacques de Molay had a reputation for parsimony; he would not waste money nor take risks with it. For him to bring so much Temple treasure into France was calculated showmanship, as was the whole flamboyant manner of his entry. He knew what he was doing, only that he happened to miscalculate. Had events fallen out differently, it would not have been called miscalculation. We should have congratulated him on his far-seeing courage and on his clever use of the fearless gesture, as valuable in tactics as war paint and battle cry.

Meanwhile he had formulated his memorandum on the questions to which the Pope had invited his answer. He gave his opinion that sailing ships were superior to galleys for military transport, that the first landing place should be Cyprus, but that the landing plans for Palestine itself should be kept secret — he would not so much as commit them to paper. Likewise he would reserve for verbal communication his proposals as to finance and leadership. Regarding amalgamation of the military orders, he had much more to say. To begin with he would remind the Pope that this proposal was not new and that it had been invariably dismissed in the past no sooner than it was mooted. The orders had done invaluable work as separate units, and to compel them to combine would cast undeserved aspersions on them. Internal jealousy and discord would be the result, while the rivalry admittedly existing between Templars and Hospitalers to date was only a symptom of healthy competition, continually stimulating both to greater prowess. Also, the Templars were the mightier and wealthier of the two and could not be expected to consent to a pooling of resources without compensation. Further, the poor pilgrims, alas, would surely suffer, since in places where heretofore both orders had kept hostelries going, one or the other would have to be closed down. To be sure, there would be one advantage: the combined orders would be so powerful that *no one* could then hope to interfere with them, ever again. . . . He held himself at the Pope's disposal and would be glad further to confer with him whenever convenient — and of course decision lay entirely with the Holy Father.

The memorandum was sent on to Philip after perusal at the Curia, not so that of the Hospitaler Grand Master Fulk de Villaret which, though bearing mainly on the wherewithal for the intended expedition, evidently was judged to be of no interest to the King of France.

At last Jacques de Molay paid his visit to Pope Clement. Few details are known except that socially it was a success and that the grand master returned to Paris shortly after with his complacency apparently undiminished. He must have got on very well with the Pope, who was glad to admire one so widely traveled and so enviably sure of himself, only too glad to let himself be convinced that there was absolutely nothing in those dreadful rumors about the Temple. For, whatever Jacques de Molay had heard or not heard before he went to Poitiers, there he was apprised of everything King Philip had told Pope Clement about the Templars. He proudly demanded an official enquiry to quash the evil rumors once for all, and went back to take up his friendly commerce with King Philip where he had left off.

On October 12, 1307, he enjoyed a signal honor. He acted as pallbearer to the Princess Catherine of Constantinople, late wife of Charles of Valois. The obsequies over, he retired to rest at his apartments in that impregnable stronghold, the Temple of Paris.

Jacques de Molay came of the Burgundian nobility. He joined the Templar Order in 1265 at the age of twenty or thereabouts, and soon went out to the East, where he saw combat in the rearguard actions of Outremer. He took part in the retreat to Cyprus. It was in Cyprus that he first attracted notice, with a statement before an assembly of four hundred knights, concerning certain reprehensible practices which, he said, were corrupting the order and would prove its ruin unless rectified. He did not say what these practices were, presumably everybody knew. Not long after he was appointed provincial master of

England. The date of his return to Cyprus and election to the grand mastership is not precisely known, but by 1295 he was in office.

How this came about is another of those stories which may or may not be true in detail, although something of the sort must have been behind a given occurrence.

There were at the time two factions in the Temple roughly definable as the Burgundian and the Provençal — which in some degree had existed, always so definable, ever since the first serious-minded founders of the order had been joined by ardent romantics from the South. There is always antagonism between North and South, not only as regards continents and nations, but also within each individual country: how much more so in France, where the South represented intellectual curiosity, fertile unorthodoxy and a heritage half classical, half Saracen, while in the North barbarian materialism had become the more hardheaded and efficient as it settled down. The regional antipathy with all that it implied was accurately reflected inside the Temple with its predominantly French membership.

When Tibald Gaudin died and a new grand master had to be chosen, the Burgundian party was in the minority, as it evidently had been for some time. The candidate of the Southerners was Hugh de Peraud, and there seemed little hope for anybody else. However, Jacques de Molay was the candidate of the Burgundians. According to the deposition of a witness later on, de Molay secretly approached the Southerners and pretended that he would vote for his opponent provided he were put on the electoral commission. This was done. He then contrived to become the commission's president, and used the influence thus obtained to have himself elected. The quarrel arising out of this must have been heated indeed, for as a matter of attested fact the Grand Master of the Hospital was dragged in to act as a peacemaker. One cannot believe that Hugh de Peraud was ever the grand master's friend, thereafter. Bitterness would be one key to his conduct during the darkest hour of the Temple.

As soon as he had established himself, de Molay set about suppressing the Southern trend within the Brotherhood. There was to be no more of the dominance of "learned men." He was "unlearned" himself, illiterate and proud of it — he would speak of himself as a *"simple* unlearned warrior" with that well-known humility of unqualified self-satisfaction. Books in private possession among the brethren were confiscated. Nor did these books fall solely in the category of entertainment — if one can so describe the edifying matter that found its way into bound manuscript. Some of these books were copies and abstracts of the Temple statutes. It was not good for brethren to be too versed in the rule — what became of *unquestioning* obedience if they were? Besides, what was the point — since at any time the grand master could pass new enactments, sometimes to meet conditions *after* they had arisen, and always without any obligation to inform anyone but those to whom the new ruling applied? Studying the rule was as bad as reading the Scriptures or the heathen authors of antiquity. Reading the Scriptures encouraged independent thinking; reading the pre-Christian classics encouraged tolerance.

Lay Bible reading was another mark of heresy, as it was in truth a preliminary to rebellion, whether against Church or state. For the next three hundred years every revolutionary movement would find a pivot in the right of access to the Word of God. Translating it into the vulgar tongue ranked almost with sorcery. Priestly latinists alone might be considered proof against the temptation to interpret God's Word for one's self.

Yet knowledge of Latin was no longer exclusive to the priesthood, and even ordination was ceasing to act as a dependable prophylactic. To have read the pagan masters was fast becoming the mark of superior erudition, so much so that writers on quite other subjects began to sprinkle their pages with gratuitous references to *"Ovidius noster," "Vergilius noster,"* to show what highly educated persons they were. While this did not necessarily betoken actual familiarity with the works of those big names, actual familiarity was no longer such a heinous thing, and even a nodding acquaintance could not but beget an awareness of the relativity of religious ethics. As regards ordinary day-to-day morality, pagan and Christian ideals of virtue squared sufficiently to substantiate the discovery of the Crusades, that honorable conduct was no Christian monopoly. Thus tolerance corroded absolute convictions and vitiated the aggressive spirit. There was some practical sense underlying the taboo.

The books were called in and many of them burned. Among those which escaped this fate was, of all incriminating objects, a volume of extracts from the Bible translated into French. (It comprised abridged versions of Genesis, Joshua, Kings, Maccabees, Tobias, Judith and Judges, with a rhymed preface obliquely boasting of the literary difficulties the translator had had to overcome; also some rationalist commentary and anecdotal material borrowed from Moslem and Talmudic texts.) This book had been made for two patrons who commissioned it in partnership: Master Odo and Brother Richard of the English Temple.

Master Odo and Brother Richard, then stationed at London, who were such fast friends that even when one displaced the other as provincial master their relationship was not affected, were Odo de Saint-Amand and Richard de Hastings. It may seem surprising that the man who eventually became one of the most aggressive grand masters in the history of the Temple should have inspired a literary production — but not when we remember that the "Templar bible" consisted mainly of tales of war, and that its very existence was illegal, an act of defiance.

Rumors of corruption had assailed the Temple from outside since almost its earliest days; and from within, those dark hints of evil "learned" influences at work had been seeping for some time past. Again, it is possible that there was something in it. The structure of the Temple, where the various grades of initiates were admitted to graded degrees of revelation, bore some similarity to that of the Assassins, with whom the Templars had once stood in lively intercourse. There was much to appeal to the intellectual in the Assassin pattern of zones of progressive sophistication, ranging from childlike literal faith through symbolical interpretation to pure abstraction, around an inner circle of rarefied, irreligious philosophy; and it has been suggested that the "learned men" then in power at the Temple borrowed from this.

Tolerance can beget indifference, laxity, the feeling that nothing matters very much apart from one's personal well-being, the couldn't-care-less attitude of a society without positive beliefs. It is true that in the latter half of the thirteenth century the famous discipline of the Templars was no longer what it once had been. There were the nameless scandals under Thomas Bérard, grand master between 1256 and 1272, against which Clement IV had inveighed; the pro-Moslem policy of his successor William de Beaujeu who had kept the order out of war for fifteen years; the repeated petitions of provincial masters for outside help against groups of rebellious subordinates; not to mention the questionable behavior of de Molay's immediate predecessor, Tibald Gaudin, who had deserted his brethren at Sidon in order to get aid which never materialized.

Simony had come to be as common in the Temple as at the papal court. The original Temple rule had made no provisions for this offense, the possibility of which had not entered the heads of the founders. In the revised criminal code of the Temple, however, simony had pride of place among thirty-one misdemeanors listed. In every shape or form, however mild, it was punishable with expulsion. The statute was never rescinded, only the interpretation of what constituted permissible extra donations had become more and more liberal. Under the Grand Master Armand de Périgord a group of knights came to the conclusion that at their entry into the order they had been guilty of simony. They informed the master, to whom this was a bitter blow, as they were the best he had. The Pope was asked to arbitrate by special messenger, and in the end the virtuous knights were expelled and immediately readmitted, this time gratis. Extra donations became an enduring custom.

About this form of lawlessness Jacques de Molay did nothing. It might be averred that the dowry every recruit had to supply was itself an entrance fee. If every Templar who had paid more were to have been expelled the remaining membership would have been small indeed, and besides the glory of the Temple might have been lessened, had the price of belonging to it fallen.

The glory of the Temple and the welfare of the Temple were all Jacques de Molay cared about. He tightened the grip of discipline; but either he did not curb his knights in their relations with the rest of the world, or else their attitude was a straight projection of his own. Any obstacle in their path was ridden down; softness was weakness; indifference to other people's sufferings and to their opinions was the mark of strength.

At Eperstoun in Midlothian one Robert the Scot held a piece of land, which on his death went to his daughter Christiana, wife of William Simple. The couple had three sons. The husband, "being given more to ease than labor," made over his life interest in his wife's property to the Templars at Balentrodach, in order to live as a pensioner in their preceptory, while his wife and children subsisted on a bare maintenance, in a house granted her on her own property. On William's death the Master of the Temple claimed the property. Christiana was ordered to leave, and refused. A troop of Templars forced an entry and dragged her bodily to the door. She clung to the lintel so that they could not pull her away, whereupon one Templar drew his knife and hacked off one of her fingers, and threw her out screaming. She appealed to the King of England, the country's sovereign lord by recent conquest, who promised that she should have justice. Her property was restored to her. But when war broke out anew in Scotland, the Master of the Temple returned with a body of Welsh mercenaries in English pay, and evicted her once more. Four days before the battle of Falkirk (1298) her eldest son approached the master, who "spoke him fair" and asked him to act as guide to his army corps. The young man agreed, and on the march was murdered by the soldiers in Rosebery Wood. The Templars kept possession of the land until in course of time — less than twenty years later, to be exact — they were themselves dispossessed.

This was only one incident, not exceptional but characteristic of what was happening all over Europe. Rapacity and avarice had joined courage and wealth as proverbial attributes of the Templar. As long ago as 1188 the Templar Gilbert of Hoxton, as one of the collectors of the "Saladin Tithe," had shocked the world by his attempt at embezzling funds destined for the Holy Land in its desperate plight; the Templars did nothing to expunge that memory. The Emperor Frederick II, exhorted to rid himself of his pride, greed and profligacy, had with malicious formality bequeathed these qualities to the Templars in his will; the Templars did everything to remind the world of this inheritance. They kept green the title of a bull of Innocent III, a Pope who was their friend and at one time had been himself a Templar — *De insolentia templarorium*.

Mothers of the people told their children, "Beware the Templar's kiss!" On Cyprus there was a saying that a woman who had never had relations with a Templar could not call herself a lady. "Everybody knew" of men who, caught spying on the secret proceedings of the Temple, had tracelessly disappeared.

Individual Templars gave as good as they got. Taxed with the suspicious secrecy of their regimen, they boasted of the frightful fate which would overtake spies and traitors. To imputations of sodomy they made flippant answer: there was no need for them to resort to this, since plenty of pretty Associate Sisters were available. Accused of denying God, they replied, "And do not all of you deny Him a thousand times a day, even for so small a matter as a louse?" Perhaps so, but in the case of ordinary people all of it was not assiduously noted, every word and deed and fabrication.

In the night of October 12, 1307, every Templar in France was arrested, including the Grand Master Jacques de Molay and the sixty knights he had brought with him from Cyprus, at their impregnable fortress of Paris.

Part Four

The Question of Guilt

17 The Charges

ESQUIU OR LE SQUIN OR SEQUIN DE FLORIAN OR FLOYRANO WAS A NATIVE of Béziers, who at an unknown date had joined the Knights Templars and risen to the office of prior at the preceptory of Montfaucon — Montfaucon in the diocese of Périgueux, not the other Montfaucon where stood the gallows of Paris, which would have been a neater omen. He lost his command for reasons unknown and began to follow the provincial governor about with petitions for another post. Rebuffed, he waylaid the governor, stabbed him to death, and fled into hiding. This was at some time between 1303 and 1305.

The intricate warren of Paris was a good place to hide, where, too, the chances were good for a fugitive from justice to find employment, and to Paris Esquiu eventually made his way. However, first of all he took a detour across the Spanish frontier, to intercept King James II of Aragon during the latter's annual springtime sojourn at Lérida, which was not far from Esquiu's native haunts. The King of Aragon subsequently denied their meeting, but a résumé of it which Esquiu sent him through semiofficial channels and which was filed without especial comment in the royal archives, gives some positive evidence.

"You, Sire, were the first whom I approached with my disclosures concerning the Templars," Esquiu recapitulates reproachfully, "which I submitted to you *in the presence of your confessor*.* You being unwilling at the time to place full confidence in my deposition, I put it before the King of France who upon enquiring into the matter found it clear as the sun. . . ." He proceeds to dun his royal correspondent for a reward of a thousand livres in rents and three thousand in cash out of the property of the Aragonese Templars, which he says King James promised him in the event that the truth of his charges against the order were proven.

It would have been a very large reward indeed. We do not know whether it was ever paid. In a way it sounds not unlike a rhetorical bet

* My italics.

—like the promise to eat one's hat, or alternatively like the rash vows made by characters in folktales and legends. For if the King of Aragon found it impossible to believe Esquiu's presentation of *"factum Templarorium,"* he — unlike Philip — had no special incentive for wishing it to be proved true. In Spain the Templars were in a different position from that obtaining everywhere else. Here their autonomy had never been complete; they ranked as subjects of the sovereign, who ratified any master-elect and received his oath of fealty. For the most part the Spanish Templars were Spaniards by birth; in Portugal only Portuguese nationals were admitted to the order, and no property might be sent out of the country without royal permission, not even the preceptories' contributions to headquarters in the East. It is a point worth noting that where the Templars throughout their career had done most for the realm — as in Aragon, Portugal and Castile — their power was smallest, and their threat to the state nonexistent.

Why, then, did Esquiu go first to the King of Aragon? Merely because it was a long way to Paris and Lérida was within easy reach? But he did go to Paris afterwards. Because he hoped, through the King of Aragon, to blackmail the Aragonese Templars into protecting him from the consequences of his crime against their French brethren? But neither he nor King James brought the Aragonese Templars into it at all.

We have no answer. There may not be any. The whole story of Esquiu's part in the plot, as we shall see, is most odd and tortuous — for no apparent reason, or none that strikes the present-day mind. It is important to remember that we are dealing with a very different mentality. Tortuousness was no reproach to it, ideally the roundabout way was best, as the shortest way seems ideally best to us; subtlety would make certain, complication was the aesthetic mode.

If in this whole context we are so frequently reminded of the fairytale or of some idiom mimed with the literalness of absurdity, it is because many a fairytale and idiom have their roots in the Middle Ages, when having to eat one's hat would not necessarily be mere hyperbole. There was no lack of the bizarre in the most ordinary everyday affairs. In

Esquiu's native Périgueux, for instance, a woman marrying for the second time was required to present the municipality with an earthen pot containing twelve sticks of different woods, a woman marrying for the third time must bring a barrel of cinders passed thirteen times through a sieve and thirteen spoons carved from the wood of fruit trees, and one who had not been deterred by past chicanery and wished to marry for the fifth time could only do so on producing a small tub containing the excrement of a white hen. A *white* hen — it is the detail which to us provides the ultimate touch of fantasy, whereas to the dauntless bride's contemporaries it was the very thing which firmly anchored regulation to reality.

Esquiu's motives, of self-protection coupled with vindictiveness, seem plain; his usefulness to King Philip would be obvious. Simply to take down his deposition and use him as a straightforward witness, however, would not do; it would be too plain; without the fancy arabesque it would not be official.

Esquiu goes to Paris, where he disappears from sight. Next he is arrested and thrown into prison — but in Toulouse, right at the other end of France (the inference being that he had got into touch with Nogaret who arranged for his comedy to be staged at a suitable distance from the capital). Esquiu is locked up in one cell with a malefactor under sentence of death. Both are denied a priest to confess them. In accordance with the Church's provision for confession when a priest is unobtainable, the two prisoners confess to one another. Esquiu confesses to such diabolical iniquities, to which he had been party as a Templar, that the other gives the guards no rest until he is taken to unburden himself before the King. The King is appalled, and cannot do otherwise than tell the Pope. There is no further mention in the prison records of Esquiu or the other man.

And who was the other man? Not, as one would suppose, a convincing random sample of convict, but one Noffo Deghi, a professional blackguard of Florentine origin, who had served the French Crown as an informer before and was shortly to do so again in a different affair (i.e. he must have been released this time).* In due course he ended on the gallows for some swindle on his own account.

Esquiu de Florian did better out of the transaction. By 1313 he is found snug in possession of Montricot, previously Templar property.

He did not figure in the investigations which began immediately after the mass arrests of October 12, 1307.

On that one night, over an area covering roughly one hundred and fifty thousand square miles, a total of about fifteen thousand persons was taken: knights and serjeants and foot, chaplains, artisans, laborers and other dependents. There was no struggle, anywhere. The King's officers hammered at the gates, the gates were opened — though numbers of Templars afterwards showed injuries sustained, after the approved formula, while resisting arrest, none of the King's men suffered a scratch — the inmates were taken off to prison or thrust under guard into their own dungeons, the royal officials searched the premises, made a complete inventory on the spot, and confiscated everything. At the Temple of Paris, Nogaret himself was in charge of the royal posse, and personally secured Jacques de Molay, Hugh de Peraud and the other leading dignitaries of the order. We may speculate whether his presence had anything to do with the fact that they all went quietly, but beyond the bare facts nothing has so far come to light.

It is all very strange. If this was a surprise attack, what could have caused every single preceptory to surrender? If it was no surprise, what could have caused the leadership to instruct them all to surrender? The Paris Temple was equal to any amount of siege, certain to win allies among the townsfolk, moreover — before the royal propaganda got its head start. With or without allies, in the provinces too their fortresses were strong, their armaments exemplary, and their tradition one of supreme confidence in the face of far greater odds than handfuls of soldiers hastily collected by rustic seneschals.

---

* The Temple also had employed him as a business go-between at various times, but this connection was not utilized in any way by either party.

Perhaps specious promises were made to the grand master, perhaps he was tricked. Perhaps it was put to him that allowing the entire order to be rounded up would be the surest way to refute the charges. But would he have been foolish enough to fall in with that? Unlettered he might be, but Jacques de Molay was a man of wide experience, forty years a Templar, and for at least half that time in the top stratum of the hierarchy. He knew Nogaret, he knew King Philip, and he had met the Pope. He could not but know what to expect of each. Arrogance, miscalculation are insufficient to elucidate his course. That he was bribed to cast the order to the wolves is too unlikely — what had anyone to offer the Grand Master of the Temple (within reason) that he had not got? Who in his place would carry out his engagement *before* he was safely in possession of the bribe? One might speculate endlessly without hope of filling in the tantalizing blank.

There are many such blanks at this point. Nogaret, for example, had become Chancellor of the realm just three weeks before, and the circumstances of his promotion are equally inviting of guesswork.

The royal seneschals throughout the kingdom had received their sealed orders about mid-September, and on the day of despatch Philip also sent letters to the other rulers of Europe, informing them of the abominations of the Temple and urging that all follow his proposed example. (The response, when at last it came in, was unsatisfactory.) All the while heated discussions continued in the Privy Council. In the course of one of these — of which the minutes have not been preserved — on September 22, the Archbishop of Narbonne, who was then Chancellor, resigned his post and returned the Great Seal. In his place the King appointed Nogaret. An excommunicate occupied the highest secular office in the state, next to the throne itself.

Meanwhile there had been further correspondence on the subject between King and Pope. Clement's letters over this period have been variously construed, but on the face of them they agree, at least in principle, to an indictment of the Templars.* ("There is so much that still

---

* And why not, since Jacques de Molay himself had demanded an enquiry?

appears impossible to credit," Clement writes diffidently. "However, since We attach great weight to your communications in this matter . . .") Philip, at all events, took it so, and ever after claimed as much.

Philip also claimed that before taking any action he had first informed the Inquisition, and that he had acted entirely upon the request of the Inquisition. This was untrue. The Inquisition was informed after he had acted, when its practiced interrogators were needed to work on the prisoners. As stated, the secular ruler had no right to touch members of a religious association, unless asked to do so by the Church. Having secured the Templars, King Philip went through the motions of securing the antedated command of the Inquisition.

His ministers did not even wait for this to start the propaganda campaign. On the day after the arrests the most serious charges against the Templar Order were broadcast to the nation. Preaching friars and spokesmen of the civil service addressed the people of Paris in the gardens of the Palais Royal, in the market place and in the streets, to nip any possible popular sympathy with the accused before it could so much as bud, and whip up hatred. They were completely successful. The friars, always among the Temple's most outspoken opponents, carried every detail of the charges into every corner of the country, and other agents passed the word that on the abolition of the Temple *all debts owing to it would be wiped out.*

The examination of prisoners was begun, and testimony was quickly forthcoming.

The charges made by Esquiu de Florian came under these main heads:

1. That the Templars put their order and its welfare before every moral and religious principle, and took oath to defend and enrich it, whether right or wrong;

2. That they kept up a secret correspondence with the Moslems;

3. That novices on admission were required to spit on the cross, to renounce Christ, and to take part in a mock ceremonial;

4. That any who attempted to expose the order were secretly murdered;

5. That the Templars despised the sacraments of the Church, omitted the words of consecration in the canon of the Mass, and practiced lay absolution and idolatry;

6. That they were addicted to immorality and sodomy;

7. That they had betrayed the Holy Land;

8. That they worshiped the devil, usually in the form of a cat.

Within a few days of October 12 these charges were known to every man, woman and child in the kingdom, and on these precise points every Templar prisoner was put to the question.

In the procedures of the Inquisition, suspicion was sufficient accusation. The accused was not allowed to know who his accusers were and he was not permitted an advocate, even had he been able to find one brave enough — for consorting with heretics rendered a person "violently suspect" and thus himself subject to interrogation. The accused was styled *witness,* and torture was used to obtain his evidence. The theory was that torture could not but extract the truth; if the witness be innocent, God would give him strength to bear any amount of pain.* To apply torture more than once was forbidden, but this prohibition was evaded by *continuing* the torture on successive days. No evidence was valid but that of the witness himself. A forced confession was invalid; therefore the witness who had confessed under torture was made to confirm his statement "voluntarily" three days later. He would then swear that he had told the truth, without omission or misrepresentation, and that he had spoken of his own free will and not from fear of torture or for any other reason. Thereupon as a repentant sinner he was reconciled to the Church, readmitted to the spiritual community, and handed over to the secular arm for temporal punishment while his immortal soul was safe. Refusing to take his oath, recanting his confession, made of him a relapsed heretic and confirmed subject of the devil. Nothing further could be done for him and he was burnt at the stake. Clerics were not permitted to inflict torture; so the friars who composed the Inquisition absolved one another that they might do so. Under canon law, too,

---

* The same theory underlay the legal device of trial by ordeal.

members of religious associations were exempt from torture. The interrogations of the Templars, however, were conducted in the presence and on the authority of royal officials — sometimes the King and Nogaret were in attendance — and not at first formally under the auspices of the Inquisition.

One marvels, not that almost everyone confessed, but that most confessed only to a part of the charges, and that even then there were stubborn cases who had to be interrogated two or three times to complete their confessions. Leading questions were asked and, according to the records, "mild arguments" employed to shape the answers. In Paris alone, thirty-six Templars died of the persuasion in the first few days after the arrests. Several had to be carried before the examiners for their subsequent "voluntary" confirmations, having lost their feet or merely the use of their limbs. Others had only been shown the instruments of torture.

The inquisitors for the most part were sincere, God-fearing men; like physicians, they had to harden themselves to the agonies of the patient, on whom they operated for the health of his sick soul.

The consensus of confession was that in the secret ceremonies of reception into the Temple, novices were required to spit and urinate on a crucifix or trample it underfoot, to deny Christ as a false prophet who had been crucified for his own crimes and not for the salvation of mankind, to kiss the receiving brethren on the mouth, on the navel, and below the spine; that they were enjoined to satisfy any sexual cravings with each other, and that the psalm sung in conclusion of the rite, "Behold how good and joyful a thing it is for brethren to dwell in unity," was used with appropriate obscene significance.

At other secret meetings the Templars worshiped:

1. A head (a) having three faces, (b) having four feet, (c) having one face only and no feet, (d) being a human skull embalmed and encrusted with reliquary jewels, (e) being carved out of wood, (f) being the remains of a former grand master, (g) being named Baphomet.

2. A cat (a) black, (b) gray, (c) brindled, (d) red.

And also present at these mysteries were (*a*) tender young virgins, (*b*) demons in female form.

The idols were anointed with the fat of roasted infants, the cat had to be kissed below the tail. The bodies of deceased brethren were burnt and the ashes mixed into a powder which was administered to the younger members in their food to make them hold fast to these ,abominable ways (shades, once again, of the Assassins and their ritual drug). For the same purpose they had to wear a cord next the skin which had acquired magic properties by being brought in contact with the idol (or idols).

All Templars were bound on oath to put the wealth and power of the order above everything else, and taught that no sin was too black to serve this end — be it buying up corn in time of famine, or selling the Holy Land to the Infidel. The grand master, the visitor and the preceptors, all laymen, were in the habit of giving absolution to the brethren, and Templars were forbidden to confess to any priests save their own chaplains.

The tribunal had taken over the Paris Temple, and there from October 18 to November 24 examined nearly one hundred and forty witnesses. (This was not counting the examinations elsewhere.)

Prison conditions in themselves were enough to break the spirit — and the prouder the spirit, the more shattering the humiliations to the body that housed it. To say that the Templars were warriors, inured to hardships, is irrelevant; hardships encountered, sword in hand, cannot compare with suffering in utter helplessness pain and indignities imposed of deliberate cruelty, without sight of the sun, without a breath of untainted air. Not a few of the Templars taken at Paris were old men, past the prime of physical endurance.

The change in their fortunes had been horribly sudden. One night they went to bed members of the most powerful organization in Christendom, to which all men aspired to belong — even King Philip, whom they had had power to reject — and in which they were secure to the end of their days and beyond, Amen. The next morning they were miserable captives, cut off from the world, which made no slightest move to help them. Their own familiar home and stronghold was part of the nightmare transformation, become prison to them overnight, and inferno.

The individual confessions did not all cover exactly the same ground, and gaps in the testimony may signify denials, since the records, concerned only with admissions and the most lucid way of setting these out, would often pass over what did not fit in. Verbatim transcriptions were not made. The recording clerks customarily worked their notes into well-constructed, easily digestible fair copies. Thus we get no cross-examination, only the result, and that in form of compact narrative. We do get the various reservations — such as, that witnesses having been induced to spit on the cross deliberately missed or contrived to put a hand in the way; that they had pronounced the abnegation of Christ with their lips but in their hearts canceled it; that they yielded only to the most dire threats; that they had never been actually forced to commit homosexual acts or availed themselves of the license to commit such.

Of all the thousands of Templars examined altogether over the next seven years, only *three* confessed to homosexual acts — which is the more surprising as homosexuality was so widespread, particularly among superior classes of men.*

Again, one does not know what to think.

If one accepts the "evidence" as the result of torture, one is forced to ask how the victims were able to stand firm on some points yet not on others. If, on the other hand, they confessed only to what was true, why did different witnesses confess to *different parts* of the same charges? And if King Philip's ministers had gone to the trouble of drawing up so comprehensive a bill, would they not pursue every item with equal energy?

---

* In England, since the accession of Edward II, it was almost as a patent of nobility. Perhaps King Philip, whose daughter's marriage to King Edward was about to be solemnized, was not so anxious to see this charge brought home?

The only witness who admitted all the charges without reservation was the Treasurer Hugh de Peraud.

One more point of speculation, before we stop pursuing what leads only to another impervious question mark.

The Grand Master Jacques de Molay was among the first witnesses to be examined. He admitted having denied Christ on his reception forty-two years before, and having been ordered to spit on the crucifix, though he had spat on the ground near it. He himself, he said, had received only a few recruits into the order, and at the end of the first, formal part of the ceremony had usually asked some other brethren to take the newcomer away and perform the rest of the initiation by themselves. Saying that "he thought nothing exceptional was done with himself," he implied that he had assumed the same was done with everybody else. He had an explanation, too. Desecration and abnegation were a test — akin to the test set Abraham in the sacrifice of Isaac — an earnest of absolute obedience, an earnest of renunciation, too, since the novice, having stripped himself of every worldly tie and possession, should show himself ready to give up the last thing he had left, his faith. Regarding the remainder of the charges, he declared that he knew nothing.

But then there came his most decisive departure. He sent a circular letter to all the Templars held in France, commanding them to make full confessions as required *despite their vow of secrecy* (i.e., for what it may be worth, he did not rescind the rule of secrecy as such).

This might explain what torture and terror, perhaps, do not entirely account for. Jacques de Molay had reinvigorated Templar discipline, all too successfully. The grand master commanded, the knights obeyed. Meanwhile there was not a living soul in France ignorant of the charges, and witnesses everywhere knew what questions to expect. The only matters left to their discretion were circumstantial details concerning the idol and the cat, and so here they contradicted each other most.

Letters can be forged — particularly when the sender cannot read or write. But Jacques de Molay never denied his authorship of this letter and it is generally accepted as his. Records also can be forged, or falsified. It is generally accepted that the grand master was at no time subjected to torture. When Jacques de Molay recanted (as he did, in course of time), it was on the grounds that confession had been forced from him by torture. With righteous scorn the royal publicists retorted that this was not so; he had *asked* to be tortured, yes, because he felt embarrassed by his confession and his circular letter asking everyone else to confess, and so that he might be able to *say* that only torture had brought him to it.

Then why *not* say so? Why stick at this of all lies? To be sure, guilt and shame may drive a man to masochistic expiation — his would not be the first example, especially in the Middle Ages. In that case, however, why did he pursue it no further at that stage? At any time between 1307 and 1314 he would have found martyrdom very easy to attain. It is generally accepted, also, that Philip and Nogaret were prepared to stop at nothing to destroy the Temple; it is accepted that the records contain hiatuses, prevarication and distortions. Then why give categorical credence to this one particular statement, that no sort of physical pressure was applied to Jacques de Molay? We cannot have it both ways.

True, there are other forms of pressure. We are back at the possibility of bribes and trickery. A man who had obtained the grand mastership by double-dealing might not shrink from treachery on a larger scale. Or he might have pursued an ingenious scheme of his own.

The latter is the more likely — not merely because deviousness rather than simplicity is to be looked for, but also because elaborate miscalculation was evidently his strong suit, and because the one ingenious scheme here applicable would alone accord with the interests of the order and the similar endeavors, as it turned out, of the Holy See.

It was of the utmost importance to both the head of the Templars and the head of the Church that the order as such should not be convicted of heresy. Firstly, unless so convicted, the order could not be dissolved. Secondly, the property of convicted heretics was lost to the Church, since forfeit to the state. Individual Templars, however, possessed no property whatsoever, and what did not exist could not be confiscated. Individual Templars might freely admit to their individual guilt; they would then be individually punished and expelled, that was all. The order would be unaffected and its assets remain intact at the disposal of its overlord, the Pope. Whether or no this had occurred to the Pope before he gave his qualified consent to an investigation of Esquiu's charges (when Clement was as yet convalescing and perhaps not fully compos mentis), it was incontrovertibly clear to him afterwards, when the investigations had started. For this was what the ensuing tussle between Clement and Philip the Fair was all about.

Once the whole Brotherhood was under restraint, the Templars' only hope was to be transferred from the clutches of the King into the jurisdiction of the Pope, which in any event was where they belonged.

Since the Inquisition, technically merely an executive branch of the Church, had in practice become more or less a separate institution — like any body of secret police, to which one may loosely compare it — the Templars were legally justified in denying the Inquisition's right to deal with them. Besides, the Inquisition commanded nothing like sufficient prison space to accommodate fifteen thousand people, and had to ask the Crown to continue lodging the prisoners on its behalf. Thus even after the Inquisition had consented to assume titular responsibility for the investigations, the prisoners remained in the hands of the King and his jailers.

In this light, it becomes clearly apparent that the grand master's every effort was in fact bent on achieving the transfer. The offenses which he admitted, combined with his suggested explanation of the mock ceremonial of reception, did not fall in the category of heresy, but they decidedly were of a kind which only the head of the Church himself should deal with. We then realize also that nearly all the Templar witnesses who were so specific about their own evil courses took refuge in the secrecy of the rule and carefully professed total ignorance as to whether these evil courses were enjoined by rule.

Again Hugh de Peraud was the exception. He alone succinctly stated that the iniquities to which he confessed were enforced throughout the order.

Very soon, therefore, the question ceased to be simply one of guilt or innocence. Rather, it turned on the distinction of individual as against corporate guilt. The Crown was committed to establishing the latter — else from the Crown's point of view the entire proceeding would be rendered futile. The Crown was inextricably committed to going on the way it had started; there was no going back, and no stopping, now. If after all that had been done to them the Templars were to get away unscathed, they would never rest until they had vengeance of the King, of the Crown and of France. Now Philip really had fashioned the Temple into a sure threat to himself, and for his part might not rest until it was destroyed.

It may be irksome that there are impenetrable passages in this, the most profusely documented period of the Temple; but at least we get a serviceable taste of the oppressive fog in which the contestants strove and labored.

18 Tug of War

IT WAS LESS THAN TWO HUNDRED MILES FROM PARIS TO POITIERS. IT WAS autumn, shading into winter, and no doubt the roads were deep in mud. But the mails were not bulky; the mails were private, delivery was at any time of day or night, and the constant correspondence of Philip and Clement had created fixed channels permanently open for speediest transmission. It had taken no more than three days for the news of the arrests to spread all over France. Over two weeks passed before Pope Clement lodged a protest.

To do him justice, it was a vehement protest when it came, and in the nature of a last-minute rescue. Already hundreds of Templars had confessed and confirmed their confessions; the next step would be for the Inquisition to hand them over to the secular arm for punishment. The state already had custody of them and of their property, so there was no occasion for delay. Clement's intervention abruptly halted the process.

He had agreed to an enquiry — but so, far that matter, had Jacques de Molay: neither had dreamt that such an enquiry would ever go beyond the closed courtroom of the Curia. Why, the Pope demanded, had he not been consulted? He was near enough at hand. He was the order's sole bishop and sole judge, and Crown proceedings even against individual Templars were an infringement of their privileges, privileges conferred by the Papacy: the Papacy itself was being flouted. The Temple's wealth, of particular importance for the next Crusade, said the Pope, had been seized by a King renowned for his financial troubles and despotic temperament: clearly the intention was to injure the Papacy materially as well as in its rights. The Pope went on to castigate the Grand Inquisitor of France, William Imbert, for having taken on the task of interrogation without asking papal permission, and removed him from office for contempt of the Holy See and abuse of his powers. The Pope ordered the cessation of proceedings conducted in an altogether uncanonical manner.

The uncanonical proceedings were continued, uncanonically employing torture as before, and under the continued uncanonical supervision of the civil power. The Pope renewed his strictures, with even greater sternness.

Popes had been stern with Philip before, and thus had helped the King to rally the French nation behind him. While Nogaret appealed to the Faculty of Theology of the University of Paris for a ruling as to whether civil officers were competent to take such action as they had been taking; the same maneuver that had served so well in the past was set in motion again — part methodical slander, part plebiscite. Parallel with the nationwide campaign against the Templars, a second one was launched against Pope Clement, with a first broadside of pamphlets to blacken his character.

Clement V was no better than Boniface VIII: selfish, greedy, petty, designing, tyrannical. He refused to prosecute self-confessed heretics for no better reason than that he wanted to keep their money to himself. He allowed the bones of a madman and base usurper (Boniface) to rest inviolate in the crypt of St. Peter's. His leniency, nay, favoritism towards the Church's most noxious enemies was placing her in terrible danger.

The Estates General would shortly be convened again and it would be seen what they had to say about all this. For it was manifest to all right-thinking men that the actions of the King of France were inspired by a most pure desire to help the Church — at the request of the Inquisition, moreover (never mind the date of that request); and who was the King of France to contest a law laid down by the Papacy * (notably under Boniface VIII!); who was he to disobey the Grand Inquisitor of France, appointed directly by the Holy Father (and incidentally Philip's confessor)? Any criticism of King Philip could only spring from tepidness in the faith, if no worse. Was not the Gallican Church in its entirety behind its royal defender? Were not the Templars abject criminals — otherwise would they be in prison? Let others, like the Kings of England and Spain, delay and equivocate. Perhaps the peoples of those other nations were content with their present burden of taxation — a burden which in France would be appreciably diminished once the state ceased to be defrauded of its due by the vast Templar exemptions.

A few weeks of this, and Clement broke down. Rome was still closed to him by reason of the Italian disturbances. He had been placed in the onerous position of seeming to protect heresy, when all he had asked was to judge for himself as was his right. A whole nation was being incited to dislike him. That most alarming demand for the posthumous trial of a Pope was being renewed, and so were Philip's importunities regarding the Imperial claims of Charles de Valois. Everything was coming down upon his head at once; he must gain a breathing space, silence the tumult with the cheapest sop he could find, and if forced to choose between granting the trial of Boniface, committing himself irrévocably as to the Imperial succession, and sanctioning the proceedings against the Templars which were going on anyway — why, he would let Philip have his way with the Templars.

Clement reinstated the Grand Inquisitor although, he pointed out, the latter had incurred just censure by his precipitate action — however, since "his dear son Philip" asked it, the Pope had decided to be merciful.

---

* Namely, that the temporal power was to comply with any request for assistance by the Inquisition.

In the bull *Pastoralis preëminentiae* he declared himself convinced by the evidence against the Templars, handsomely retracted his harsh words about Philip, and called on all Christian sovereigns to arrest the Templars in their territories.

This bull was published on November 22. On November 20 and 23, the King of England had written to his father-in-law the King of France and various other princes, making light of the charges and affirming his belief in the innocence of the Templars. On December 4 he wrote to the Pope, rather more forcefully, asseverating that the order had been atrociously maligned and that the Supreme Pontiff ought to protect it. But this letter came too late to help uphold Clement's resolution. It crossed with *Pastoralis preëminentiae,* upon receipt of which King Edward II metaphorically shrugged his shoulders and gave up any further effort on behalf of the Templars. To do otherwise would stamp him a heretic by association, and when all was said and done no harm but only profit could come to him on obeying the papal edict.

Nowhere save in Portugal was the edict ignored; though in Cyprus it did not arrive until the following May, maritime traffic being at a standstill during the winter months — or so the Governor of Cyprus averred: it so happened that he owed his position to the Temple. But while everywhere else the Templars were duly arrested, Philip's holy zeal found little echo. No other sovereign shared his monomaniac intensity, none was so near bankruptcy, and no one possessed a propaganda machine such as the French Crown had built up.

The Pope had second thoughts, and Philip unwisely spurred that mental process. No sooner had he got his way than he resumed pressing for the trial of Boniface, which Clement thought to have indefinitely deferred by his sacrifice of the Templars. Not for the first time, Philip had gone too far in driving home his advantage; not for the first time, a docile Pope, cornered and tormented, turned and fought back. When Philip least expected it, Clement came out at last with an absolute refusal to arraign the dead Pope, now or ever, and over and above that once more withdrew his consent to the proceedings against the Templars.

The game began all over again. The Pope demanded extradition of the Templars to the Holy See, the King demanded a guarantee that the Templars would not then go free. The decision of the Faculty of Theology came in after months of discussion. It proved possible to distill from the completed questionnaire the point that in an emergency and as a temporary measure the secular power was justified in arresting heretics without previous authorization by the Church. Thereupon the royal publicists got well and truly into their stride, fresh volleys of scurrilities were discharged against Pope Clement, the Estates General assembled and sonorously called for the extirpation of the Templar Order. The people had spoken — *vox populi, vox dei*. The King carried his divine mandate to the Pope in person.

Arriving at Poitiers, the King knelt to kiss the Pope's foot. The Pope raised him up and kissed him on the lips. All around was the King's great and splendid retinue, his sons, his brothers, the most distinguished of his counselors — and an army. The eminent visitors went into conference with the Curia. The army encircled the town.

The conference lasted some time, although the verbal arguments were doomed to be only a matter of rhetoric, in view of King Philip's strong physical argument, his soldiers.

The standard of rhetoric was high. Nogaret kept in the background, his intimate colleague William de Plaisians spoke for the Crown. He started with a trumpet blast of *"Christus vincit, Christus regnat, Christus imperat!"* (opening words of the coronation anthem) since, he went on to say, in causing the Templars to be unmasked Christ had won a victory unparalleled since the Crucifixion. Thus King Philip had come to Poitiers, not in the role of accuser, but even as an angel of annunciation, to acquaint the Holy Father with the joyful tidings of this, Christ's victory, whereat every living creature on this earth was in transports of gladness. William de Plaisians then reviewed the whole series of events, beginning with the miraculous coincidence that the Grand Master of the Temple and its treasure had happened to be in France at the very moment of unmasking. No less miraculous was the simultaneity of the Templars' confessions, all over France. In conclusion he pointed out (trusting the

Holy Father would not take it amiss) that the Church owed a far greater debt to the King of France than to the Pope. Many of King Philip's royal forebears had shed their blood for the faith, as had also the barons and the people of the realm. Upon the blood of these Kings, these nobles and this people was the Church enthroned. In this glorious kingdom there had been nurtured the study of theology unto the Church's illumination. When now, therefore, King, nobles, prelates and commons of this same kingdom urged speedy settlement of a perfectly simple religious matter, it behoved the Pope to heed them — unless he wanted them to adopt a rather more peremptory tone in future.

Indignantly the Pope replied that the blood upon which the Church had been founded was the blood of Christ, of the Apostles and a multitude of other saints and martyrs, including the Popes of the first four centuries A.D. True, he himself had not as yet had the chance to make a like sacrifice for the Church — so far having merely been elevated to a position of high dignity which, however, was not by any means without its drawbacks. They might take it from him, the pleasure of beautiful vestments, honors and ceremonial were far outweighed by the heavier cares upon his spirit. Nevertheless he was fully prepared to show how dear he held the Church and would gladly suffer a martyr's death for her sake.

Well, well, said William de Plaisians, seeing that Saints Peter and Paul had been permitted to set Jesus right on occasion, one would have thought that His Vicar might stomach a little gentle admonition even from the lowliest of his flock. The Pope ought to realize that the Templars were worse than Saracens and Jews, wherefore it was meritorious to exterminate them.

The Pope returned that even in the flagrant case of Sodom and Gomorrha, the Lord had sent an angel to make exhaustive enquiries under the proper authority before taking final steps.

William de Plaisians answered by reciting, to the Pope's face, all the aspersions on the Pope's character which had been disseminated throughout the kingdom.

Step by step Clement was forced back, on the defensive for his rights, his character and — remembering the fate of Boniface, and the soldiers massed outside — his person. Soon he ended every speech with honeyed references to the disinterested piety of the King of France. The King of France for his part moderated his tone, and by minute haggling over a period of weeks a compromise was reached. Clement agreed in principle to support Charles de Valois' pretensions to the Empire. Philip agreed that in the event the Temple were dissolved its forfeit property should be used exclusively for the next Crusade (most of the liquid assets of the Temple having been absorbed already into the royal exchequer). Clement agreed that the Templars in bulk, though as individuals, should be tried in the episcopal courts and under the supervision of the Inquisitors of all the countries concerned, and Philip agreed that the grand master and other leading officials were to be reserved to the Holy See. It was agreed that the charges against the Temple as a whole should be judged by a special commission, to be appointed by the Pope. This commission should have ample time, its verdict to be delivered at a General Council of the Church in October 1310 — two years hence. Yes, two years appeared an ample term, in which anything might happen. Provisionally Clement agreed also to the trial of Boniface before that same General Council. Philip offered him a Pope for a Pope; the canonization of Boniface's victim, Celestine V, was included in the program.

The French army withdrew, and in further token of mutual goodwill a selected group of seventy-seven Templars was sent to Poitiers for the Pope to interview. Among them were Jacques de Molay and the preceptors of Normandy, Aquitaine and Cyprus, all four personal acquaintances of Pope Clement.

These four men, having made more than three-quarters of the long journey from their Paris prison, were left behind at Chinon, a mere forty miles from Poitiers, on the grounds that poor health prevented them from traveling farther. Either their guards believed them yet too healthy in body and spirit, or else Pope Clement felt unable to face them. The Pope was in poor health himself; when it came to the point, he did not take his opportunity to speak with the seventy-two other Templars either.

He saw them, at a distance, while their confirmatory depositions were read out to an assembly of clergy, lords and commons, over which he presided, and at which the penitents were merely on silent exhibition.

The untrimmed beard was a distinguishing mark of the Templar (so much so that when the rounding-up of Templars began in England, passes had to be issued to harmless citizens with beards). The gaunt, unsavory prisoners, therefore, were not defaced with unshaven stubble lending a corroboratively villainous air to the suspect's visage. But after the terrors and privations of nine desolate months, with all the filth of prison and ill-tended wounds upon them — whether they glowered or cringed at the recital of their crimes, they would not arouse pity so much as disgust. Those other four, whom the Pope had known in their full might and glory — they might perhaps have shaken him in their debasement. But they were out of sight at Chinon.

A delegation of cardinals was sent to see them there, and in the presence of King Philip's officers obtained from them confirmation of nearly all the previous confessions. On making their report, the delegates emphasized the repentance of the prisoners and recommended that their jailers be told to treat them humanely. For all this kindly thought, they played straight into King Philip's hands again, since confessed and repentant heretics who had received the absolution of the Church, might be submitted to temporal judgment without further ado. However, Clement was awake to this and very insistent that nothing must be settled before October 1310, a date to which he clung with a tenacity worthy of a less ancillary object. Yet the exposition of the seventy-seven Templars enabled him to declare to the world that a number of Templars of all categories had personally admitted their guilt before the Holy See, and on this basis he carried out his undertaking to empower the bishops everywhere to try the individual Templars in their dioceses.

Thus it came to pass that the Templars were wholly delivered up to their enemies. The papal commission of enquiry, which alone was to have authority to investigate the order as such, took almost a year to form up, while the episcopal courts started their work at once. The bishops as a class had never loved the Templars. As a class, hitherto they had been antagonistic to the Inquisition, whose powers cut across their own, more and more. Now over the body of the Templars there was the first rapprochement. Especially the bishops of France co-operated sedulously with the erstwhile rival institution, even to the extent of inflicting gratuitous torture on Templars who had already confessed all that was asked of them.

The time lag between summer 1308 and autumn 1309, which was when the papal commission began its work, was no period of grace for the French Templars.

In England, King Edward II had signed the order for the Templars' arrest on December 15, 1307, the day after *Pastoralis preëminentiae* was received. In emulation of Nogaret's methods, the Templars of England were taken at one swoop on January 7, those of Wales, Ireland and Scotland on the 10th.* But the net was not drawn tight, the haul was incomplete. Unpopular as the Templars were, the measure aroused no enthusiasm in the realm. The order was executed as a matter of duty; fanaticism, persecution did not enter into it. Also, in England torture was illegal, and the testimony of outside witnesses, so far from being considered irrelevant, was an integral part of judicial procedure. There was no fixed time limit for collecting evidence; there was no hurry. Eighteen months passed before any serious investigations were begun, by which time many prisoners had somehow regained their freedom. Hardly any were recaptured, in spite of the threat of excommunication for giving aid to fugitive Templars.

The first hearings started in November 1309. Not one of the Templars examined admitted to anything save the rule of secrecy, which was no new disclosure, and in itself no crime. Outside witnesses established nothing but rumors and hearsay, often at fourth and fifth hand. About

---

* Both this King and his father had raided the Temple of London in the past, on two separate occasions. But then they had only carried away large sums of money, having sought admittance under peacable pretexts; and soon after, Crown and Temple had amicably combined in arms against Scotland.

the least grotesque testimony produced was that recruits newly received into the Temple commonly looked pale next morning.

In Aragon, King James made haste so slowly, that by the time he moved to carry out the papal edict, the Templars of his dominions had withdrawn into their two strongest fortresses. Only one group, attempting escape by sea, fell into the hands of the royal officials. For well over a year the rest defied an army continually reinforced by auxiliary levies until, starved out, they surrendered in late spring 1309. The primary examinations lasted until the end of that year, when the examining commission professed itself still unconvinced of the Templars' guilt, a conclusion it was forced to repeat another nine months later. The prisoners remained in protective custody, however.

The Kings of Aragon, Castile and Portugal concluded a pact by which none would allow the Pope to dispose of the Templars' property, should the order be abolished. Yet the King of Portugal distinguished himself from first to last, protecting the Temple from the Inquisition. In Castile the investigations petered out before very long.

In Italy, Sicily and French-controlled Naples many confessions were obtained. But they were anything but uniform and made scant material contribution to the end result.

In Cyprus, where *Pastoralis preëminentiae* was not officially received for several months, information had nevertheless reached the Templars of the island, who as in Aragon were found to have completed all preparations for armed resistance. The governor, being indebted to them for his position, probably tried to work in with both sides. Although eventually he, too, did his duty as a good son of the Church, the Templars' surrender was obtained by negotiation and they were held in relatively light internment.

The situation of the Templars in Germany was roughly analogous to that in the Spanish peninsula. Their power here was balanced by the Teutonic Knights, and most of the nobility had kinsmen attached to both orders. The central authority of the Emperor was not at that time strong enough to co-ordinate the nobles or the prelates, a majority of whom came out boldly in sympathy with the Templars. At their trials in this part of the Empire the Templars appeared fully armed and honorably escorted; on at least one occasion the indictment merely spoke of "terrible charges, with a detailed repetition of which we will not weary this assembly," and invariably the verdict was acquittal.

Matters were not going well for Pope Clement V. Having entered the quagmire of compromise, he was bogged down in it. Whichever foot he put forward, it was a false step he took. Whatever path he tried was to the ultimate detriment of the Papacy. Once he had publicly identified himself with King Philip's attack on the Temple, it was for him a case of heads you win, tails I lose. Exoneration of the Templars must spell defeat for the Holy See as well as for the French Crown, for the Holy See had declared itself satisfied of their guilt and authorized international prosecutions. Abolition of the Temple would be a defeat for the Holy See though victory for the French Crown. Only the Church which had created it could dissolve a religious association; only by dissolving the Temple could the Pope honor his promises to the King of France in whose territory he was caught. It would be the first time that a religious association was dissolved, creating a precedent scarcely less ominous than the trial of Boniface. Even the cardinal question of the Templars' individual or corporate guilt was growing blurred and, as time went on and more and more of the Temple's property disappeared in the hands of the royal officials who were holding it, threatened to become a purely academic one.

Pope Clement, too, was on the rack.

19 The Defense of the Temple

KING PHILIP HAD ACHIEVED RATHER MORE THAN HIS ORIGINAL OBJECT. HE had not merely got the consent of the Holy See to his procedure against the Templars, but their trials were finally instituted under Church auspices.

A papal bull, *Faciens misericordiam,* directed all Templars, individually and collectively, to hold themselves ready to appear before the Inquisitors once more and answer all questions truthfully. They were also informed of the General ·Council which should pronounce judgment in 1310. *Faciens misericordiam* was made available in an unusually large number of copies, that it might reach every prospective "witness" in even the most remote of prisons.

The papal commission which was to report on the order as such was composed of three bishops and three archdeacons, with an archbishop for president. The archbishop was Giles Aiscelin of Narbonne, the whilom Chancellor who had resigned his office in 1307 during King Philip's secret preparations for the mass arrests, which steeped him in the odor of impartiality. The first task the commission set itself was to create a firm representation of the order, to avoid confusion of the issue. An invitation was sent out for all Templars in France wishing to act as defenders of their order to come forward on November 12, 1309.

At first none responded, it was thought because they did not fully understand the new terms of reference and suspected a trap, or because the invitation had not been sufficiently publicized. This having been remedied, six Knights Templars agreed to appear before the commission at Paris, but it soon became clear that they were still under the impression that they had been offered the chance to defend themselves as individuals. On comprehending at last, they asked leave to consult together and then refused, saying that they lacked the ability, the training and the means to serve as advocates. Communication between the Temple leadership and the rank and file was necessarily somewhat impeded, and the latter presumably wanted to observe the last directive of which they were so far aware, to obstruct all endeavors towards a collective indictment.

The next prisoner to have himself taken before the commission was Hugh de Peraud. He no sooner confronted the court than he pleaded to be excused. Asked why, then, he had come, he replied, rather oddly, "Just to have a look at the commission" (*ad videndum eos*). Without any indication as to tone of voice or the niceties of contemporary colloquial usage, one cannot tell whether he had wished to show contempt or to satisfy himself that any hope of succor from that quarter, too, was vain. It is improbable that the balance of his mind was gone, for he still had the wit to ask that he be taken before the Pope — when he might be prepared to make an additional statement — and to display praiseworthy anxiety, not for himself, not for his order, but for the next Crusade. He was returned to his dungeon.

Meanwhile, however, interprison communications had been repaired, and a wave of hope and confidence swept over the Templars; the Holy Father had at long last taken their affairs in hand, and at long last their helpless passivity was ended. Numbers of prisoners forwarded their desire to speak for the defense. The first knight to withdraw his confession appeared, on the same day as the grand master himself, November 26, 1309. He was the Preceptor of Paris, named Ponsard de Gisi, and, testifying that his previous admissions had been extracted by torture, declared himself willing to undertake the defense of the order. On being shown a note he had once addressed to the provost of Poitiers and containing charges of simony and sexual immorality against his order, Ponsard de Gisi explained that he had written this in an access of spite after a quarrel with Hugh de Peraud.

A great change had come over Jacques de Molay, or rather, he showed a return to all the haughty dignity associated with the Grand Master of the Temple. He did more than retract his previous confessions.

"I challenge your jurisdiction over the Order of the Temple," he told the commissioners. "As it is under the sole authority of the Pope, he alone can be its judge. . . . The Emperor Frederick, charged with great crimes against the Church, was allowed plentiful time to prepare his defense, and judgment on him was suspended for thirty-two years. . . . I have neither the knowledge nor the ability adequately to present a defense, yet I shall do my best. . . . I should be acting the part of coward and ingrate, were I to abandon the cause of my noble Order. I realize the difficulties which face me. I realize how helpless I am — a man who is the prisoner of Pope and King and who has no more than a single shilling to his name. Let me be given aid and counsel enabling me to meet the charges. It is not only the Templars who will show the falsity of the accusations, but the kings, the princes, the prelates, the dukes, the counts and barons of the world will testify in its favor. . . . I shall be glad to assist in the examination and depositions of kings, princes, prelates, dukes, counts, barons and clergy, and all honest men. . . ."

One cannot say what the commission might have expected. However, it appears they were much taken aback, and there was great commotion among the officers of the Crown who crowded the courtroom (ostensibly to protect the papal commission against the *truculence* of the prisoners!). When this subsided, the grand master was sternly bidden to reconsider his offer: could it be that he did not fully remember the grave nature of those confessions he wished to recant? If so, perhaps he would like to have his memory refreshed. (This was deliberate intimidation, unlawful and irrelevant since the commission had no power to deal with individuals and since defenders had been called for, threatening the grand master with the classification of relapsed heretic and candidate for the stake.)

The records were read back to him, and only now did Jacques de Molay realize just what he was up against. Remarks he might have made at different times, in different contexts, had been strung together, elaborate statements had been condensed and shorn of qualifying clauses, so that, unable to disclaim them roundly, he could only rage at their misleading import. He cried out aloud: though the rulers of the Church might deem themselves safe from the wrath of man, let them beware of the wrath of God! Had the like of this been done to him by lay men, his sword should make answer. O that it were the custom in this land, as it was the custom among Saracens and Tartars, to cut off the heads of perjurers!

The commission contented itself with urging him once more to reconsider his *recantation* and ponder the statutory fate of relapsed heretics. De Molay became confused. The Grand Inquisitor suggested that they two talk things over in another room. De Molay accepted, and on his return asked the court for an adjournment, which was granted.

When two days later he appeared again at the tribunal, he thanked the commissioners for having saved him from acting rashly. He would now like to withdraw his hasty offer to defend his order. On further consideration, too, he would not now retract his previous confessions entirely, but merely attempt to extenuate them somewhat. He would ask everyone to bear in mind that no order had done more to beautify its churches or held more splendid services there than the Temple in its time; no other Order had equaled the Temple's generosity in almsgiving and none had done greater service to the Holy Land. In reply the commission pointed out that merit could not avail where the foundations of orthodoxy were lacking; and the witness replied hastily, true, true, and he for his part always had adhered most firmly to the Creed of the Holy Catholic Church of Rome. In that connection, might he ask to be allowed to hear mass again and partake of the sacrament? The commissioners said they would see what they could do. Thereafter at all interrogations to which he was submitted Jacques de Molay maintained his refusal to defend the order, unless it be before the Pope himself.

There was a halt in the onrush of defenders. The other prisoners must have thought that their chief had returned to the notion of blocking the trial by refusing to recognize it — for a short time everybody declined to defend the order without express authority from their grand master. This was not forthcoming, but neither was there any contrary guidance. The grand master relapsed into inactivity and nothing at all was heard from him.

Whether inspired by terror or miscalculation, deliberately silent or held incommunicado, the leadership had broken down. Templar knighthood at large rose to the occasion.

After two and a half years in the unspeakable jails of their time, where fetid night reigned twenty-four hours of the day; starved with cold and hunger, rotting in perpetual damp and foulness, chafed and ulcerated from the load of iron chains, robbed of their accustomed uniforms, crippled and debased by torture — the old warriors regained their old élan at the chance of battle. They had the whole winter to work themselves up to it, for the tribunal suspended sessions until February, 1310.

Between February 14 and March 28 five hundred and forty-six prisoners out of six hundred and fifty in central Paris offered to defend their order, and in a matter of days the number rose to seven hundred. They were brought together in the garden of the Bishop of Paris. In such fettle were they that, although told merely to signify their willingness or otherwise to stick by their offer, many could not so contain themselves and raised a great uproar. Never, they shouted when the charges were detailed once more — never would they countenance such revolting and unfounded lies. They would fight for their order to the death. They regretted nothing and had nothing to regret save the falsehoods they themselves had uttered under pressure of the Inquisition and King Philip's henchmen — and they did not mind who heard them, for they built their trust in God, Pope, Holy Church and justice.

They did not prove so trusting, however, when asked to choose their spokesmen. It took much persuasion and deliberation before a part of them agreed on six men to represent them, three priests and three knights. The names of the knights were William de Charbonnet, Bertrand de Sartiges and Robert Viguiers. The priests were Peter de Boulogne, Reynald de Pruino and Matthew de Clichy; the King might have been glad to count them among his lawyers and own them among his new chivalry, for their alert intelligence and amazing valor. The intellectuals, the "learned men," denounced in the past for their corrupting influence, and without whose rallying influence in the last few months of waiting the spirit of resistance might well have flagged again — the men whom their unlettered grand master had put down, showed their worth.

The six in turn chose Peter de Boulogne as their foreman. He went into action immediately, with the vigor of a free man in prime condition. He began by stating once more that the Templars' willingness to plead did not mean that they acknowledged the jurisdiction of any body other than the Curia. Once more and in the name of all his brethren he declared the accusations untrue and unbelievable by any sane person. He then proceeded to put forward their demands. He demanded the release of all Templars from the power of the royal officers who, he said, were doing their best to suppress all genuine evidence and to render effective defense impossible. For effective defense money, writing materials and the like were required; he demanded a grant from Temple property. He demanded that all former Templars, who had left the order and testified against it, be arrested and interrogated in his presence before the papal commission. He asked that the last religious confessions previous to any admissions of guilt, of Templars deceased in the course of interrogation, be presented in evidence. He asked that all lay men be henceforth excluded from the court, where they had no business other than to intimidate witnesses. He asked for an increase of prisoners' maintenance allowances. He presented a memoir affirming the purity and the great merits of the order and describing its treatment at the hands of the royal seneschals and the Inquisition, which he asked to have sent on to the Pope.

His real gains were small — two promises and one assurance: his memoir should be sent, the jailers were to be instructed to be more gentle with the prisoners, and witnesses need not fear to testify.

The trial proper began on April 11, and without pause the defense protested, objected, demanded, argued: evidence obtained previously by the Inquisition, and all confessions extracted by torture, should be ruled inadmissible; no further publicity prejudicing prospective witnesses should be given to the present hearings, also, witnesses who had already testified and others yet to be heard should be segregated; the defense should be provided with a list of the witnesses, and so on, irrepressibly. On nearly every point Peter was overruled, but that did not stop him.

He had offered to prove the use of torture, bribery and forged letters * by the prosecution, and was able to make good at least a part of his promise — that pertaining to torture. Witness after witness gave the most frightful details, and the visible evidence of their bodies was not lacking. The details are available elsewhere and I will not go into them. As one Templar, Vincent de Villers, later shrieked in anguish, had he been called upon to swear that he had personally slain the Saviour, he would have confessed to that too. We can believe him.

It seems the papal commissioners also were not unimpressed. The prosecution was not doing very well, even though the defense had

* Jacques de Molay's early circular letter?

no right to cross-examine witnesses. A lot of hearsay was produced and much that was inconclusive, even manifestly dubious. Someone had once known a man who became a Templar and spoke of "terrible things that went on in the order." Someone else had once heard the prior of Laon hint at an awful secret within the Temple which he dared not reveal. Yet another outsider, who, however, at least had an uncle who had once been a Templar, remembered a similar story about the prior of Laon. Several former Templars testified; they had abjured their errors, cut off their beards and appeared in secular dress. According to one, it was common practice to tie a crucifix to one's stirrup so as to spurn the sacred emblem with the foot. According to another, crosses were often sewn to the seat of the trousers. The idol allegedly adored at the Temple proved a frequent stumbling block: it was "a friend of God" who conversed with the Deity whenever it wished; * it was the embalmed head of Hugh de Payens, or of the demon "Baphomet." † Descriptions, as already noted, were widely divergent; it is the more surprising that a former serving brother who affirmed every one of the charges, including that of idolatry, was unable to describe the head *at all*. Many others got around that difficulty, stating that they had heard about it but had never personally set eyes on the head.

It appeared that often a novice had been on the point of obeying the command to spit on the cross, when there had come some sudden intervention and he was hustled away. Some deposed that they had understood the renunciation of Christ to be symbolic of St. Peter's denial of his Master, some thought it an efficiency test, as it were — those who refused were sent overseas ahead of those who had done as they were told — not in punishment, but because they had shown that the Saracens would be unable to shake their faith.

There is one query obstinately nagging the onlooker after the event, to which at the time little or no attention was given. If for a half-

* The Bogomils called themselves the Friends of God.

† Clearly a corruption of "Mahomet," which appears so in several medieval poems as the name of The Prophet of Islam.

century or longer the Temple had carried on its infamous transactions unchecked, there *must* have been others, outsiders, implicated by default, constant accessories to the persistent crime. In that connection the most interesting story is told by a Templar of Carcassonne. He testified that he had been received into the order under observance of all the reprehensible ceremonies; he had then been immediately sent to the East, where he had remained until the fall of Acre. As early as 1280, however, he had relieved his conscience in confession to the Augustinian hermit Julian. The hermit at first refused to believe what he was told, saying repeatedly that it was impossible. When at length he was convinced, he imposed a fasting penance on the Templar, which the latter declined since undue fasting was forbidden in the order and would attract notice. The hermit took the penitent's point and suggested that wearing an iron girdle under his tunic might be better. The Templar bore it for four years, and in 1284 he confessed again, this time to the Patriarch of Jerusalem. The Patriarch wept bitter tears, gave him absolution purposely framed in general terms, told him to fast on bread and water every Saturday of his life, and to bear his cross and loyally guard the interests of the Holy Land. There the matter ended.

The penances strike one as absurdly light — quite apart from the friendly discussions as to suitable forms of mortification and the lachrymose acceptance of the Patriarch. And that is the least of it. The secrecy of the confessional could not excuse the priest from doing something about revelations of this order; and there were ways which would not involve him in violation of his trust — such as making arrangements for the penitent to repeat his confessions before a higher authority. In fact it is doubtful whether anyone but the Supreme Pontiff would have power to give absolution in a case like that. Remembering Clement IV's strictures on the Templars for evil practices "best unnamed," one is forced to wonder whether the Papacy had not in truth received some such information. If so, a mere warning would seem a feeble countermeasure indeed. In any event, there are only two accounts altogether of worried Templars seeking outside spiritual advice.

There are stories of the thriller type, a good example being that of a renegade knight who said he had fled the order for its abominations and recounted sundry hair-breadth escapes from subsequent recapture and assassination; his own father had made common cause with the Temple and had tried to return him to the brotherhood by force.

A variety of opinion was submitted as to how and when the abominations had been first introduced into the Temple. The Grand Masters Thomas Bérard (1256–1272) and William de Beaujeu (1272–1291), the much maligned, were respectively accused of it, also a Grand Master Roncellinus, said to have been released from Moslem captivity against a promise to impose these vile customs on his brethren. The particular tenuity of this version apart, there never was a Grand Master Roncellinus, nor is there any trace of any other Templar of that name. The name Roscellinus, that of a minor functionary, occurs in a twelfth-century document of the London Temple — too early to fit the charge, which was generally placed a hundred years later. Above all, none of this was evidence, for all that it might have been effective in fortifying prejudice.

Only one category of circumstantial inference bears a perplexing likeness to the stamp of truth, a homespun trivial sort of truth mirroring common human experience, from which it is as hard to escape as it is hard to be convinced by the greater farrago. Templars who told of their horror at the conditions of their reception were asked why, then, they had gone through with it. The reply was that they had been ashamed to back out, having said good-by to family and friends, with a grand send-off advertising their envied future avocation, newly fitted out from head to foot, and all the rest. Who does not know of incompatible marriages completed under the same stress? Again, however, this could hardly be cited as conclusive evidence, even with the best will in the world to convict.

The papal commission, it must be admitted, was determined to make up its own mind and to hear every single witness. The witnesses for the defense began to appear. The recantations multiplied, the accounts of frightful tortures came thick and fast; and still there were hundreds of prospective defenders. It became clear that the General Council would have to be postponed for a year; soon even 1311 appeared as an overoptimistic deadline. Optimism, for that matter, grew daily upon the defenders as those who had already given evidence returned to hearten those still waiting their turn. The Crown had reason to be disquieted.

Two and a half years had gone by. Two and a half years, without anything positive happening, was too long to keep popular feeling at the requisite pitch. Tales of the tortures endured by the Templars and of their magnificent resilience were spreading over the country, and sympathy for them was steadily growing. The mob, which could be so useful under skillful manipulation, had shown itself capable before now of taking the bit between its teeth. Not so very long ago, it had driven the King himself before it; and that he had found asylum at the Temple, which he had been persecuting ever since, did not in the present circumstances endear him to a people which had plentiful grievances of its own — given latitude for recollection.

The diocesan bishops of France, having visited their malice on the Templar prisoners in their power, had put themselves into the same position as the King. They could not afford to have the order vindicated and the prisoners released. But an international order could not be condemned unless it was shown that the crimes of which it stood accused had been practiced internationally. Too little progress had been made outside France.

From all sides pressure on the Pope was reapplied — a whole engine of interlinked and cumulative pressures.

Whatever one's opinion of Clement V and his conduct, he had not been entirely idle, he did not merely drift. His weaknesses — of character, physique and situation — made delaying tactics the only kind he could employ, and employ them he did. Failing a truly granite backing by the rock of St. Peter, time was the Templars' best ally, and it was due to Clement's systematic shilly-shallying that they got it.

The French Crown saw it was high time to raise the question of

Boniface again. The dilatoriness of the papal commission in the matter of the Templars need not affect the trial of the dead Pope, the King's ministers argued. Philip and Nogaret paid another visit to the Curia. To keep the prelates on their toes meantime, another bishop had come in for the same treatment as first meted out to Saisset of Pamiers. Bishop Guichard of Troyes had been placed under arrest and indicted for witchcraft, also for having caused the death of the late Queen Jeanne by (long-distance) poisoning. The person who had acted as informer for the Crown was the Florentine Noffo Deghi, one-time accomplice of Esquiu de Florian.

The threatened swing in popular sympathy pressed on the King, the King pressed on the Pope and on the Gallican bishops whose pressure was thrown likewise upon their Supreme Pontiff. There was nowhere for Clement to turn, nothing to stay him and no way out — excepting the way of martyrdom, to be sure. Had Clement been of the stuff of martyrs, he would have challenged martyrdom long before the situation became such that martyrdom was the only step left to him, morally justifiable and aesthetically pleasing. Clement was no longer master of his soul, his will, his actions. He stumbled whither he was pushed; he did what he must do.

He wrote around frantically to the rulers of those Christian countries where the investigations had so far borne no fruit at all, accusing them of shirking their duty and demanding greater rigor. His timing was not in his hands, either; his injunctions for more efficient torture were dated the day before Christmas. In particular the King of England, as well as the English clergy, came in for a severe attack on their stubborn adherence to the prohibition of torture under English law.

King Edward's position was then somewhat vulnerable. One point on which he had obeyed papal instructions to the letter was the confiscation of Temple property. He had confiscated everything and refused to surrender any particle to the Church, saying he himself knew how to deal with the Templars' riches in the manner most acceptable to God. At length, compelled to hand over what was not his, he could no longer lay his hands on and restore the whole, and he gave in on the subject of torture. In this way, by the injunction of Pope Clement V, at Christmas, 1310, this method of interrogation became legalized in England. Even so, it was as yet distasteful. Torturers had to be imported from the Continent, and their scope was limited by the King's proviso that there were to be no mutilations, no incurable wounds and no violent hemorrhages.

Upon the whole, the upshot was as disappointing as before. All that the English tribunals ever established was the rule of secrecy, the fact that Templars were supposed to make confession only to their own priests, the *probable* practice of lay absolution, and the wearing of a mysterious cord which, however, corresponded to the "belt of Nazareth," defining the "zones of chastity," as recommended by St. Bernard.

So much for England.

In Cyprus, the pro-Templar governor had recently died by assassination, and the exiled King returned, eager to assist in the suppression of the order which had been instrumental in deposing him. Nevertheless the Templars were acquitted. Cyprus being still the order's official headquarters, this was awkward, and the Pope ordered a retrial. The records of the retrial were lost, and so the final verdict is unknown.

In Aragon, the renewed investigations were more successful; in the Papal States of Italy and French-controlled Sicily, Naples and Flanders the result left little to be desired. But the aggregate number of Templars examined in these places, and consequently the proportion of confessions, were greatly inferior to those in France. The main weight of evidence and the burden of proof remained the lot of the French Crown.

20 The Trials

THE YEAR 1311 BROUGHT A SUDDEN ACCELERATION ON ALL FRONTS. PHILIP'S comparative patience was at an end. The royal publicists took up their pens again and inundated the kingdom with another flood of pamphlets against the Pope. The air was thick with charges of bribery, forgery, intimidation and unlawful torture sent up by the Templar defense against the Crown; the ministers of the Crown, adept at turning any available material to account, made brilliant diversionary use of those specific accusations by fastening them on Clement. They now described him as a kind of master secret agent of heresy. All his procrastination stood revealed for what it was. He had paid some of the witnesses against the arch-heretic Boniface to disappear, had tortured and murdered those whom he found incorruptible, and even now was working further to postpone the promised trial in the hope that any witnesses he had been unable to secure would die of old age before they were called. Clement and Boniface, indeed, were birds of a feather: it was very doubtful whether Clement for his part had attained the tiara by legitimate means, and had he not developed simony from a fine art into common custom?

Clement threw in his hand. He agreed to hold the enquiry on Boniface, immediately: but it should be conducted, not by a General Council (with a probable majority of prelates under French domination), but by a curial committee. Philip in his turn agreed. Nogaret accommodatingly showed that to pass sentence on Boniface no General Council would be needed — since Boniface was dead and therefore not now head of the Church.

The enquiry started in March, 1311, at Avignon, with Nogaret and William de Plaisians acting for the prosecution. Before leaving Paris, Nogaret made his will, a thing he had not previously troubled to do in the face of longer and more dangerous journeys. He wished to be buried at the Dominican church of Paris or, should he die "elsewhere," at Nîmes (close to Avignon). But any premonitions he might have had were erroneous.

At first, the proceedings were slow to move. Prosecution and defense were both in the hands of professionals, civil and canon lawyers, and the preliminaries were drawn out by learned bickering. The defense objected to King Philip's representatives as men who had been personally active against the deceased Pope and one of whom, moreover, was under the ban. The prosecution objected to the composition of the tribunal because several of the chosen cardinals were reputedly biased against France. Nogaret for the first time submitted a *request* for absolution plus recognition that he had acted in good faith at Agnani; the defense was quick to side-step what would be tantamount to condemnation of Boniface. After that the quibbling took a turn for the more esoteric, and Pope Clement in the chair contributed his mite of obstruction, variously in the shape of headaches, stomach aches, nose-bleeding and the like. But this could not go on forever. At length the witnesses were called.

The prosecution presented its case with the adroitness born of ample practice. There were witnesses for every aspect of the charges, and they never contradicted each other. Their information was exact in the smallest details, down to the extraction of blood from a black cock Boniface was alleged to have used for necromantic purposes. They were word-perfect in his blasphemous sayings: such as that the Virgin Mary was no more a virgin than his own mother and that he himself was mightier than Christ, for he could raise poor men to wealth and power and cast down princes, whereas Christ had lived lowly and despised; and that life after death was a myth, useful enough for keeping the unlearned people in subjection, but otherwise a matter of contempt to any educated man.

There are two significant features about these depositions. One, whether or no the allegations were correct, the fact that such dicta had evident currency shows how much religious belief had deteriorated. Two, although some of the witnesses for the defense complained of having been put to the torture, not one of the many whom the French lawyers produced, did so. Whatever the truth, we see which side commanded the most support, or which inspired the healthier respect.

The trial was going ill for Boniface. Then all at once it stopped.

Nobody knows what happened. We are up against another impenetrable veil. The likeliest explanation which has been suggested is that Clement, in mortal terror at the way matters were shaping, had yielded to the last turn of the screw and given Philip the desired guarantee that the Temple should be destroyed.

The trial of Boniface was wound up hastily and in a manner giving satisfaction all around. The tribunal found that Boniface had been lawfully elected Pope, that his memory stood unsmirched, and that the King of France, his enemy and accuser, was a decent fellow too, his good faith incontestable. What might have been the one flaw in the arrangement was merely a face-saving device: the ban on Nogaret was only conditionally withdrawn. Nogaret was ordered to go on (the next) Crusade, not later than 1314, and if not he, his descendants should fulfill his vow for him, else his excommunication would stand after all. Pending his pilgrimage, the ringleader of Agnani was readmitted to the community of Christians. He returned to Paris and to his activities as Chancellor of the realm.

Some little time before, the Archbishopric of Sens had fallen vacant. The King desired it to go to the Bishop of Cambrai, brother of Enguerrand de Marigny, the Crown's present superintendent of finances. The reputation of this prelate was not of the best, and Pope Clement had been resisting the appointment because, as he tactfully put it, the candidate was too young — only twenty-two years old. All opposition was now set aside, and the gay young spark of an ecclesiastic took up his high office in the month of April.

The lurking, quintessential importance of this appointment was that one of the suffragans of Sens was the Bishop of Paris. Thus the newly invested archbishop had control of the diocese of Paris, where the papal commission of enquiry into *Factum Templarorium* had its seat. The ultimate significance of the commission was that sentence could not be passed, whether on the order or its individual members, until the commission had announced its verdict. But this had never been explicitly laid down; it had been taken for granted — a loophole on which the royal ministers had hit at last.

While the commission continued its sessions, while aspiring defenders of the Temple continued to send in petitions and declarations and their elected advocates continued the valiant quick-fire of objec-

tions and demands, while there was yet no end in sight to the long
file of witnesses, the new primate, hand in glove with the Crown,
convoked his own archepiscopal council. As if the papal commission
did not exist, the business before the Council of Sens was to decide the
guilt of the Templars examined in the ecclesiastical courts of the see,
*and especially the guilt of those who had since come forward as de-
fenders of the order.* The summons was for Monday, May 11, and,
if not secret, it was kept fairly quiet. Technically there was no necessity to inform anyone not a member of the council. The papal commission got no word of it, but somehow the news reached the Templars,
though not until the eleventh hour, that is, May 10, which was Sunday.

The papal commission did not sit on Sundays. But the defense committee set up sufficient clamor to obtain speech with some commissioners and persuaded them to hold an extraordinary session. The
commission agreed and assembled hurriedly, with two of its members
missing, the presiding Archbishop of Narbonne and the Bishop of
Trent, who sent word that they had had to go and say mass.

The protest drawn up in haste by the defense was lengthy and involved, but did not lack telling thrusts. Peter de Boulogne read it
out. Not only was the action of the Archbishop of Sens unjust and
illegal, but, the defense shrewdly submitted, it was also an attack on
the authority of the papal commission itself. If permitted to succeed,
this would pull the ground entirely from under the commission. The
commission had to have time to digest this. The defenders were
marched back to their prison, while the commissioners conferred. After
some hours they gave their answer.

"We are deeply grieved for you," they told the Templars, "but, having no jurisdiction over the Archbishop of Sens, and since provincial
councils have been operating under papal sanction, we fear·that we
are powerless to intervene."

The King's advisers had finally found a way of profiting from that
very distinction between individual and corporate offenses, which the
Templars and the Pope had labored to maintain at all costs.

Next morning, Monday, the commission met as usual. In the middle of the hearings, the session was interrupted by a message from the Archbishop of Sens, announcing the decision of his council, already. The Pope had long ago decreed that Templars who had been previously questioned by the Inquisition need not be examined again (as to their individual guilt) by the episcopal courts. As we have seen, the bishops had been ignoring this clause; but on it the Council of Sens based its verdict.

According to that, the Templars fell into four categories:

1. Those who had confessed to lesser offenses — these were to be released once they had done penance;

2. Those who had confessed to more serious crimes — these were to be kept imprisoned for varying stretches of time;

3. Those who had made no admissions — so there must have been some such, though the records are otherwise silent about them — and who were sentenced to perpetual imprisonment;

4. Those who had retracted their confessions — relapsed heretics, to be handed over to the temporal arm and put to death.

By this division, the professed defenders of the Temple fell into the fourth category. To make a start, fifty-four of them should be handed over to the royal officers immediately.

The papal commission protested; it even availed itself of some of Peter de Boulogne's arguments. The Archbishop of Sens replied, unruffled, that nothing could be farther from his intentions than to interfere with the work of the commission — which good work should most certainly go on. His own work was quite unconnected with it. He was not dealing, as was the commission, with the order as a whole, but merely with the persons of individual Templars, and he had no alternative but to consign recanting and impenitent heretics to the flames.

The commission was paralyzed. The royal officers seized the fifty-four Templars allocated to them and set up fifty-four stakes by the Porte de Saint Antoine, that same day.

That same day, the fifty-four Templars were taken to the place of execution, in tumbrils which were the most dishonorable mode of conveyance for a knight, though their white mantles had been restored to them for the occasion. Friends and relatives of theirs were brought along to join in a last attempt at persuading them to swear to the heresies of the Temple and thus save their lives. None of the fifty-four made use of the offer. Their white mantles with the eight-pointed red cross were torn off them, they were bound to their stakes and the fires lit. A great multitude stood watching, among them other Templar prisoners under guard. The fifty-four lifted up their voices and proclaimed their innocence and the glory and purity of their order, over and over, until the noise of conflagration drowned all other sound.

As a public demonstration, the burnings were not an unqualified success. In France the processes of the Inquisition were not, and would never become, festive popular entertainments on a scale such as they attained in Spain. They struck the hearts of men with terror right enough, but pity is close kin to terror. Dislike of the Templars wavered under the sheer numerical weight of fifty-four simultaneous victims, and dissolved in admiration of their fortitude. Many in the crowd of spectators had seen the crosses worn by some of the burned Templars shine imperishably with a strange light not of fire. The executioners raked the ashes and cast what was left into the Seine, but before long charred fragments of one sort and another turned up in the possession of humble relic-hunters. Doubtless there were still people who unreservedly applauded the wretched end of knights not long ago so insolent and rich; yet they, too, could hardly escape the lesson that no one was safe, no one at all, under King Philip.

As a means of intimidating the defenders of the Temple, the executions succeeded fully. The defense collapsed.

Not Peter de Boulogne, not Reynald de Pruino — who stood up in court the next day, and the next, denouncing the burnings as illegal, making protest after protest just as ever, level-headed, indomitable, letting no conceivable advantage slip. But every single day Templars, literally by the score, in fear and tears and trembling, gave notice that they wished to withdraw from the defense of the order. Soon the representatives who were left would represent none but their own four selves. Yet, strangely, those who were in fact taken to the stake — and they presently numbered a hundred and twenty in all — met their agonizing death with unfailing courage. Out of a hundred and twenty-two, only two retracted their recantations at the last moment and swore as desired that the order was guilty of every crime.

Powerless as they were to avert the fate of their brethren, the two most eloquent advocates of the defense still had power to irritate. The papal commission received an order from the Archbishop of Sens to hand over Reynald de Pruino for examination by the council. This could not be allowed to pass without a murmur, since, as Peter de Boulogne had foretold would be the case, such an order completely ignored the right and functions of the commission, rendering its status farcical, and violated the legal assurance of immunity under which the spokesmen for the defense had performed their task. Like the defense, the commission protested, and appealed to the Curia. The Curia preserved unbroken silence, while the Archbishop of Sens asserted himself with all the resonance of one who knew the whole armed might of the secular power was behind him.

Fear fell upon the commissioners themselves. At the next session no prisoners appeared and only three commissioners. Then Reynald de Pruino and Peter de Boulogne, both, were given up to the Council of Sens. William de Charbonnet and Bertrand de Sartiges asked to be allowed to desist from the defense — the remaining two, Robert Viguiers and Matthew de Clichy, had faded into the background some time since — and so there was no one left to conduct it.

The commission was adjourned.

The Council of Sens, however, continued briskly. The prisoners were now in such a state of terror, so anxious not to depart from their earlier confessions and share the fate of the hundred and twenty martyrs, that many prefaced their statements before this tribunal with an advance disclaimer of any error in recital they might unwittingly commit.

The proceedings of the papal commission were formally closed in May. The minutes were worked up in concise form, attested, and deposited in the treasury of Notre Dame of Paris. The original records remained the property of the commissioners, who signed and sealed them, every one. Their official verdict was that on the whole the charges of the indictment were not proven, although undoubtedly some nefarious practices had been carried on in the Temple, which certainly ought not to go unpunished.

On October 1, 1311 the Ecumenical Council, which to Pope Clement had once seemed so far off, and which King Philip at one time had almost despaired of, met at the small town of Vienne on the eastern bank of the River Rhône, a few miles south of Lyons. Vienne was packed to overflowing. In addition to the papal court, there were over three hundred high dignitaries of the Church with their retinues, droves of monks and friars, the entire households of visiting nobles, and the living newspapers of the day, jongleurs and trouvères. Prices rose steeply, and the harvest stocks of the countryside sank with alarming rapidity.

On the agenda were: (1) The next Crusade, (2) sundry minor Church reforms, (3) *Factum Templarorium*.

Items 1 and 2 received only cursory attention. Interest was concentrated on the fate of the Temple and the destiny of its wealth. Until these were settled, nothing else could be decided with any finality.

Pope Clement V assumed the role of prosecutor — in its way a not altogether disagreeable change for him. He delivered a major oration on the iniquities of the order, concerning which he was in possession of such overwhelming proof, including confessions by two thousand Templars as well as numerous outside testimony, that no further investigation was needed to abolish it.

But now he was given another taste of what a weakened Papacy had to swallow. He was dealing with the ecclesiastics of Christendom in its entirety, not merely with the friends of France, whose strength was not as expected. Only the three French archbishops, one Italian bishop and a few cardinals declared themselves satisfied — Clement himself estimates the opposition at five or even six to one. The opposition would not agree to the condemnation of the Templars without first hearing their defense. The Pope replied, more than a little disingenuously, that defenders had been invited, but that none had come forward. Unmoved, the General Council asked that the invitation be repeated now, and repeated it was.

The response was sensational. Seven Knights Templars rode into Vienne — Knights Templars in uniform, unshackled and unescorted, like apparitions of the past. They told the council that they were the representatives of between fifteen hundred and two thousand Templars who had escaped arrest and gone underground in the hills about Lyons — the French Crown had only recently acquired control of this province, where covert hostilities against the central authority had not yet died down. The seven had been charged to convey the earnest desire of their brethren to attend the council and defend their order.

The Pope was thunderstruck. What to do? What he did was to double his bodyguard, giving out that he had sure intelligence of a contemplated raid upon his person by the Templar Resistance, and to have these seven representatives of it placed under arrest. The council voiced disapproval, strongly, and the seven knights were freed. Not being submitted to immediate public examination as desired, they prudently took themselves off while they might. For simultaneously with their release the Pope had adjourned the council — until April 3, 1312, nearly six months hence.

Time was no longer on the side of the Templars, but the ally of their enemies.

For most of the council members and attendants traveling home and back again next spring was out of the question. The extreme overcrowding of Vienne was unallayed through the winter months. The visitors complained of tedium, cold and damp, primitive living conditions and rheumatism; the native population was on the verge of famine. They were none of them much better off than prisoners, themselves. Principles began to sag, justice to appear secondary to a speedy end.

About the middle of March, 1312, the small provincial town became an even more uncomfortable place to stay in, by the arrival of King Philip the Fair with his three sons, his brother Charles of Valois, several of his most distinguished advisers, and the usual stately train befitting such a company, meaning an army. It looked much like a repetition of the Poitiers conference of 1308 — except in that the consistory meeting which the King had caused the Pope to call was not public, but a very private one. The cardinals forming the main body of it were summoned under observance of every precaution of secrecy. The Pope presided, the King sat next to him on a throne only slightly lower. *In camera,* under the eye of the King, by apostolic provision, the Order of the Temple was abolished there and then, on March 22, twelve days before the General Council reassembled. The end would be more speedy than any one had dreamt.

April 3 came, the public session opened — the French military still surrounding the town — and the council was presented with the accomplished fact. The bull *Vox in excelso* proclaimed the dissolution of the Temple to the world.

The General Council took it quietly, which was more than Clement had dared hope, for he had prepared a ponderous speech of justification. He would be candid, he said, and admit that the evidence obtained against the Templars was insufficient for canonical condemnation. However, he, the Holy Father and High Pontiff, himself was absolutely convinced of the order's guilt. That should be enough. Even were it not, the Templars had been so discredited by the events of the last three years that their moral standing in the world was nil. It was impossible that they should now play a leading part in the next Crusade. Their usefulness was over. Furthermore, by agreement with the King of France, their property had been assigned to the Holy Land, but could not be made available so long as their fate hung in suspense.

There were no questions. There was no discussion. The concluding argument was in every sense unanswerable. No one would disagree that the cause of the Holy Land was always paramount; no one could be under any delusion that the Temple's wealth was still intact. Restitution might be decreed, but was genuinely beyond any power on earth to encompass. To avoid any appearance of robbery, the bull *Ad providam Christi vicarii* of May 2 awarded the property of the defunct Temple to its brother Order of the Hospital, with the exception of property situated in the Spanish peninsula.

That was the end.

But no, it was not yet the end. The Order of the Temple had ceased to exist; not so the Templars in their prisons scattered all over Europe. Also, the proceedings against the order having gone on for so long and having attracted international attention, a spectacular last act must be staged in dramatic finis. The text must needs be illustrated.

Decision as to what was to be done with the individual Templars was left to the appropriate archepiscopal councils. An exception was made of the following four dignitaries: the Grand Master Jacques de Molay, the Preceptor of Normandy, Geoffrey de Charnay, the Visitor of France and former Treasurer, Hugh de Peraud, and the Preceptor of Poitou and Aquitaine, Geoffrey de Gonaville. In reserving these for his own judgment the Pope had never wavered — and he continued unwavering also in avoiding to meet them face to face.

At regular intervals Jacques de Molay made petition for an interview, always in vain. Indeed, he must have got on famously with the Pope when last they had met in 1307, they must have harmonized too well for Clement to bear the sight of him afterwards. The Pope was often ill. The Pope was always ill at the crucial dates. Twenty months went by before the Pope so much as brought himself to appoint a commission of three cardinals who, in the unavoidable absence of the Pope through illness, were to examine the chiefs of the former order and pass sentence on them.

Most of the Templars who had confessed, maintained their confessions and abjured their calling, had been set at liberty. Some, even, had been granted subsistence allowances from the former estate of the order. The chiefs could anticipate no less. Jacques de Molay, Geoffrey de Charnay, Hugh de Peraud and Geoffrey de Gonaville repeated their original admissions of guilt before the three cardinals, declared themselves repentant of any subsequent recantations and craved pardon. The commission of three pronounced them reconciled to the Church, and sentenced them to life imprisonment. Clement need never set eyes on them again. If not dead, they would be buried.

Only once more should they appear in the light of day.

On March 18, 1314, six and a half years after that night of mass arrests, the people of Paris were called together outside Notre Dame to witness the last act. A wooden platform had been erected, together with grandstands to seat the nobles and ecclesiastics; the commonalty thronged the open space, and soldiers of the King hemmed it in.

When everybody was in place, the tumbrils were brought on, containing the Templar chiefs, four scarecrows loaded with chains, jolting over the cobbles. One by one the four were assisted from the carts and made to climb on to the platform. There they stood while first their confessions were read out and then the judgment. This being done, they were asked themselves to affirm their guilt and penitence before the people.

Two of them, Hugh de Peraud and Geoffrey de Gonaville, listened quietly with bowed heads. But the grand master straightened with a jangle of chains and raised his fettered arms, and his voice rang out of turn, trained to carry in battle, hailing the shades of thousands of Knights Templars who had died in battle for the Cross.

This was his speech:

It is only right that at so solemn a moment and when my life has so little time to run, I should reveal the deception which has been practiced and speak up for the truth. Hear me: before Heaven and earth and all of you for my witnesses, I confess. I confess that I am indeed guilty of the greatest infamy. But the infamy is that I have lied. I have lied in admitting the disgusting charges laid against my Order. I declare, and I must declare that the Order is innocent. Its purity and saintliness have never been defiled. In truth, I had testified otherwise, but I did so from fear of terrible tortures. Other Knights who retracted their confessions have been led to the stake, I know. Yet the thought of dying is not so awful that I would now uphold my confession to foul crimes which were never committed. Life is offered me, but at the price of perfidy. At such a price life is not worth having. If life is to be bought only by piling lie upon lie, I do not grieve that I must lose it.

Geoffrey de Charnay joined him and with great passion spoke in similar vein.

The audience had got its spectacle, though not as planned. The spectacle of courage in supreme adversity, which never fails to wring blood even from the stone, which sends a chill of poetry through even the most callous skin — that spectacle worked its effect as ever. Before the answering tumult of the spectators might become translated into action, the four prisoners were bundled into their carts and hurried back to jail.

They had not as yet been handed over to the civil authority, and this was quickly remedied. King Philip instructed the provost of Paris to relieve the Church of the two relapsed heretics, if necessary by force. How much force was found to be necessary is an open question.

The next morning, March 19, 1314, Jacques de Molay and Geoffrey de Charnay, strongly guarded, were taken to the little island of de Palais in the River Seine and there burnt alive. Like those who had gone before them, they cried their innocence and the innocence of their order as long as they retained power of speech.

21 *Reaping the Whirlwind*

THE ONLOOKERS WEPT AND GROANED, AND SHOOK THEIR FISTS AT THE EXECU-tioners. They fell on their knees and prayed. The soldiers of the King dispersed them. In the night some came back and under cover of darkness salvaged what they could from the remains of the pyre, and, bearing the grisly bits of coal in their mouths, swam back to the mainland, to hide and reverence what might turn out to be holy relics. Before long the relics did begin to work miracles, as told everywhere in France. But the martyrs of the Temple never became saints of the Church which had made them great and then consigned them to perdition. For Clement V, like Boniface VIII, retained his sacrosanct position. The rightful Pontiff is infallible, and whom he condemns stands convicted of guilt forever.

The infallibility of Clement V was not put under strain much longer. He died a month after the execution of Jacques de Molay and Geoffrey de Charnay, almost to the day, on April 20, 1314.

It was said that with his dying breath the burning grand master had summoned the Pope and the King of France to meet him before God's judgment seat within the year. King Philip the Fair obeyed the summons on November 29. He was struck down mysteriously on the chase, not by the common occupational hazard of kings, the hunting accident, but by a seizure of some kind. He was carried home to his palace and before the end was given grace to recover consciousness so that he made a good death, his soul departing cleansed and at peace with his Maker. He was able to express his wishes with regard to the succession and the future of the kingdom, and in his last moments on earth begged his heir to exercise moderation in tax-levying and rigid honesty in minting the coin of the realm. His heart was embalmed and sent, along with the jeweled splinter of the True Cross which he had purloined from the Temple, to repose at the monastery of Poissy. Men who in their day believed that the seat of all human emotion was the heart, informed posterity that the heart of Philip the Fair was no larger than that of an infant or a fowl. Perhaps it only shrank in the embalming.

Three grown sons survived him, and each in turn reigned for a short time, amid scandals, petty squabbles and retrogression. By 1328 the house of Philip the Fair was extinct. Some people attributed this also to the dying curse of Jacques de Molay, but some held Boniface VIII responsible, although the outraged Pope had cursed Philip's stock "unto the seventh generation," whereas it did not last beyond the second generation — in the direct line, that is. With a little juggling and sophistry, such as is customary in the interpretation of prophecies, it would be almost possible to make out a case that Louis XVI was a descendant of Philip IV in the required degree.

Nogaret conscientiously played his part in counteracting the flare of popular anger ignited by the Templar pyres, and which, unorganized and without a clear objective, soon flickered out again. Outstanding points in his relevant writings and perorations were that God had brought about the loss of the Holy Land as a punishment for the sins of the Templars, and that it was equally God who had caused Jacques de Molay to recant, since He did not wish so horrible a sinner to attain the Kingdom of Heaven by penitence and reconciliation. If Nogaret was struck at all by a similarity in the fate of the Templars to that of his parents, it would be only with grim satisfaction, for the Templars in their hale glory had been pitiless henchmen of the Albigensian persecution and had themselves escorted many a Catharan heretic to the stake. Then, before the year of 1314 was out, he followed his master to the tryst appointed by Jacques de Molay. The circumstances and the precise date of his death are obscure like his private life, and made a fertile breeding ground for legend. According to one, Nogaret went mad before he died and astonished the King and assembled courtiers by putting out his tongue at them all. Presumably only total derangement could have inspired such a gesture. At all events, his descendants were not cursed, but flourished, although not prominent in public life. In recent times his progeny were still alive in France, and may be so yet.

His friend and partner, William de Plaisians, died that same year. Possibly they were lucky; they might not have thrived in the new reign. Their colleague Enguerrand de Marigny, in that unhealthy profession of supervisor of the royal finances, was hanged in 1315, after a mock trial following the methods perfected in the trials of the Templars.

Popes have no progeny, or none that counts; they are wedded to the Church and their descendants are the Popes that come after them. Pope Clement's struggles to fight free of the toils devised by an ex-Catharan had in fact led the Papacy into the slough of the "Babylonish captivity" at Avignon, where the Holy See remained stuck fast for the best par of a century. This, broadly speaking, materially helped to estrange t'

German states of the Empire and the island of Britain, so that the Reformation might be said to have been a portion of the Templars' curse upon the Papacy.

Edward II of England, though not mentioned by name in the malediction, came to a hapless end in 1327, when he was deposed and murdered at Berkeley Castle. Under his son, grandson of Philip the Fair, the realm was devastated by revolt and plague. Altogether, it was noted, the Black Death, which reduced the population of Europe probably by four-fifths, spared not one country that had owned, and disowned, its Templars.

Of positive profit to the destroyers of the Temple there was little. The order having been merely dissolved and not convicted of heresy, the state had no claim to former Temple property, while the Church was unable to get its hands on the vanished Templar moneys. Only in Spain were the Templar possessions appropriated smoothly and wholly by the three-King coalition for the continuous war against the Moors. Everywhere else, nominally all had been transferred to the Hospital. As it was, the Hospitalers were not over anxious to accept the inauspicious windfall, and did so with the reservation that they would take over only such part of it *as would not bring them into conflict with the secular power*. The object lesson of the last seven years had not been lost on them.

It was just as well. Headed by the King of France, the Temple's debtors declared that all debts owing to heretics were automatically null and void, and soon it was discovered that, on the contrary, it was the Temple which was heavily in debt, especially to the French Crown. The Hospital was obliged to pay over large sums in compensation for expenses incurred by the state over six years of enquiries, in cost of legal proceedings, food and lodging for the thousands of prisoners, and executioners' fees and the price of materials for the pyres.

On kindred pretexts, the more valuable Templar properties in England were withheld, notably the Temple of London. When finally the Hospitalers came into what remained, the movable goods had gone and the rest was so deteriorated by reason of neglect and free-lance depredations as to be more burden than gain. In Scotland alone the abolition of the Temple was not ratified. The local branches of the order amalgamated with the Hospital's, and in that form survived until the Reformation. But then, in the Caledonian wilds there was no wealth to speak of, for anyone.

In Aragon and Portugal, too, the Temple was metamorphosed rather than eradicated. King James created a new order, that of Our Lady of Montosa, which took over the Templar uniform and in all probability enrolled former members of the Brotherhood; King Denis openly re-assembled his Portuguese Templars under their old name of Poor Knights of Christ, deleting only the subdefinition "of the Temple of Solomon."

Unofficially, the Hospital took in many former Templars. Others fled overseas to join the Saracens, or sought obscurity in sundry humble walks of life. Some married — but the Holy See soon set them right. While their order had been dissolved, they themselves had not been released from their vows, and they were urged to join any monasteries which would have them. A few old men, we are told, made frenzied efforts to compensate themselves for a lifetime of personal austerity before it was too late and plunged into a round of debauch. The debaucheries cannot have been very marvelous, on remittances equivalent to a monk's daily requirements in food and clothing.

One thing which it is pleasant to know is that Peter de Boulogne broke prison and escaped. Surely one may rejoice that this intrepid man was saved, without appearing to abandon any attempt at detachment. For whether or not the Templars were guilty of the crimes on which they had been arraigned, there is nothing problematical about the fact that they were the victims of a monstrous injustice, of glorified lynch law, of judicial murder. That is a matter for partiality; some emotion is not out of place.

And yet — and yet, emotion pulls again in two ways. The Temple was, in Western Europe, the last stronghold of feudalism in its archaic in-flexible form, citadel of reaction and the stuff of military dictatorship. Had it remained impregnable, had it been left to go on growing as it

would, what sort of outlook was there for the Western peoples? Philip
IV, or, if we prefer to speak in terms of historic forces, the French
monarchy, had to get rid of the Templars, whether of reasoned and
deliberate intent or by the blind automatic propulsion of its nature.
Hovering on the brink of annihilation as we are, we have become chary
of the word "progress," even unable to pronounce it without bitterness.
But the end of the world has been just around the corner ever since its
beginning; as we are in life, we are in death. Whatever it may lead to
at the last, progress there has been, advance in knowledge, happiness
and ease, while evil and catastrophe were with us always; and the
death-wish of the race, the ineluctable pull of self-destruction, had never
been long out of action. It was active in the Templar movement too, just
as the French monarchy in time succumbed to it. What might have been,
what ought to have been done and by what better means, makes bootless
animadversion.

Now for a last glance at the evidence and a few summary thoughts.
No documentary proof of the charges was ever found. In spite of the
surprise effect of the arrests in 1307 and in spite of exhaustive research,
the idol which thousands of prisoners confessed to having worshiped —
that head of wood, of silver, bearded, beardless, eyeless, carbuncle-eyed,
life-sized, larger than life, the size of a fist — no such idol was unearthed.
No cats were ever apprehended either.

If, as was stated by some, the Temple in France possessed one single
idol only, which traveled in rotation from house to house, it cannot have
varied so greatly in appearance. If, on the other hand, according to other
depositions, there were a great many such heads — which might account for the contradictory descriptions — it becomes the more unlikely
that all of these should have disappeared without trace. The nearest thing
to it was a certified relic, of which the prosecution did not even attempt
to make use.

Regarding the obscene and blasphemous initiation ceremonies, it is
impossible to make up one's mind. Here the confessions, though they
may have been the result of torture, show few discrepancies. On the

other hand, many witnesses stated that they had first heard the substance of the charges *after* their arrest (so that they would have been required only to answer yes or no to leading questions), and in not a few cases groups of witnesses were confined together and may have agreed on a common version, to save themselves additional "questioning."

Several witnesses said that they had treated the whole thing as a joke, several others that, though they themselves had been disgusted, the receiver and his assistants had obviously derived amusement from what they were imposing on the novice. Initiation ceremonies, ancient and modern, commonly include unpleasant rites of some sort, humiliating if not painful. All work and no play is beyond Jack's endurance; a gross age will not be squeamish where comic relief is concerned; what had started in part as a mortal joke played on the Saracen might have gone on to develop a private ritual of sacrilegious clowning.

It is well known that the most deeply devout nations tend to invent the most blasphemous colloquial oaths. One sign of our rationalist orientation is that the worst we can do in the way of swearing is to name simple bodily functions. The theory of repression and inevitable compensatory outburst is equally familiar. Besides, the warriors of the Cross felt that God had failed them, an additional incentive to venomous horseplay. Even today the custom has not quite died out, in primitive communities afflicted, say, by drought, of taking the statue of a patron saint from his niche, stripping him of ornaments and carrying him in punitive procession. That strikes the same chord.

The explanation proffered by Jacques de Molay and others, that making the recruit spit on the cross and deny the Saviour was a test of obedience (or, conversely, of fortitude), is not without point. Or it might have been an especially abstruse and ingenious device of mortification. There is no end to supposition. We do not know.

We do know that the Templars never hesitated to lay down their lives for the Cross they were alleged to defile as a routine matter, and that countless numbers of them had preferred death to renunciation of their faith when they were captured by the Moslems.

Another pointer on the credit side is the usual behavior of heretics.

By definition, the heretic was a believer, as fanatical as the orthodox, sufficiently convinced of treading the only right path to salvation to die for his belief — since to save his life all he needed to do was recant. At the stake, he would glorify his superior faith and thus affirm his guilt to the last breath — precisely as the Templars affirmed their orthodoxy and innocence.

Further, if, as deposed in adverse evidence, every member of the order had to practice the crimes of the indictment and anybody who refused was murdered, it is strange that such murders passed undetected for so long. Cowards did not enter the Temple; its ranks were full of upright men and those imbued with all the pride of noble blood. A considerable percentage of recruits might have had to be murdered, then.

On the other hand, while it is suggestive that nowhere but in France or under immediate French influence were the wholesale confessions obtained, it is also strange that the English Templars, who passed their lesser ordeal more or less with flying colors, would swear only to the purity of the Temple in England. Of other countries, they said, they knew nothing. They may, of course, merely have wished to be careful and safeguard themselves against whatever casuistry was to be leveled at them next.

In England alone, the practice of lay absolution was held to have been established; yet all the preceptors, who would have been the persons to give such indulgence, strenuously denied this accusation from start to finish. Possibly the formula used in conclusion of chapter meetings had been misinterpreted: "The sins you have, either through shame or fear, failed to confess, we, *in accordance with the authority bestowed on us by God and the Pope,* forgive you, *so far as we are able."* The chapters dealt with weekly affairs and disciplinary offenses: the "sins" of the formula therefore would have referred to the latter, and in that light the words I have italicized stand out clearly in restriction, rather than extension, of general pardon. Many witnesses stated that they had so understood it, although others had considered themselves relieved of any obligation to confess their sins at all. It is not impossible that the misconception was tacitly allowed to take root — it would be like the Templars' notorious arrogance and love of independence.

Regarding license to practice sodomy, to which large numbers of witnesses testified though only three admitted having taken advantage of it, doubts similarly arise in several directions. Many of these witnesses qualified the confession, saying they had not at the time realized what the receiver's words had meant, but had been enlightened since, *during their interrogation*.

The kiss of peace, an important rite in secular life and a statutory part of the Temple's official initiation ceremony, was normally given on the mouth. Even if it was true that recruits were forced to kiss the officiating brethren also on the navel and below the spine, this would not necessarily impart a vicious flavor to the act of reception. Priests and sovereign rulers of old were endowed with an, as it were, honorary bisexual nature: "Thou art my father and mother," was once a conventional apostrophe. No one thought anything of it when Baldwin of Flanders was adopted by the Prince of Edessa in a familiar ceremony symbolizing the act of birth: the adoptive son's hair was cut off in token of infanthood, and the adoptive father took him under the garment next his body, then folding him in a close embrace to his bared breast. The receiver of novices, acting on behalf of the Temple, adopted the recruit into the order, where a new life awaited him, and a new life must be preceded by rebirth. Those kisses, therefore, might have been symbols of a symbol, in a rudimentary, shorthand sketch of that ancient ceremony of adoption, acknowledging a mystic femaleness in the birthgiver.

Again in England, some play was made with the avowals of the rule of secrecy (which did not form part of the indictment except by implication) — perhaps to eke out the meager crop of definite evidence. It could not be twisted into a punishable offense; yet, in the last analysis, their secretiveness was perhaps the Templars' chief offense, being the medium in which antipathy, fear and accusations had proliferated.

All through the Middle Ages and beyond, religious communities of every kind were the butt of evil rumors of which sexual immorality and consequently regular infanticide were the most common theme. The other two military orders had come in for their share of defamation and suspicion, and while their constitutions, wealth, power and pride approximated to the Templars', one essential difference was that secrecy had no part in their scheme of existence. The other important particular in which the Templars stood alone was their facilities for undermining the efficacy of the ban (Nogaret, not Philip the Fair, should have applied for membership!), which had first made them independent of the Church and by the same token deprived them of ecclesiastic protection.

The contrast of nominal poverty and factual wealth, the primal flaw in the foundations of the Temple had cracked the whole superstructure, and laid the order open at once to the interior attack of degenerating purpose, and attack from without on its morals and its rights.

To the man in the street the Templars' vow of poverty would be a sham — if their property belonged to an abstract entity, the order, wherein did that entity exist, after all, save in its components, men of flesh and blood? — suggesting that the vow of chastity, surely a more difficult one to keep, was likely to have gone overboard as well.

Medieval asceticism was obsession with sex, turned inside out. St. Bernard's insistence on lighted dormitories, the occupants of which must on no account remove or even loosen their clothes, could not but insistently direct the imagination at sins evidently very hard to prevent. The insistence that the fighting monks were to shun woman even more stringently than most other religious fraternities lent added fuel to the train of thought; it was seriously submitted that the injunction to sodomy had been designed to clinch the Templar's aversion from all feminine contact. So the train of thought sped on to the final point of arrival: for a group of men obviously more sinful than the generality to be more privileged than anybody else, could not be just. Envy and greed might call themselves righteous.

Being composed of men of flesh and blood, no society is, in fact, an abstract entity. None is proof against internal jealousy and conflict of opinion. If Jesus had lived in the flesh to welcome St. Paul among His disciples, one rather wonders what would have happened. The human factor, naturally impossible to eliminate from any human dealings, is also forever unpredictable.

Almost certainly the unforgotten rivalry of Jacques de Molay and Hugh de Peraud — which a number of witnesses opined had initially turned on the corruption within the Temple — influenced the course of events in 1307. Had the leadership been united, had there been no under-currents of old scores and competition to obfuscate the mainstream of contingency, a more rational line of defense might have succeeded.

One of the main points of Esquiu's charges that the Templars had be-trayed the Holy Land, was not rigorously pursued. In the end Nogaret had had to shift it on to the metaphysical plane, saying that the Holy Land had been lost for the sins of the Templars, which was hardly the same as active treachery. The search for scapegoats is an invariable consequence of defeat, and here the Templars had served for quarry ever since they had presented a compact and prominent body to be shot at.

Belief in immortality obeys a need as deep and compulsive as the need for scapegoats. Humanity has never learned to accept the thought of total extinction, and in attributing survival alike to a prehistoric beast in Loch Ness, to legendary King Arthur on Avalon, and to the Emperor Barbarossa (whose very bones were lost piecemeal in transit to Palestine) inside Mount Kyffhaeuser, to name only a few, man has manufactured reassuring evidence for his own unending future. Sig-nificanctly, however, it is never the weak and humble who are kept in this wishful state of preservation, only the strong and puissant. The im-mortal hero will rest waiting in suspended animation for an hour of danger so grave that only he can help, when he will come forth to the rescue of his people. The concept has the further advantage of foster-ing optimism: for it follows that so long as the hero-father-protector does not break his catalepsy, matters could still be a lot worse. On this level, immortal monsters form a complementary feature, substantiating that ever-present background fear of deserved punishment, which is the price of security in parental protection.

From the destruction of the Temple onwards, men have obeyed an impulse to prove the secret survival of the Templars, rich and mighty knights who would not have allowed themselves to be immolated save for a hidden, lofty purpose: they who, in the days of the Crusades, when noble knights were always ransomed and the common foot and common civilians were always slaughtered, had scorned to buy their lives and 'died with the people; they who had every reason for undying vengefulness and for wishing to show the world what it had lost in them.

Thus the voyages of discovery, the achievements of the *conquistadors,* the supreme flowering of Western craftsmanship of the Renaissance, and finally the liberation of the peoples in the nineteenth century have been apportioned to the Temple. The great imperialist explorers were all crypto-Templars; the great trade guilds of Europe with their exclusive mysteries were of Temple pedigree; Freemasonry, which helped to pave the way for the French Revolution, was but a resurrection of the Temple.

Credit where credit is due: Prince Henry of Portugal, "the Navigator," who in the first half of the fifteenth century provided much of the impetus of maritime exploration, was a Knight of the Order of Christ, membership of which by that time had become an adjunct of the royal family, not unlike the ribbon of the Garter in modern England. Whether this makes him a Templar depends on one's dialectical enthusiasm.

Undoubtedly many Templar refugees, a large proportion of whom had been serving brothers, carried their various skills with them into anonymous exile and worked at their trades to earn their bread. Doubtless they would have spread some of their order's lore in this way. But they would in fact have been compelled to join the appropriate guilds; they did not found them. Trade and craft guilds were already flourishing in pre-Republican Rome, and uninterested in peaceful manual pursuits as were the Teutonic tribes, similar associations did exist in Barbarian society.

Undoubtedly, too, Freemasonry — which did not make its appearance until the eighteenth century — borrowed from the nomenclature and internal organization of the Temple, just as it drew on the then infant science of archaeology via the supposed priestcraft of ancient Egypt. Yet its name, its emblems, and its structure were taken directly from an actual trade guild of builders, and its aims were nonbelligerent, but rather socio-idealistic. But like the human races, all secret societies share certain basic features.

No body, whether individual or corporate, lives and dies without leaving its influence behind, and the Templars are no exception. Is not that good enough?

It is not enough. It wants to be influence of a certain kind, enabling us to retrace history always along an ascending line, which is our lifeline of hope positive: furnishing us with the means of distilling from the mass of blood and horror and injustice always some fresh surety that suffering is never in vain. If terror be kin to pity, pity and self-pity are so close as to be almost indistinguishable.

Hence yet another urge craves satisfaction: to make amends, to make it up to the victims and confound their persecutors, by posthumous award of honor. In 1917, when under General Allenby the first Christian army since 1244 entered Jerusalem, the effigies of the knights buried in the Temple Church of London were crowned with laurel — a graceful and beautiful gesture, and an accurate one, not assuming too much.

Let us be modest in our demands for comfort, let us say that without injustice the ideal of justice had never been set up, that without cruelty no humane principles would have shaped themselves in opposition, and that, but for the besetting malignity of man and life and matter, the noble phenomenon of courage had never come to birth.

Our last look at the Templars shall be through the eyes of Matthew Paris, describing a departure of knights for the Holy Land:

> They set out, passing through the town with spears held aloft, shields displayed, and piebald banners advanced, in unbroken formation, and sought a blessing from the people who crowded to see them pass. The Brethren uncovered, bowed their heads from side to side, and recommended themselves to the prayers of all.

Tables of Names

GRAND MASTERS OF THE TEMPLE

Hugh de Payens	1118 (1128)-1136
Robert de Craon	1136-1146
Everard des Barres	1146-1149
Bernard de Trémélai	1149-1153
Andrew de Montbard	1153-1156
Bertrand de Blanquefort	1156-1169
Philip de Milly of Nablus	1169-1170
Odo de Saint-Amand	1170-1179
Arnold de Torroge	1179-1184
Gerard de Ridefort	1185-1190
Robert de Sablé	119(?)-1193
Gilbert Erail	1193-1201
Philip de Le Plaissiez	1201-1208
William de Chartres	1208-1218
Peter de Montaigu	1218-ca. 1230
Armand de Périgord	ca. 1230-124-?
William de Sonnac	124-?-1250
Reÿnald de Vichiers	1250-1256?
Thomas Bérard	1256-1272
William de Beaujeu	1272-1291
Tibald Gaudin	1291-1295?
Jacques de Molay	1295-1314

LATIN KINGS OF JERUSALEM

BALDWIN I (of Boulogne — brother to Godfrey de Bouillon) 1100-1118

BALDWIN II (Le Bourg, Count of Edessa, cousin to Baldwin I) 1118-1131

MELISENDE (daughter of Baldwin II) m. FULK (Count of Anjou) 1131-1143

BALDWIN III (son of Melisende and Fulk) 1143-1162

AMALRIC I (second son of Melisende and Fulk) 1162-1174

BALDWIN IV (Leper King — Amalric's son) 1174-1185

BALDWIN V (son of Baldwin IV's sister Sibylla by William of Montferrat) 1185-1186

SIBYLLA (elder daughter of Amalric, sister to Baldwin IV, Baldwin V's mother) m. GUY (Lusignan) 1186-1190

ISABELLA (second daughter of Amalric, half-sister to Baldwin IV and Sibylla) m. HENRY (Count of Champagne and Navarre) 1192-1197

and

AMALRIC II (Lusignan — King of Cyprus) 1198-1205

MARIA (of Montferrat — daughter of Isabella by Conrad of Montferrat) m. JOHN (Brienne) 1210-1225

YOLANDA (daughter of Maria and John) m. EMPEROR FREDERICK II (Hohenstaufen) 1225-1228

CONRAD (Hohenstaufen — son of Yolanda and Frederick II; King of Germany) 1228-1254

CONRADIN (Hohenstaufen; absentee King) Regency conducted by King Hugh III (Lusignan) of Cyprus 1254-1268

HUGH III (King of Cyprus) 1268-1284

JOHN I (King of Cyprus) 1284-1285

HENRY II (King of Cyprus) 1285-1291

All dates refer to actual reigns and not necessarily to the life spans of the monarchs concerned. The year 1291 marked the factual end of the Kingdom of Jerusalem, but for many succeeding generations the Kings of Cyprus continued to have themselves crowned also Kings of Jerusalem.

POPES OF THE RELEVANT PERIOD

Urban II	1088-1099
Paschal II	1099-1118
Gelasius II	1118-1119
Calixtus II	1119-1124
Honorius II	1124-1130
Innocent II	1130-1143
Celestine II	1143-1144
Lucius II	1144-1145
Eugenius III	1145-1153
Anastasius IV	1153-1154
Adrian IV	1154-1159

Alexander III	1159-1181
Lucius III	1181-1185
Urban III	1185-1187
Gregory VIII	1187
Clement III	1187-1191
Celestine III	1191-1198
Innocent III	1198-1216
Honorius III	1216-1227
Gregory IX	1227-1241
Celestine IV	1241
Innocent IV	1243-1254
Alexander IV	1254-1261
Urban IV	1261-1264
Clement IV	1265-1268
Gregory X	1271-1276
Innocent V	1276
Adrian V	1276
John XXI	1276-1277
Nicholas III	1277-1280
Martin IV	1281-1285
Honorius IV	1285-1287
Nicholas IV	1288-1292
Celestine V	1294
Boniface VIII	1294-1303
Benedict XI	1303-1304
Clement V	1305-1314

EMPERORS OF THE RELEVANT PERIOD

Byzantine Emperors

Alexius I	1081-1118
John II	1118-1143
Manuel I	1143-1180
Alexius II	1180-1183
Andronicus I	1183-1185
Isaac II	1185-1195 (deposed)
Alexius III	1195-1203

Isaac II (restored)	1203-1204
Alexius IV	1203-1204
Alexius V	1204
Baldwin I*	1204-1205
Henry*	1206-1216
Peter*	1217
Robert*	1218-1228
John (Brienne)*	1228-1237
Baldwin II*	1237-1261
Theodore I	1206-1222
John III	1222-1254
Theodore II	1254-1258
John IV	1258-1261
Michael VIII	1261-1282
Andronicus II	1282-1328

*The Latin Emperors of Byzantium are marked with an asterisk.

Holy Roman (German) Emperors

Henry IV	1056-1106
Henry V	1106-1125
Lothar III	1125-1137
Conrad III*	1138-1152
Frederick I (Barbarossa)	1152-1190
Henry VI	1190-1197
Frederick II	1212-1250
Conrad IV*	1250-1254
Rudolf I* (Habsburg)	1273-1292
Adolf*	1292-1298
Albert I*	1298-1308
Henry VII	1308-1314

*Those German emperors who were never crowned are marked with an asterisk. Antikings and rival claimants during periods of vacancy of the Holy Roman throne are not given.

FRENCH AND ENGLISH KINGS
OF THE RELEVANT PERIOD

France

Philip I	1060-1108
Louis VI	1108-1137
Louis VII	1137-1180
Philip II (Augustus)	1180-1223
Louis VIII	1223-1226
Louis IX (Saint Louis)	1226-1270
Philip III	1270-1285
Philip IV (The Fair)	1285-1314

England

William the Conqueror	1066-1087
William Rufus	1087-1100
Henry I	1100-1135
Stephen	1135-1154
Henry II	1154-1189
Richard I	1189-1199
John	1199-1216
Henry III	1216-1272
Edward I	1272-1307
Edward II	1307-1327

Bibliography

Addison, C. G., *History of the Knights Templars*, London, 1842.

Archer, T. A. and Kingsford, C. L., *The Crusades*, London, 1894.

Arnold, T. and Guillaume, A., *The Legacy of Islam*, Oxford, 1931.

Atiya, A. S., *The Crusade in the Later Middle Ages*, London, 1938.

Burkitt, F. C., *Early Eastern Christianity*, London, 1904.

Campbell, G. A., *The Knights Templars, Their Rise and Fall*, London, 1937.

Charpentier, John, *L'Ordre des Templiers*, Paris, 1944.

Creswell, K. A. C., *Early Muslim Architecture*, Oxford, 1932-1940.

Curzon, H. de, *La Règle du Temple*, Paris, 1886.

Deschamps, Paul, *La Défense du Royaume de Jérusalem*, Paris, 1939.

Duggan, Alfred, *Devil's Brood*, London, 1957.

Encyclopaedia Britannica, 9th and 11th editions.

Encyclopaedia of Islam.

Erdmann, C., *Die Entstehung des Kreuzzugsgedanken*, Stuttgart, 1935.

Evans, Joan, *Life in Mediaeval France*, London, 1957.

Fedden, Robin and Thomson, John, *Crusader Castles*, London, 1957.

Finke, Heinrich, *Pabsttum und Untergang des Templerordens*.

Fritsche, E., *Islam und Christentum im Mittelalter*.

Gibbon, Edward, *The Decline and Fall of the Roman Empire*, London, 1896.

Grollenberg, L. H., *Atlas of the Bible*, London & Edinburgh, 1956.

Grousset, R., *L'Empire des Steppes*, Paris, 1944.

Guillaume, A., *Islam*, London, 1954.

Hammer, J. von, *Histoire de l'Ordre des Assassins*, Paris, 1833.

Heaton, Herbert, *Economic History of Europe*, New York, 1936.

Hill, G. F., *Coins and Medals*, New York, 1921.

Holtzmann, W., *Wilhelm von Nogaret*, Freiburg, 1898.

Kantorowicz, E., *Frederick the Second*, London, 1931.

Lacroix, Paul, *Manners, Customs and Dress during the Middle Ages and Renaissance*, London, 1874.

La Monte, J. L., *Feudal Monarchy in the Latin Kingdom of Jerusalem*, Cambridge, Mass., 1932.

Lawrence, T. E., *Crusader Castles*, London, 1936.

Le Strange, G., *Palestine under the Moslems*, London, 1890.

Levis-Mirepois, Duc de, *Philippe le Bel*, Paris, 1936.

Lizerand, G., *Le Dossier de l'Affaire des Templiers*, Paris, 1928.

Longnon, J., *Les Français d'Outremer du Moyen Age*, Paris, 1946.

Martin, E. J., *The Trial of the Templars*, London, 1927.

Melville, Marion, *La Vie des Templiers*, Paris, 1951.

Neumann, C., *Bernhard von Clairvaux und die Anfänge des zweiten Kreuzzuges*, Heidelberg, 1882.

Norgate, K., *Richard the Lion Heart*, London, 1924.

O'Leary, De L., *A Short History of the Fatimid Khaliphate*, London, 1923.

Oman, Charles, *A History of the Art of War in the Middle Ages*, London, 1924.

Piquet, J., *Les Banquiers du Moyen Age: Les Templiers*, Paris, 1939.

Previté-Orton, C. W., *The Shorter Cambridge Mediaeval History*, Cambridge, 1952.

Prutz, H. G., *Entwicklung and Untergang des Templerherrenordens*, Berlin, 1888.

Prutz, H. G., *Kulturgeschichte der Kreuzzüge*, Berlin, 1883.

Prutz, H. G., *Wilhelm von Tyrus*, Munich, 1883.

Röhricht, R., *Geschichte des Königreichs Jerusalem*, Innsbruck, 1898.

Roolvink, R., *Historical Atlas of the Muslim Peoples*, London, 1957.

Runciman, Steven, *A History of the Crusades*, Cambridge, 1951-1954.

Scholz, R., *Die Publizitsik zur Zeit Philipps des Schönen und Bonifaz's VIII*, Stuttgart, 1903.

Smith, G. A., *The Historical Geography of the Holy Land*, London, 1935.

Strakosch-Grossmann, G., *Der Einfall der Mongolen in Mitteleuropa in den Jahren 1241 und 1242*, Innsbruck, 1893.

Usama ibn Munqidh (editor and translator, P. K. Hitti), *Memoirs: An Arab-Syrian Gentleman and Warrior in the Period of the Crusades*, New York, 1929.

Viollet-le-Duc, E. E., *Dictionnaire Raisonné du Mobilier Français*, Paris, 1858-1875.

Index

DATE DUE